SECURITY ISSUES FOR WIRELESS SENSOR NETWORKS

SECURITY ISSUES FOR WIRELESS SENSOR NETWORKS

Parag Verma, Ankur Dumka,
Anuj Bhardwaj, Navneet Kaur,
Alaknanda Ashok, Anil Kumar Bisht,
and Raksh Pal Singh Gangwar

CRC Press
Taylor & Francis Group
Boca Raton London New York

CRC Press is an imprint of the
Taylor & Francis Group, an **informa** business

First Edition published 2022
by CRC Press
6000 Broken Sound Parkway NW, Suite 300, Boca Raton, FL 33487-2742

and by CRC Press
4 Park Square, Milton Park, Abingdon, Oxon, OX14 4RN

© 2022 Taylor & Francis Group, LLC

CRC Press is an imprint of Taylor & Francis Group, LLC

ISBN: 978-1-032-18904-8 (hbk)
ISBN: 978-1-032-19085-3 (pbk)
ISBN: 978-1-003-25760-8 (ebk)

DOI: 10.1201/9781003257608

Typeset in Times
by MPS Limited, Dehradun

Contents

1 Introduction to Wireless Sensor Networks   1
Introduction   1
Issues and Challenges   2
Architecture for WSNs   3
Types of Sensors   4
Components of WSNs   5
Types of Wireless Sensor Networks   6
Applications of WSNs   7
Protocols in WSNs   7
    SPINS: Security Protocols for Sensor Networks   7
    LEAP: Localized Encryption and Authentication Protocol   9
       Gradient-Based Routing (GBR)   11
       Active Query Forwarding in Sensor Network (ACQUIRE)   11
    Probabilistic Key Distribution Schemes   11
    Deterministic Key Distribution Schemes   12
References   14

2 Security in Wireless Sensor Networks – Background   15
Introduction   15
Constraints in Sensor Networks   17
    Unreliable Communication   17
    Node Constraints   17
       Battery Power/Energy   18
       Recharge Ability   18
       Sleep Patterns   19
       Transmission Range   19
       Memory Limitations   19
       Unattended Operations   20
    Network Constraints   20
       Ad Hoc Networking   20
       Limited Preconfiguration   20
       Data Rate/Packet Size   20
       Channel Error Rate   21
       Intermittent Connectivity   21
       Unreliable Communications   21
       Higher Latency in Communication   21

Frequent Routing Changes   21
Unknown Recipients   22
Physical Limitation   22
Characteristics of Sensor Networks   22
Power Efficiency   22
Scalability   23
Responsiveness   23
Reliability   23
Mobility   23
Compact Size   23
Physical Security   24
Memory Space   24
Bandwidth   24
Security Goals for Sensor Networks   24
Confidentiality   25
Integrity   26
Authentication   26
Data Freshness   27
Availability   27
Self-Organization   28
Secure Localization   28
Time Synchronization   28
Security Classes   29
Attacks on Sensor Networks   29
Passive Information Gathering   30
Attacks Against Privacy   30
Monitor and Eavesdropping   31
Traffic Analysis   31
Camouflage Adversaries   31
Active Attacks   32
Routing Attacks   32
Node Subversion   33
Node Malfunction   33
Node Outage   33
Physical Attacks   34
False Node   34
Node Replication Attacks   34
Layering-Based Security Approach   34
Physical Layer   35
Data Link layer   36
Network Layer   36
Transport Layer   37
Application layer   37
Conclusion   38
References   38

3 QoS as a Means of Providing WSN Security   41
   Introduction   41
   Quality of Services in Wireless Sensor Networks   43
      QoS Concept and Security Effect   44
      QoS Challenges in Sensor Networks   45
      QoS Metrics in WSN Layers   47
         Application-Specific QoS Parameters   47
         Network-Specific QoS Parameters   48
   Related Studies   49
   Reliability, Availability and Serviceability (RAS)   53
   Calculating Probability of Node Availability in a WSN   56
   Experiments and Evaluations   57
   Conclusion   60
   References   61

4 The Security Framework for Wireless Sensor Networks   65
   Introduction   65
   Security Requirements in WSNS   66
   Wireless Sensor Networks' Security Framework   68
      The Secure Triple-Key Management Scheme   68
         Base Station to Node Key Calculation   70
         Nodes to Cluster Leader Key Calculation   70
         Cluster Leader to Next Hop Cluster Leader Key Calculation   71
         Cluster Leader to Base Station Key Calculation   72
         Analysis of Secure Triple-Key Management Scheme   72
      Secure Routing   74
         Node Algorithm   74
         Secure Localization   77
         Determining the Node Location   77
      Securing the Node Location: An Analysis   78
      Malicious Node Detection Mechanism   79
   Threat Model   81
   Trust Model   82
      Trust Evaluation Model   83
         Trust Evaluation of the Sensor Node   83
      Trust Evaluation of the Relay Node   88
         Data Trust   88
         Trust List   88
   Conclusion   89
   References   90

5 Secure Key Management Scheme (SKMS)   93
   Introduction   93
   Key Management in a Wireless Sensor Network   94

Key Management Schemes   95
Pre-Distribution Key Management Schemes   97
   Key Pool-Based Pre-Distribution Key Management Schemes   97
   Pair-Wise Key-Based Pre-Distribution Key Management
   Schemes   98
   Key Space-Based Pre-Distribution Key Management Schemes   99
   Group-Based Probabilistic Pre-Distribution Key Management
   Schemes   99
   Grid-Based Pre-Distribution Key Management Schemes   102
   Deployment Knowledge-Based Pre-Distribution Key
   Management Schemes   103
   Polynomial-Based Probabilistic Pre-Distribution Key
   Management Schemes   104
   Matrix-Based Pre-Distribution Key Management Schemes   104
   Tree-Based Pre-Distribution Key Management Schemes   105
   Combinatorial Design-Based Pre-Distribution Key Management
   Schemes   106
   Hypercube-Based Pre-Distribution Key Management Schemes   106
   ID-Based Pre-Distribution Key Management Schemes   107
   Energy-Aware Pre-Distribution Key Management Schemes   107
   Location-Based Pre-Distribution Key Management Schemes   109
   Cluster-Based Pre-Distribution Key Management Schemes   110
   Other Pre-Distribution Key Management Schemes   111
In Situ Key Management Schemes   115
Challenges Faced by Key Management in a WSN   116
   Evaluation Metrics for KMS in a WSN   116
   Security Metrics   117
   Efficiency Metric   117
   Flexibility Metric   117
Proposed Advanced EG Scheme for WSN Security   118
Key Pre-Distribution Phase   118
Shared Key Discovery Phase   119
Path Key Establishment Phase   119
Analysis and Simulation Result   119
   Connectivity   120
   Safety Analysis: Resilience against Attack Capture Nodes   121
Conclusion   122
References   122

6 **Secure Routing Algorithms (SRAs) in Sensor Networks**   131
Introduction   131
Challenges of Design Tasks of Routing Protocol for a WSN   132
Classification of Routing Protocols in a WSN   133
   Attribute-Based or Data-Centric Routing Protocols   133

Flooding and Gossiping   133
SPIN   135
Directed Diffusion   135
Rumor Routing   138
Gradient-Based Routing   139
Hierarchical-Based Routing (Clustering) or Node-Centric
Routing Protocol   140
LEACH   141
PEGASIS and Hierarchical-PEGASIS   142
TEEN and APTEEN   143
Energy-Aware Cluster-Based Routing Algorithm   146
Location-Based Routing (Geographic Protocol)   149
MECN and SMECN   149
GEAR (Geographic and Energy Aware Routing)   150
GAF and HGAF   150
Fermat Point-Based Energy-Efficient Geocast Routing
Protocol   152
Multi-Path Routing Protocol   152
N-to-1 Multi-Path Routing Protocol   153
Multi-Path Multi-Speed Protocol (MMSPEED)   154
Braided Multi-Path Routing Protocol   154
Energy-Aware Routing   155
Comparison of Routing Protocols   156
Routing Attacks in Wireless Sensor Networks   156
Sybil Attack   158
Black Hole Attack   158
Denial of Service Attack   159
Wormhole Attack   159
Hello Flood Attack   159
Grey Hole Attack   160
Conclusion   160
References   166

7 **Secure Localization Technique (SLT)**   169
Introduction   169
Operational Challenges in WSNs   170
Secure Localization Process   171
Classification of Localization Techniques   174
Direct Approaches   175
Indirect Approaches   175
Range-Based Localization   175
Range-Free Localization   179
Attack Model   181
Elementary Attacks   182

Range Change Attack   182
False Beacon Location Attack   182
Combinational Attacks   184
    Impersonation   184
    Sybil Attack   184
    Replay Attack   184
    Wormhole Attack   185
    Location-Reference Attack   185
Existing Solutions of Secure Localization Systems   187
    Node-Centric Secure Localization   187
        The Prevention Method   187
        The Detection Method   187
        The Filtering Method   188
    Infrastructure-Centric Secure Localization   189
Existing Secure Localization Systems   190
    SeRLoc   190
    Beacon Suite   190
    Attack-Resistant Location Estimation   191
    Robust Statistical Methods   191
    SPINE   192
    ROPE   192
    Transmission Range Variation   193
    DRBTS   193
    HiRLoc   194
Proposed Secure Localization Technique (SLT)   194
    Network Model and Assumptions   196
    Results and Discussion   203
Summary   207
References   207

8 Malicious Node Detection Mechanisms   213
Introduction   213
Security Threats against Wireless Sensor Networks   214
    Abnormality Detection   215
    Misuse Detection   215
    Specification-Based Detection   215
Literature on Malicious Node Detection   216
Suspicious Node Detection by Signal Strength   223
    The Model   223
    Suspicious Message Detection by Signal Strength (SMDSS)   225
    Suspicious Node Information Dissemination Protocol (SNIDP)   225
Proposed Malicious Node Detection Mechanism   226
    Feature Extraction   226
        Link Stability Features (LSFs)   227

        Probabilistic Features   228
        Randomness Features   229
        Credit Features   230
     Classification   230
     Result and Discussion   232
  Notes   237
  References   238

9 The Distributed Signature Scheme (DSS) Based on RSA   241
  Introduction   241
  Related Work   242
     Threshold Signatures   243
     Distributed Signatures   243
     Mesh Signatures   243
     Attribute-Based Signatures   243
  RSA-Based Secure Schemes   244
  RSA-Based DSS   245
     Distributed Signature Features   246
     RSA-Based Secret Key Distributions Main Approaches   246
  Our Approach on Scheme Establishment   248
     Scheme Initialization   249
     Generation of Distributive Signature   250
     Key Projection Distribution to New User   250
  Summary   251
  References   251

Index   255

Introduction to Wireless Sensor Networks

1

INTRODUCTION

There is a need to collect the environmental parameters from a remote location and send the collected data to base station for processing of the data. For this purpose, a wireless sensor network (WSN) is used, which is a network consisting of a number of sensors connected to a base station in order to collect the information of any environmental parameters. A wireless sensor network can be defined as a self-configured and infrastructure-less network that can be used for monitoring different physical and environmental parameters based on the type of usage and applications. Environmental parameters like pressure, temperature, etc. are collected by sensors that are sent from node to node to a mail location, termed a *sink node*, for observation, processing and analyzing. Thus, sink node acts like an interface between user data and network. The processed data can be collected from sink nodes through queries. Thus, a WSN network consists of hundreds to thousands of nodes connected in a form of network that communicate with each other using radio signals to process any information from a remote location to a base station for processing. The nodes are set using different types of topologies like star, mesh, hybrid, etc., depending upon the type of usage and structure needed.

The work of a WSN is divided into four basic steps:

1. Sensing unit
2. Processing unit
3. Transceiver unit
4. Power unit

The addition of any other unit is based on the type of application and usage.

The sensing unit is used for sensing any environmental parameters that are used to pick data and collect information of interest. This sensor unit is further subdivided into

DOI: 10.1201/9781003257608-1

subunits as sensor subunits and analog-to-digital converters. These sensors generate analog signals that are converted into digital signals using an analog-to-digital converter that is fed to a processing unit for processing. The processing unit contains a small memory with a management procedure that carries assigned sensing tasks by coordinating sensing nodes with other sensing nodes. The transceiver is used for sending the information, whereas the power unit consists of power supplies used for providing power to different components.

ISSUES AND CHALLENGES

A wireless sensor network can solve problems based on issues and applications. While implementing a wireless sensor network, there are many issues, which are discussed in this section. One of the prime issues in wireless sensor networks is communication by means of a wireless medium for transferring data within the network. Other issues involve energy consumption using a non-renewable form of energy for data transfer from node to node. Some major issues covered in this section are as follows.

Security: One of the major issues of WSN is security and this issue is covered in this book. The issue of security is also discussed by Zia et al., who divided the security of a WSN into four major pillars: confidentiality, integrity, authentication, and availability. Another issue of security was discussed by Sharma et al., who added one more pillar to the existing structure proposed by Zia. In a WSN, network security is one of the important parameters that is needed in each and every layer of a WSN.

Power Consumption: Power management in a WSN is one of the important issues, as all the nodes of a WSN need power for operation and these nodes depend on a non-renewable source of energy to work. Another issue with nodes of a WSN is the size of the battery, which is small and needs more power. As the process of data compression by these nodes needs energy that require bigger batteries, there is limited energy of the nodes.

Fault Tolerance: Another issue of a WSN is fault tolerance, i.e., failure of nodes, that is due to the fact that nodes of a WSN are frequently being deployed in dangerous and unconditional environment locations like under water, terrain, etc. for the purpose of collecting the data and may cause the hardware failure of these nodes, physical damage of these nodes and also the exhaustion of these nodes.

Latency: Latency in collecting the data from a WSN is also an issue as data is needed from the source node to the base station with minimum delay and latency for which suitable protocols and network topology is required.

Throughput: Throughput or increasing the efficiency of a WSN is always a challenge and an issue, which is an area of research from the past and currently. Since a WSN uses radio and packet transmission as a means for communication from one node to another, and the rate of successful transmission of these data and packets from the source to the destination node should be high, there is a need for efficient and fast transmission.

Data Suppression, Aggregation and Fusion: Data suppression suppresses the data of a WSN to send it from the source node to the destination node, whereas data aggregation is used for combining the data from different nodes and changing that data into meaningful information by reducing the data and removing any redundancy and thus also saves energy. Thus, data suppression, aggregation and fusion minimize the redundancy of data by reducing the load of traffic within the network, which also increases the bandwidth utilization of the network.

Production Cost: The frequent failure of sensor nodes may lead to a heavy cost of a WSN. The sensor node cost should be kept in mind before deploying nodes in a WSN.

Scalability: A number of sensors are used in a WSN and, in order to have high resolution of data, the node density varies from place to place. There are many protocols used for retrieval of data to be scalable and it also maintains adequate performance of the system as per the scalability of the network.

Topology: Selection of topology based on the type of applications and requirements is necessary for an efficient WSN, which is required for saving energy consumption in a WSN. Maintenance of topology is also an important aspect that needs to be addressed in view of reducing the consumption of energy within a WSN.

Transmission Media: For transmission of data from one node to another, radio communication is used over popular Industry, Scientific and Medical (ISM) bands. There are some WSNs that might use optical-based communication or infrared-based communication, so selection of a transmission medium in such a case is of utmost importance.

ARCHITECTURE FOR WSNS

A WSN uses a five-layered network architecture of an open systems interconnection (OSI) reference model (Table 1.1).

The five layers of a WSN are controlled by means of three cross layers for working efficiently. These three layers are power management, connection/mobility management and task management layers.

TABLE 1.1 Layered architecture of wireless sensor network

Application Layer
Transport Layer
Network Layer
Data Link Layer
Physical Layer

Application Layer: The application layer is the topmost layer of WSN architecture that involves the concept of management of traffic, providing software for different applications. These applications send queries for obtaining the information of the system.

Transport Layer: The transport layer is responsible for internetwork communication. This layer uses multiple protocols for providing reliability to the system and avoiding the congestion within the network. A WSN uses node-to-node communication and hence it does not use a TCP-based connection for the transmission of data. It uses a user datagram protocol (UDP) connection for node-to-node transmission within a WSN.

Network Layer: The network layer of a WSN deals with routing protocols that are responsible for parameters like power consumption, reliability, memory and redundancy factors, etc. Routing protocols can be classified into three factors: flat routing; hierarchical routing; and event driven, query-driven or time-driven based upon the type of applications or deployment. Routing protocols can also use the data aggregation concept for providing redundancy within a WSN in order to provide redundancy and save energy. Data fusion can also be used for aggregation of data, which also removes noise from aggregated data.

Data Link Layer: The data link layer is used to provide reliability of data from point to point to multipoint. The data link layer is also used for error control and multiplexing of data. This layer supports a media access control (MAC) address, which is a hardware address of nodes. This layer is used to provide higher reliability, low delay, higher efficiency and throughput.

Physical Layer: The physical layer of a WSN is used as an interface for transmission of a data stream over a physical medium. The physical layer also supports the frequency of data transmission, including parameters like frequency, generation of carrier frequency for modulation, signal detection and security, etc.

TYPES OF SENSORS

The heart of a wireless sensor network is the type of sensors we are using and that is based on the type of applications we are using for these sensors. The individual nodes of the wireless sensor network are often termed Motes. These sensors can broadly be divided into three groups as follows:

1. Microelectromechanical system (MEMS): This category includes magnetometers, acoustic sensors, pressure sensors, pyroelectric effect sensors, etc.
2. Complementary metal oxide semiconductor (CMOS) based sensors: This category consists of humidity sensors, temperature sensors, capacity proximity sensors, etc.
3. LED sensors: This category includes proximity sensors and light-based sensors.

Based on demand and requirements, combinations of sensors can be deployed to create a network. For example, for environmental conditions we can use a combination of MEMS, CMOS and LED sensors for measuring environmental conditions like humidity, temperature, pressure, light, etc. On similar grounds for tracking people or devices at any place, we can use a combination of all sensors like proximity sensors, pyroelectric sensors or acoustic sensors. Thus, these systems will be used for preparing the smart system using sensor-based technology, which reduces human efforts for any system and makes the system intelligent and smart.

COMPONENTS OF WSNS

A wireless sensor network can be customized based on the requirements and applications required, but a basic WSN consists of the following components for setting a communication among networks.

Microcontroller: The microcontroller of a WSN is used for processing data, controlling the functionality of components within a node and performing tasks within a WSN.

Transceiver: The transceiver is responsible for sending and receiving data from a single device.

Sensors Nodes: Sensor nodes use an ISM band that provides a free radio spectrum allocation and global availability. These radio frequency bands are used for communications among nodes of a wireless sensor network. A wireless sensor network uses license-free communication frequencies of 173 MHz, 433 MHz, 868 MHz, 915 MHz and 2.4 GHz. The transceiver can be in different states of sending, receiving, idle and sleep. These are often termed radios that are used for transmission of data or signals.

Sensors: Sensors are devices that activate with any change in the physical state of a system and then converting that signal in the form of measuring an analog signal. These analog signals are changed to digital signals by means of an analog-to-digital converter that is then sent for further processing. These sensors can be passive omni-directional, passive narrow-beam or active sensors depending upon the type of usage and applications.

Passive omni-directional sensors sense data without manipulating the environment. They are self-powered and require energy to amplify analog signals and have no notion of direction in measurement. Passive narrow-beam sensors have a well-defined notion of direction while measurement (e.g., camera). Active sensors actively probe the environment (e.g., SONAR or RADAR, etc.)

Memory: Most of the microcontrollers contain on-chip memory for storage of information. The requirement of memory depends from application to application. These memories are used for storing application-related data. The size of memory is constrained with a few kilobytes only.

Battery/Power Source: Energy is one of the important aspects in terms of a wireless sensor network. The sensing nodes need power for sensing, communication and processing of data. The power source needed for a wireless sensor network varies

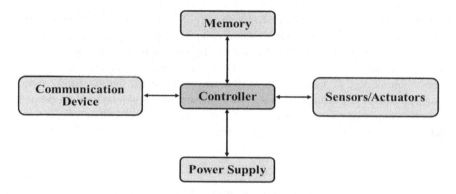

FIGURE 1.1   Components of a wireless sensor network.

from a 1.2- to 3.7-volt battery. A lot of research is going in this direction for laying stress on green energy for nodes. The power source can be AA, coin batteries or solar panels (Figure 1.1).

TYPES OF WIRELESS SENSOR NETWORKS

The types of wireless sensor networks depend upon the type of usage for a WSN. A WSN can be deployed underwater, underground, on land, etc. Based on the area where it can be implemented, WSN types are specified as:

1. Underground WSNs
2. Underwater WSNs
3. Terrestrial WSNs
4. Multimedia WSNs
5. Mobile WSNs

In underground WSNs, nodes are deployed under the ground for monitoring conditions within the ground, whereas the sink node is placed above the ground and collects all information from the nodes under the ground and sends it to the base station. Since the nodes are situated under the ground, this system is difficult and more costly in terms of maintenance, deployment, recharge and attenuation and signals lost are also a major issue in these WSNs.

Underwater WSNs deploy nodes under the water for collecting information of underwater conditions. The signals collected are sent to the sink node and from there to the base station for further processing. This network suffers problems of long propagation delay, bandwidth and faulty sensors due to sensors always immersed in water. Charging or replacement of batteries is again an issue in these types of networks.

Terrestrial WSNs deploy sensors in air that can be deployed in an ad hoc manner or structured manner depending upon the type of usage or application. Changing batteries is easy and these networks are less expensive compared to the above networks. These networks can make use of green energy by using solar energy. Energy conservation can be achieved in these networks by means of minimizing delays, low duty cycle operations, optimal routing, etc.

Multimedia WSNs are used for tracking and monitoring of multimedia events like audio, video, etc. This network makes use of low-cost sensor nodes that are equipped with cameras and microphones, etc. The data is transmitted by interconnecting nodes. The data is processed by compression, retrieval and correlation of data through these sensor nodes. This network faces major issues of high-energy requirements, high bandwidth requirements and innovative techniques for data compression and processing as sensor nodes of this network have to carry multimedia that require high bandwidth and advanced processing techniques.

Mobile WSNs consist of mobile network nodes that can be moved from one place to another on their own to interact with the physical environment. These mobile nodes can compute senses from the physical environment and communicate with neighboring nodes. This wireless network provides better coverage than other static networks and provide better energy efficiency, channel capacity, etc. compared to a static wireless network.

APPLICATIONS OF WSNS

WSNs can be used in many applications, as summarized in Table 1.2.

PROTOCOLS IN WSNS

There are many protocols used for processing information within WSNs where security is one of the important concerns. We are discussing major protocols in brief in this chapter and will be discussing other protocols in detail in subsequent chapters.

SPINS: Security Protocols for Sensor Networks

SPIN protocol is responsible for data confidentiality, data authentication, data integrity, data freshness and broadcast authentication. For ensuring data confidentiality, authentication, integrity and freshness, it uses one protocol sensor network encryption protocol (SNEP) and for authenticated broadcast it uses μTESLA.

SNEP: In SNEP, two communicating parties, A and B, share a master secret key, K_{AB}, and they derive independent keys using the pseudorandom function F: encryption

TABLE 1.2   Applications of WSNs

Area of Application of WSN	Use
Asset Management	Tracking of containers
Air Traffic Control	Controlling air traffic pattern
Home Automation	Multiple home system control like conservation, convenience, safety, etc., electric, water and gas utility usage data, home security
Military Application	Battlefield management, battlefield reconnaissance, surveillance, management, combat field surveillance, detecting structural faults in aircraft, detecting structural faults in ships, detection of enemy vehicles
Electricity Management	Automatic meter reading, smart grid management, electricity load management
Biological Field	Biological monitoring for agents, detecting toxic agents
Medical	Biomedical applications, smart ambulance, real-time monitoring of patient, wireless body area networks, collecting database for clinical data, heart beat sensor, telemedicine
Road Safety and Management	Bridge and highway monitoring and management
Construction	Building and structure monitoring, building automation, building energy control and monitoring, detecting structural faults in buildings
Disaster Management	Earthquake detection, tsunami detection and response, disaster emergency response
Business	E-money applications, kiosks, monitor and controlling workspaces, intruder detection
Habitat	Habitat monitoring, sensing
Industry	Industrial and building monitoring and automation, manufacturing monitoring and automation, asset management, process control, inventory management, manufacturing control, material processing system
Power System	Monitoring of electrical distribution system, smart grid sensor and actor network application, automated remote meter reading, thermal rating monitoring of conductor in power system, monitoring sag clearance in overhead conductor
Transportation	Traffic monitoring, transportation-based application, VANET-based application, road-based application, car parking, underground railway tunnel monitoring
Gas Monitoring	Sewage gas monitoring, gas pipeline monitoring, gas meter monitoring, air pollution monitoring
Other Purposes	Commercial applications, consumer application, consumer electronics and entertainments, tracking of belongings like pets, etc., heating control

keys $K_{AB} = F(1)$ and $K_{BA} = F(3)$ for each direction of communication, and MAC keys $K_{AB}^0 = F(2)$ and $K_{BA}^0 = F(4)$ for each direction of communication.

The encrypted data has the format $E = D_{(K;C)}$, where D is the data, the encryption key is K, and the counter is C. The MAC is $M = MAC(K^0, C\|E)$.

The complete message that A sends to B is

$$A - \to B: \{D\}(K_{AB}, C_A), MAC(K'_{AB} C_A\|\{D\}(K_{AB}, C_A))$$

In the above communication, one node will be a base station and another will be some other node. The present SNEP protocol provides semantic security by using a counter and data authentication by using MAC in the message, replay protection by using a counter, weak freshness and it has low communication overhead by keeping a counter state at each point.

If communicating parties know that they do not have the counter values synchronized, then they will exchange the counter using a counter exchange protocol. This scheme has a loophole that somebody may utilize this fact and may insert a DoS attack by sending fake messages and keeping both nodes busy in the counter exchange protocol. In that case, both parties may start sending counters with each message and defending the attack.

μTESLA: SPINS use μTESLA, which is a multicast stream authentication protocol. It uses a delayed key disclosure mechanism where the key used to authenticate i^{th} message is disclosed after the $(i + 1)^{th}$ interval at some time.

SPINS employs a base station as a key distribution center. μTESLA provides authentication for data broadcasts, and requires the base station and sensor nodes be loosely time synchronized. Basically, a base station (BS) randomly selects the last key, K_n, of a chain, and applies a one-way public function H to generate the rest of the chain $K_0, K_1, ..., K_{n-1}$ as $K_i = H(K_{i+1})$. Given K_i, every sensor node can generate the sequence $K_0, K_1, ..., K_{i-1}$. However, given K_i, no one can generate K_{i+1}. At the ith time slot, BS sends an authenticated message MAC_{Ki} (Message). Sensor nodes store the message until BS discloses the verification key in the $(i + 1)^{th}$ time slot. Sensor nodes can verify a disclosed verification key K_{i+1} by using the previous key K_i as $K_i = H(K_{i+1})$.

Advantages of this scheme are its one memory efficient scheme, it provides strong security features by ensuring data confidentiality, it provides data authentication and data integrity and it is also responsible for data freshness and broadcast authentication.

Disadvantages of this scheme include μTESLA overhead from releasing keys after a certain delay and possible message delay. In μTESLA, nodes are required to store a message until the authentication key is disclosed. This operation may create storage problems and encourages DoS types of attacks. An adversary may jam key disclosure messages to saturate storage of sensor nodes.

LEAP: Localized Encryption and Authentication Protocol

LEAP protocol is a key-based algorithm that provides different keys for different messages for separate security requirements. It assumes that the packets exchanged by the nodes in a sensor network can be classified into several categories based on different criteria, e.g., control packets vs data packets, broadcast packets vs unicast packets, queries or commands vs sensor readings, etc. Here, authentication is required for all type of packets, whereas confidentiality may be required for certain types of packets. For example, in the routing control, information usually does not require confidentiality, whereas readings transmitted by a sensor node and queries sent by the base station may need confidentiality. LEAP protocols can be classified into four different categories based on keys:

- **Individual key:** In individual keys, a key is shared by every node with the base station and used for communication between the base station and an individual node.
- **Group key:** In group keys, a global shared key is used by the base station for encrypting messages that are broadcasted to the whole group.
- **Cluster key:** In cluster keys, a key is shared by a node and all of its neighbors, and it is mainly used for local broadcast.
- **Pairwise shared key**: In pairwise shared keys, a key is shared by a node with each of its immediate neighbors. In LEAP, pairwise keys are used for securing communication that requires privacy or source authentication.

Establishing individual keys, pairwise keys and multi-hop pairwise keys in the key setup phase, nodes receive a general key, K_I. A node S_u can use K_I and a one-way hash function H to generate its master key: $K_u = H_{K_I}$. In the shared key discovery phase, node S_u broadcasts (ID_u, RN_u) and a neighbor S_v responds with $(ID_v, MAC_{K_v} (RN_u/ID_v))$.

Node S_u can then generate the key $K_v = H_{K_I} (ID_v)$, and both nodes S_u and S_v can then generate the session key $K_{u;v} = H_{K_v}(ID_u)$. A multi-hop pairwise key may be required to reach the cluster heads. In that case, node S_u generates a secret K_{uc} and finds m intermediate nodes. It divides the secret into shares $K_{uc} = sk_1 sk_2 \dots sk_m$, and sends each share through a separate intermediate node S_{vi}; (1 i m). Basically, node S_u sends $ENC_{K_{u;vi}} (sk_i)$, $H_{ski} (0)$ to node S_{vi}, and S_{vi} sends $ENC_{K_{vi;c}} (sk_i)$, $H_{ski} (0)$ to cluster head S_c.

This solution has a high communication cost because S_u sends m messages through m intermediate nodes to increase resilience. However, security of the system depends on the general key, K_I, which can be compromised by capture of a sensor node. It is possible to compromise all the session keys generated by LEAP once K_I is compromised.

LEAP provides a mechanism to generate group-wise keys, which follows the LEAP pairwise key establishment phase. The node S_u, which wants to establish a group key with all its neighbors $v_1, v_2, \dots, v_m$, first generates a unique group key, K_u^g. It then sends K_u^g to its neighbor v_i as $ENC_{K_{u;vi}} (K_u^g)$. The security of the scheme depends on security of the pairwise keys, which in turn has very low resilience.

For establishing a group key, it uses a mechanism similar to μTESLA. Advantages of this scheme are as given: it offers efficient protocols for supporting four types of key schemes for different types of messages broadcasted, reduces battery usage and communication overhead through in-network processing and uses a variant of μTESLA to provide local broadcast authentication.

Disadvantages of this scheme are presented: it requires excessive storage with each node storing four types of keys and a one-way key chain and computation and communication overhead dependent upon network density (the more dense a network, the more overhead it has).

Gradient-Based Routing (GBR)

A GBR protocol is proposed that works on the concept of hop counts, where each node calculates the height with the base station, which is the number of hops or number of counts of sensor nodes taken to reach the base station. This protocol uses the concept of data aggregation and traffic distribution to optimize the resource utilization for maximum throughput within the network. In order to distribute traffic in a balanced manner within the network, three different techniques are used: stochastic scheme, energy-based scheme and stream-based scheme depending upon different parameters need to be kept in mind.

Active Query Forwarding in Sensor Network (ACQUIRE)

ACQUIRE protocol was proposed by Sadagopan et al. (2003), which uses the same concept of COUGAR of a distributed database for dividing complex queries into several sub-queries for forwarding data within the WSN. This is achieved by allowing several nodes to respond to queries all together. The performance of this protocol is better than directed diffusion as directed diffusion protocol may not be used for complex queries due to consideration of energy consumption; also, directed diffusion protocol uses a flooding mechanism for continuous and aggregation of queries. On the other hand, the ACQUIRE protocol uses efficient querying by adjusting the values of look-ahead parameter d, where d is equal to the diameter of the network. In case the network diameter is small, that is if the value of d is too small, then the number of hops the query has to travel will be more.

An ACQUIRE Base Station (BS) sends a query that is forwarded by each node to those that are receiving the query. Each node that is receiving the query will respond to a query partially by means of pre-fetched data it gathers and forward the data to other sensor nodes. For updating pre-fetched information, the node depends on its neighbor and gathers updated information from its neighbor by means of look-ahead of d hops. After resolving the query received from BS, it sends it back through the shortest reverse path back to BS.

Probabilistic Key Distribution Schemes

In a probabilistic key distribution scheme, a probabilistic key pre-distribution scheme is for pairwise key establishment. For each sensor node, a set of keys is chosen from a big pool of keys and given to each node before deployment. In order to establish a pairwise key, two sensor nodes only need to identify the common keys they share.

Thus, every pair of nodes in the network share a key with certain probability. Since keys are randomly chosen from the key pool, they are not related. Hence, it is not possible to calculate other keys by knowing some of the keys from the key pool. When a node is captured, its keys are disclosed to the adversary. So, all the keys captured by the adversary must be removed from the network. This leaves the network disconnected after a certain number of node captures. This is the main drawback of this scheme. Space overhead is also more in this scheme because more keys than required need to be stored in each node to ensure a certain probability of key sharing. The addition of a node also has the same probability of key share with its neighboring node.

Chan et al. further extended this idea and developed two key pre-distribution techniques: q-composite key pre-distribution and random pairwise scheme. q-composite key pre-distribution also uses a key pool but requires two sensors to compute a pairwise key from the q pre-distributed keys they share. In the random pairwise keys scheme, random pairs of sensors are picked and assigned a unique random key. In both schemes, resilience is improved because the probability that a link is compromised when a sensor node is captured decreases. But, the probability of key sharing also decreases because a pair of sensor nodes has to share q keys instead of one. This scheme achieves good security under small-scale attacks, while being vulnerable to large-scale attacks.

A similar mechanism is proposed by the pairwise key establishment protocol, which uses threshold secret sharing for key reinforcement. SA generates a secret key $Kr_{A,B}$, $j-1$ random shares ski, and $skj = Kr_{A,B} \oplus sk1 \oplus ... \oplus skj - 1$. SA sends the shares through j disjoint secure paths. SB can recover $Kr_{A,B}$ upon receiving all shares. In cooperative pairwise key establishment protocol, SA first chooses a set $C = \{c1, c2, ..., cm\}$ of cooperative nodes. A cooperative node provides a hash $HMAC(Kc1,B, IDA)$. A reinforced key is then $Kr_{A,B} = K_{A,B} \oplus L_c \in C$ HMAC (Kc,B, IDA), where $K_{A,B}$ and $K_{c,B}$ are the established link keys. Node SA shares set C with node SB; therefore, SB can generate the same key. This approach requires nodes SA and SB to send and receive c more messages. Moreover, cooperative nodes have to send and receive two extra messages. In addition to increased communication cost, each cooperative node has to execute the hash message authentication code (HMAC) function twice for SA and SB. The key reinforcement solutions in general increase processing and communication complexity, but provide good resilience in the sense that a compromised keychain does not directly affect the security of any links in the WSN. But, it may be possible for an adversary to recover initial link keys. An adversary can then recover reinforced link keys from the recorded multi-path reinforcement messages when the link keys are compromised.

Deterministic Key Distribution Schemes

Deterministic key distribution schemes have the advantage that the graph is fully connected because every node in the network can establish a key with any other node. Basically, deterministic algorithms are of three types:

- Master key based

- Matrix based
- Polynomial-based key distribution scheme

Broadcast session key negotiation protocol (BROSK) is based on single master key that is pre-deployed in each sensor node. This master key is used to establish a key between a pair of sensor nodes. A master key based scheme is very simple to implement but it has resilience. Once the master key is known to the adversary, it is possible to derive all the link keys. A lightweight key management system proposes a solution with slightly better resilience where more than one master key is employed. It also does not give full resilience to node capture.

Blom proposed a key pre-distribution scheme that allows any pair of nodes in a network to be able to find a pairwise secret key. As long as no more than t nodes are compromised, the network is perfectly secure (this is called the t-collusion resistance property). We briefly describe how Blom t-secure key pre-distribution system works. During the pre-deployment phase, the base station first constructs a $(t + 1)$ N matrix G over a finite field GF(q), where N is the size of the network and q is a prime number. G is considered public information; any sensor can know the contents of G, and even adversaries are allowed to know G. Then, the base station creates a random $(t + 1)$ $(t + 1)$ symmetric matrix D over GF (q), and computes an N $(t + 1)$ matrix $A = (DG)^T$, where $(DG)^T$ is the transpose of DG. Matrix D needs to be kept secret, and should not be disclosed to adversaries or any sensor node, although one row of $(DG)^T$ will be disclosed to each sensor node. Because D is symmetric, it is easy to see:

$$\mathbf{AG} = (\mathbf{DG})^T\mathbf{G} = \mathbf{G}^T\mathbf{D}^T\mathbf{G} = \mathbf{G}^T\mathbf{DG} = (\mathbf{AG})^T:$$

This means that AG is a symmetric matrix. If we let $K = AG$, we know that $K_{ij} = K_{ji}$, where K_{ij} is the element in K located in the ith row and j^{th} column. We use K_{ij} (or K_{ji}) as the pairwise key between node i and node j. To carry out the above computation, nodes i and j should be able to compute K_{ij} and K_{ji}, respectively. This can be easily achieved using the following key pre-distribution scheme, for $k = 1 \ldots N$:

1. Store the kth row of matrix A at node k.
2. Store the kth column of matrix G at node k.

Therefore, when nodes i and j need to find the pairwise key between them, they first exchange their columns of G. Then, they can compute K_{ij} and K_{ji}, respectively, using their private rows of A. Because G is public information, its columns can be transmitted in plain text. It has been proved that the above scheme is t-secure if any $t + 1$ columns of G are linearly independent. This t-secure property guarantees that no nodes other than i and j can compute K_{ij} or K_{ji} if no more than t nodes are compromised.

Merkle proposed a digital signature system that is "precertified", generates signatures of 1–3 kilobytes, requires a few thousand applications of the underlying encryption per signature and only a few kilobytes of memory. If the underlying encryption takes 10 microseconds to encrypt a block, generating a signature might take 20 miliseconds. The signature method is called a "tree signature".

REFERENCES

Aslan, Y. E., Korpeoglu, I., & Ulusoy, O. (2012). A framework for use of wireless sensor network in forest fire detection and monitoring. *Computers, Environment and Urban Systems*, 36(6), 614–625.

Guevara, J., Barrero, F, Vargas, E, & Becerra, J. (2011, April). Environmental wireless sensor network for road traffic application. *IET Intelligent Transportation Systems*, 177–186.

Khan, R. A., Shah, S. A., Aleem, M. A., & Bhutto, Z. A. (2012, April). Wireless sensor networks: A solution for smart transportation. *Journal of Emerging Trends in Computing and Information Science, 3*.

Ramson, J. (2017). *Applications of wireless sensor networks – a survey.* 10.1109/ICIEEIMT.201 7.8116858.

Sadagopan, N., Krishnamachari, B, & Helmy, A. (2003, May). The ACQUIRE mechanism for efficient querying in sensor networks. In *Proceedings of the first IEEE international workshop on sensor network protocols and applications (SNPA)* (pp. 149– 155), Anchorage, AK.

Zu, X., & Li, D. (2009). CDMA based wireless water quality monitoring syste m for Intensive fish culture. In *International Conference on Communications and Mobile Computing* (pp. 380–385).

Security in Wireless Sensor Networks – Background

2

INTRODUCTION

Wireless sensor networks (WSNs) are special types of networks. WSNs consist of hundreds or even thousands of small devices, each with sensing, processing and communication capabilities to monitor the real-world environment. They are envisioned to play an important role in a wide variety of areas ranging from critical military surveillance applications to forest fire monitoring and building security monitoring in the near future (Akyildiz et al., 2002). In these networks, a large number of sensor nodes are deployed to monitor a vast field, where the operational conditions are most often harsh or even hostile. However, the nodes in WSNs have severe resource constraints due to their lack of processing power, limited memory and energy. Since these networks are usually deployed in remote places and left unattended, they should be equipped with security mechanisms to defend against attacks such as node capture, physical tampering, eavesdropping, denial of service (DoS), etc. Unfortunately, traditional security mechanisms with high overhead are not feasible for resource-constrained sensor nodes. Moreover, threats to sensor networks are different from threats to mobile ad hoc networks. A traffic model in WSNs is many to one, unlike in mobile ad hoc models where it is many to many. Sensor nodes are prone to failure due to harsh deployment environments. The number of nodes in WSNs can be several orders of magnitude higher than the nodes in the ad hoc network. Sensor nodes may not have global identification.

The sensor networks based on an inherently broadcast wireless media are vulnerable to a variety of attacks. Security is of prime importance in sensor networks because of the absence of central authority and random deployment of nodes in the network and nodes assume a large amount of trust among themselves during data aggregation and even detection. From a set of sensor nodes in a given locality, only one final aggregated message may be sent to the base station, so it is necessary to ensure that the communication links are secure from data exchange. A cryptographic solution based on symmetric or public key cryptography is not suitable for sensor networks due to the high processing requirements of the algorithm, so there is a need of special types of protocols for ensuring security in sensor networks. Though WSN holds promise for a large number of applications, the problem of securing these networks has been a roadblock to their large-scale adoption and deployment, and the research field of securing WSNs is still in its infancy. While WSNs are prone to the security threats of conventional networks, these networks are subject to additional threats; these additional threats result from the sensor nodes' intrinsic characteristics, mainly the limited communication bandwidth, computation power, memory and battery capacity and deployment environment. Traditional safety mechanisms for providing confidentiality, authentication and availability are not efficient in WSNs where network sensor nodes have limited communication bandwidth, CPU cycles, memory and battery capacity. These traditional safety mechanisms come at the cost of computation complexity of encryption algorithms, memory usage for storing security information and network bandwidth for key synchronization and certificate distribution and revocation. Moreover, wireless sensors networks are deployed in open, unattended and physically insecure environments where an adversary can easily capture nodes and subsequently use these nodes to attack the whole network. Building tamper-proof sensor nodes is not a viable solution since these nodes are deployed in large numbers, and adding to the building cost of these nodes is not a welcome solution. Finally, the radio communication between network sensor nodes makes these networks susceptible to all possible attacks on wireless communication environments.

The researchers in WSN security have proposed various security schemes which are optimized for these networks with resource constraints. A number of secure and efficient routing protocols (Deng et al., 2006; Karp & Kung, 2000; Papadimitratos & Haas, 2002; Tanachaiwiwat et al., 2003), secure data aggregation protocols (Estrin et al., 1999; Hu & Evans, 2003), etc. have been proposed by several researchers in WSN security. In addition to traditional security issues like secure routing and secure data aggregation, security mechanisms deployed in WSNs also should involve collaborations among the nodes due to the decentralized nature of the networks and absence of any infrastructure. In real-world WSNs, the nodes cannot be assumed to be trustworthy apriori. Researchers have therefore, focused on building a sensor trust model to solve the problems which are beyond the capabilities of traditional cryptographic mechanisms (Ganeriwal et al., 2008; Liang & Shi, 2005). Since in most cases the sensor nodes are unattended and physically insecure, vulnerability to physical attack is an important issue in WSNs. A number of propositions exist in literature for defense against physical attack on sensor nodes (Hartung et al., 2005; Hu & Evans, 2004). In this chapter, we present a comprehensive overview of various security issues in WSNs. First we outline the constraints of WSNs, security requirements in these networks and various possible attacks and the corresponding countermeasures. Then a holistic view of the security issues is presented. These issues are classified into six categories: cryptography, key management, secure routing, secure data aggregation, intrusion detection and trust management. The advantages and disadvantages of various security protocols are discussed, compared and evaluated. Some open research issues in each of these areas are also discussed. The remainder of the chapter is organized as follows. In Section 2, various constraints in WSNs are discussed. Section 3 presents the security requirements in WSNs. Section 4 discusses various attacks that can be launched on WSNs. Section 5 presents the numerous countermeasures for all possible attacks on WSNs. Finally, Section 6 concludes the chapter, highlighting some future directions of research in WSN security.

CONSTRAINTS IN SENSOR NETWORKS

All security approaches require a certain amount of resources for implementation, including data memory, code space and energy to power the sensor. However, currently these resources are very limited in a tiny wireless sensor.

These nodes have limited processing capability, very low storage capacity and constrained communication bandwidth. These constraints are due to limited energy and physical size of the sensor nodes. Due to these constraints, it is difficult to directly employ the conventional security mechanisms in WSNs. In order to optimize the conventional security algorithms for WSNs, it is necessary to be aware of the constraints of sensor nodes (Carman et al., 2000). Some of the major constraints of a WSN are discussed below.

Unreliable Communication

Unreliable communication is another serious threat to sensor security. Normally the packet-based routing of sensor networks is based on connectionless protocols and thus inherently unreliable. Packets may get damaged due to channel errors or may get dropped at highly congested nodes. Furthermore, the unreliable wireless communication channel may also lead to damaged or corrupted packets. Higher error rate also mandates robust error handling schemes to be implemented leading to higher overhead. In certain situation even if the channel is reliable, the communication may not be so. This is due to the broadcast nature of wireless communication, as the packets may collide in transit and may need retransmission (Akyildiz et al., 2002).

Node Constraints

A sensor is a tiny device with only a small amount of memory and storage space for the code. In order to build an effective security mechanism, it is necessary to limit the code size of the security algorithm. For example, one common sensor type (TelosB) has a

16-bit, 8 MHz RISC CPU with only 10K RAM, 48K program memory, and 1024K flash storage (Liang & Shi, 2008). With such a limitation, the software built for the sensor must also be quite small. The total code space of TinyOS, the de-facto standard operating system for wireless sensors, is approximately 4K (Slijepcevic et al., 2002), and the core scheduler occupies only 178 bytes. Therefore, the code size for the all security-related code must also be small. The capabilities and constraints of sensor node hardware will influence the type of security mechanisms that can be hosted on a sensor node platform.

Battery Power/Energy

Energy is the biggest constraint to wireless sensor capabilities. We assume that once sensor nodes are deployed in a sensor network, they cannot be easily replaced (high operating cost) or recharged (high cost of sensors). Therefore, the battery charge taken with them to the field must be conserved to extend the life of the individual sensor node and the entire sensor network. When implementing a cryptographic function or protocol within a sensor node, the energy impact of the added security code must be considered. When adding security to a sensor node, we are interested in the impact that security has on the life span of a sensor (i.e., its battery life). The extra power consumed by sensor nodes due to security is related to the processing required for security functions (e.g., encryption, decryption, signing data, verifying signatures), the energy required to transmit the security related data or overhead (e.g., initialization vectors needed for encryption/decryption) and the energy required to store security parameters in a secure manner (e.g., cryptographic key storage). Energy is perhaps the greatest constraint to sensor node capabilities. We assume that once sensor nodes are deployed in a sensor network, they cannot be recharged. Therefore, the battery charge taken with them to the field must be conserved to extend the life of the individual sensor node and the entire sensor network. Various mechanisms within the network architecture, including the sensor node hardware, take this limitation into account. When considering implementing a cryptographic function or protocol within a sensor node, the impact on the sensor node's available energy must be considered. When applying security within a sensor node, we are interested in the impact that security has on the life span of a sensor (i.e., its battery life). The extra power consumed by sensor nodes due to security is related to the processing required for security functions (e.g., encryption, decryption, signing data, verifying signatures), the energy required to transmit the security related data or overhead (e.g., initialization vectors needed for encryption/decryption) and the energy required to store security parameters in a secure manner (e.g., cryptographic key storage). Since the amount of additional energy consumed for protecting each message is relatively small, the greatest consumer of energy in the security realm is key establishment.

Recharge Ability

We assume that once sensor nodes are deployed in a sensor network, they cannot be recharged. Therefore, the battery charge taken with them to the field must be conserved to extend the life of the individual sensor node and the network. Security functions must minimize energy consumption in order to extend sensor network life.

Sleep Patterns

In order to conserve energy, we assume that sensor nodes spend a majority of their operational time in low-power sleep modes and only awake when required to processes an event (e.g., a tank detected). For this reason, a node's availability within the sensor network may be limited. This includes its availability to receive cryptographic key updates. In mobile computing environments, PDA devices like the Palm Pilot have low-power modes that are used to conserve energy. The result of these sleep patterns is potential unavailability of a node to receive data. In particular, we are concerned about receiving security-related commands (e.g., zeroize) and key material. Failure to maintain or update to the correct keys could isolate a sensor node from communications with the rest of the network.

Transmission Range

The communications range of sensor nodes is limited in order to conserve energy. Sensor nodes from Sensoria and Rockwell Collins have variable transmission power from 10 mW to 100 mW, allowing the nodes to restrict their transmission range as necessary. Reducing the transmission power saves sensor node energy and provides a lower probability of detection. The actual range achieved from a given transmission signal strength is dependent on various environmental factors. We assume that locally sensor nodes have a transmission range of approximately 100 meters. Long-haul communications capabilities of greater than 1 km are available gateway nodes. In order to support ad hoc networking, we assume that the assignment of gateway nodes is determined at deployment and can be supported by any node in the network. Gateway nodes may contact relay points that transmit the signal even farther (e.g., over a satellite link).

Memory Limitations

A sensor is a tiny device with only a small amount of memory and storage space. Sensor processors require different types of memory to perform various processing functions. Memory is a sensor node that usually includes flash memory and RAM. Memory ROM or EPROM is needed for storing the general purpose programming such as an embedded operation system, security functions and basic networking capability. RAM is needed for storing application programs, sensor data and intermediate computations. Programmable memory such as EEPROM and FLASH are needed for storing downloaded application code and data between sleep periods.

In the SmartDust project, for example, TinyOS consumes about 4K bytes of instructions, leaving only 4,500 bytes for running security algorithms and applications (Hill et al., 2000). A common sensor type-TelosB- has a 16-bit, 8 MHz RISC CPU with only 10K RAM, 48K program memory and 1024K flash storage. The current security algorithms are, therefore, infeasible in these sensors (Perrig et al., 2002).

Unattended Operations

Depending on the mission of sensor network, the sensor nodes may be unattended for long periods of time. The likelihood that a sensor encounters a physical attack in such an environment is, therefore, very high. Remote management of a WSN makes it virtually impossible to detect physical tampering. The amount of time that a sensor is left unattended increases the likelihood that an adversary has compromised its key material. This makes security in WSNs a particularly difficult task.

Network Constraints

This section discusses constraints specific to distributed sensor networking. Distributed sensor networks have unique limitations not encountered in more typical wired LAN environments.

Ad Hoc Networking

Sensor networks are ad hoc in nature, with the composition of the network determined at the time of deployment. During the sensor node mission, the composition of the network and its routing topology may change. This constraint limits the ability to preconfigure sensor nodes for specific purposes. Sensor nodes should be able to support various roles in the network to ensure the reliability of the network.

Limited Preconfiguration

The nature of ad hoc networking requires limited preconfiguration in order to support a flexible and easily deployable network. This constraint limits the amount and type of cryptographic material that should be necessary to deploy a secure sensor network.

Data Rate/Packet Size

Both the data rate and packet size affect the overall sensor node energy consumption. We assume that packet sizes within the sensor network are relatively small, potentially as small as 30 bytes with a header. We also assume that the data rates are relatively low, less than 1 kbit/second. The packet size determines the percentage of overhead in a given message. The message header can be a larger percentage of message overhead if the message spans packets. Cryptographic services should adhere to packet size restrictions in order to limit the amount of overhead and thus reduce the transmission energy penalty associated with transmitting the extra bits. The low data rate must also be considered when implementing cryptographic services in order to minimize latency throughout the network.

Channel Error Rate

We assume that low-layer communications protocols will offer error detection and correction services. Errors that propagate into the layers where confidentiality, integrity or authentication services are applied will affect their verification and authentication processes preventing any application data from being exchanged. In particular, in some modes cryptographic modes of encryption and decryption, the effects of errors vary depending on the use of feedback or chaining with previous results (e.g., CipherFeedback (CFB) mode).

Intermittent Connectivity

Intermittent connectivity within the sensor network may arise from channel fading and the sleep patterns of nodes. We assume that channel fading may be time-dependent and a function of the weather and other battlefield conditions. The sleep patterns of nodes may change over time due to available power and event detection. The limited availability of sensor nodes may influence the mechanisms used to reliably distribute security critical messages including cryptographic keying messages and other remote keying messages (e.g., zeroize, CRLs). Because it is a requirement to reliably distribute these types of messages, the reliability mechanisms most overcome intermittent connectivity limitations. Otherwise, cryptographic synchronization issues may result and possibly isolate sensor nodes from the network.

Unreliable Communications

We assume that the packet-based routing of the sensor network is connectionless and thus inherently unreliable. Packets may get damaged due to channel errors or dropped at highly congested nodes. The result is lost or missing packets. Higher network protocols must be introduced to add reliability. Connection-oriented transport protocols such as TCP may be added. Reliability is required for the distribution of key material and security critical commands.

Higher Latency in Communication

In a WSN, multi-hop routing, network congestion and processing in the intermediate nodes may lead to higher latency in packet transmission. This makes synchronization very difficult to achieve. The synchronization issues may sometimes be very critical in security as some security mechanisms may rely on critical event reports and cryptographic key distribution (Stankovic et al., 2003).

Frequent Routing Changes

As the available energy decreases in key nodes throughout the network, the need to change the routing topology to balance the energy usage within the network becomes important. Frequent routing changes can mean that the intermediate nodes processing data for and end-to-end session can change. Also, since many security services instead will be provided on a hop-by-hop basis, cryptographic key establishment will occur with local neighbors in the routing topology. If the routing changes, the set of local neighbors may change and thus cryptographic key establishment may need to occur again.

Unknown Recipients

When a packet is routed through the sensor network, the packet's source may not know the path the packet takes to its final destination if the packet traverses multiple hops. For this reason, a node may assume that once the packet is transmitted, the intermediary nodes are unknown and may be untrustworthy. For this reason, security services may be applied at either an end-to-end or on a hop-by-hop basis, depending on the sensitivity and type of data exchanged.

Physical Limitation

Sensor networks deployment nature in public and hostile environments in many applications makes them highly vulnerable to capture and vandalism. Physical security of sensor nodes with tamper-proof material increases the node cost.

CHARACTERISTICS OF SENSOR NETWORKS

The characteristics of a good WSN include power efficiency, scalability, responsiveness, reliability and mobility, compact size, physical security, memory space and bandwidth; these characteristics make them an attractive choice for many applications, and also present the researchers with distinct security challenges.

Power Efficiency

Sensors in WSN contain non-renewable power resources, thus causing an energy-starved wireless network. Sensors cannot be recharged because of the volume and distribution of the network, which makes recharging of the nodes a laborious and expensive task. Power limitations in a WSN are considered the major constraint to the performance of the network. As all the nodes do local processing, they are always in need of power. Thus, the inclusion of security features like encryption, decryption, authentication, etc. comes at the price of a decrease in the overall performance of the nodes because of the energy consumed during these cryptographic algorithms and schemes. Security is vital for a WSN, so there is always some compromise to make between the secure communication and allocation of energy resources for implementing cryptographic schemes.

Scalability

The ability for a network to grow in terms of the number of nodes attached to the WSN without causing excessive overhead can be termed its scalability. There is a higher chance of communication links being broken as the network size increases.

Responsiveness

The ability of the network to quickly adapt itself to change in the topology is considered its responsiveness. There are, however, downfalls to a highly responsive network; compromises need to be made. The latency of packet delivery in a dynamic environment as well as scalability will decrease in a highly responsive network.

Reliability

Like all other wireless communications, channels in the WSN are subject to unpredictable environmental conditions, state of channels, interference and many other factors that usually deteriorate the quality of service of the wireless links and induce errors in the information being transmitted. Error correcting codes, MAC and cyclic redundancy check (CRC) are sometimes used to cope with these problems. They are widely being used in wireless links to ensure better service at the expense of extra bits added to the original messages.

Mobility

It is the network's ability to handle mobile nodes and changeable data paths. The way the design goes it is necessary for WSN to be highly responsive in order for it to deal with mobility. As a result, it becomes harder to design a large scale as well as mobile WSN.

Compact Size

As discussed earlier, a sensor network may contain hundreds or probably thousands of autonomous nodes. For such a huge network, size does matter. Sensors are kept small, which also limits the components on the main chipboard of the sensor and only the most crucial parts are installed on it. Small sizes of sensors may be considered a positive attribute, as sensors can be deployed so that they are not visible.

TABLE 2.1 Sensor node and its required memory space

SENSOR NODE	MICROCONTROLLER	PROGRAM AND DATA MEMORY	EXTERNAL MEMORY
IMote 2.0	Marvell PXA271	32 MB SRAM	32 MB Flash
Mica 2	ATMEGA 128L	4k RAM	128k Flash
TelosB	TI MSP430	10k RAM	48k Flash
Ubimote2	TI's MSP430F2618	8k RAM	116k Flash

Physical Security

Sensors usually get information about the environment and perform their designated operations. They have to interact with exposed surroundings, which poses hazards to the physical protection of the sensors.

Memory Space

Sensors have small memory space, which accounts for their low cost and power consumption. Memory is a precious asset for any sensor; thus, keeping the size of the security algorithm source code small. Sizes of the keys that need to be stored are also kept at a minimum length because of scarcity of memory storage. Table 2.1 lists some of known sensor nodes and their memory spaces.

Bandwidth

A WSN is a low-bandwidth network compared to other wireless networks; the quantity of data transmitted and received by the nodes is very low. This helps the nodes in saving the crucial power for other functions. As an estimate, each bit transmitted consumes as much power as executing 800–1,000 instructions. This is one of the reasons why cryptographic schemes with large key sizes (i.e., public key cryptography) are not preferred for these sensor networks.

SECURITY GOALS FOR SENSOR NETWORKS

A WSN is composed of sensors. Due to the attributes of being a network and utilizing wireless communications, the security demands for a WSN are unique. Security requirements in a WSN to ensure trustworthy and secure connections and communications are a combination of the specifications for a computer network and wireless communication security. A WSN has its own distinct features, as discussed in

Section 3, which make these networks unique. Their anomalous character is due to their large volume, pattern of distribution and resource restrictions. All of these aspects give rise to some particular security necessities. We will discuss some basic security specifications for a WSN.

Simplicity in a WSN with resource-constrained nodes makes them extremely vulnerable to a variety of attacks. Attackers can eavesdrop on our radio transmissions, inject bits in the channel, replay previously heard packets and many more. In order to secure a WSN, the network needs to support all the security properties, mainly confidentiality, integrity, authenticity and availability. Attackers may deploy a few malicious nodes with similar hardware capabilities as the legitimate nodes that might collude to attack the system cooperatively. The attacker may come upon these malicious nodes by purchasing them separately, or by "turning" a few legitimate nodes by capturing them and physically overwriting their memory. Also, in some cases, colluding nodes might have high-quality communications links available for coordinating their attack. Sensor nodes may not be tamper resistant and if an adversary compromises a node, user can extract all key material, data and code stored on that node. While tamper resistance might be a viable defense for physical node compromise for some networks, we do not see it as a general-purpose solution. Extremely effective tamper resistance tends to add significant per-unit cost, and sensor nodes are intended to be very inexpensive (Boyle & Newe, 2008; Sharma, 2009).

These networks are kept inexpensive; thus, introducing many constraints in the performance parameters. Low-cost sensors incorporate shortcomings in their storage capacity, power requirements and processing speed. This poses a unique dilemma for researchers as they have to design efficient and distinct information security schemes that work seamlessly with the resource-constrained sensor networks.

Sensors in the network are mostly exposed to an open environment as they have to interact with either other sensors or human beings. Physical security of these sensors is always vulnerable and thus poses an unprecedented threat to the overall security of the network. Advances in power analysis and time-based attacks enable the malicious entities to perform various hazardous activities.

Wireless channels are still considered unreliable and the same is the case with WSNs, which may contain a very large number of nodes and sinks, thus giving rise to concerns about the validity of the communications in the network. Trust models for the nodes have to be developed to make sure that all the nodes taking part in the communications are trustworthy.

All these unique features of WSNs changes the way we look at their security.

Confidentiality

Data is communicated between the sender and the recipient, sometimes being routed through many nodes. This data may also be kept in memory for further processing. This data can be sensitive enough to be known only by the sender and the recipient. Sometimes, the adversary can access this information by eavesdropping between wireless links, gaining admission to the storage or by other attacks. To keep the privacy of significant data transmitted among sensor nodes, confidentiality is a fundamental security service. Data confidentiality means that the data can only be accessed, and thus utilized, by only those entities that are authorized for this purpose.

If any data is lost by negligence and weak security measures, it can lead to identity thefts, loss in business, privacy breaching and many other malicious activities. This makes data or message confidentiality the most important feature of any security protocol.

In a WSN, data confidentiality can be observed by making sure that

1. A sensor network should not leak any data to other networks in vicinity, thus retaining the message completely within the network.
2. Data is sometimes routed through many nodes before reaching the destination node. This causes a rise in need for secure communication channels between different nodes and also between nodes and base stations.
3. Encryption is one of the most commonly used procedures to provide confidentiality of data. Critical information such as keys and user identities should be encrypted before transmission. Sensitive information can be characterized from the kind and type of protocol being used, i.e., symmetric or asymmetric cryptography, mutual authentication, identity or nonce-based encryption.
4. Steps can also be taken towards encrypting the sensitive data before storing them in memory. This is particularly important if the nodes are exposed to user interaction, or in military applications.

Integrity

Provision of data confidentiality stops the leakage of data, but it is not helpful against insertion of data in the original message by adversary. Integrity of data needs to be assured in sensor networks, which solidifies that the received data has not been altered or tampered with and that new data has not been added to the original contents of the packet. Environmental conditions and the channel's quality of service can also change the primitive message.

Data integrity can be provided by Message Authentication Code (MAC). For this purpose, both the sender and receiver share a secret key. The sender computes the MAC using this key and contents of message, and transmits the message along with the MAC to the receiver. The recipient recalculates the MAC by using the shared secret key and message. Absence of irregularity in composition of a calculated MAC establishes integrity in the received message.

Authentication

Authentication is used in sensor networks to block or restrict the activities of the unauthorized nodes. Any disapproved agent can inject redundant information, or tamper with the default packets carrying information. It is particularly important in case of decision making chunks of information. Nodes receiving the packets must make sure that the originator of packets is an accredited source. Nodes taking part in the communication must be capable of recognizing and rejecting the information from illegitimate nodes. In the case of two-party communication, data authentication can be achieved through a purely symmetric mechanism: the sender and the receiver share a secret key to compute the MAC of all communicated data.

Data Freshness

Data freshness means that the data is recent and any old data has not been replayed. Data freshness criteria are a must in case of shared-key cryptography where the key needs to be refreshed over a period of time. An attacker may replay an old message to compromise the key.

Some of the messages are critical enough that extra precautions need to be taken to ensure their correction. Confidentiality and authentication may not be useful when any old message is replayed by any attacker. Data freshness implies that the received messages are recent, and previous messages are not being replayed. The importance of data freshness becomes evident in networks using shared-key operations. During the time taken for transmission of a shared key in a WSN, a replay attack can be carried out by an adversary.

Data freshness is categorized into two types based on the message ordering: weak and strong freshness. Weak freshness provides only partial message ordering but gives no information related to the delay and latency of the message. Strong freshness, on the other hand, gives complete request-response order and the delay estimation. Sensor measurements require weak freshness, while strong freshness is useful for time synchronization within the network.

To accommodate data freshness, nonce, which is a randomly generated number or a time-dependent counter, can be appended to the data. Messages with previous nonce and old counter numbers are rejected. This guarantees acceptance of only recent data, and thus the freshness in data is achieved.

Availability

Introduction of a security scheme in a WSN comes at the expense of computational storage and energy costs. Security features in the network may be considered as extra feature by some because of the restrictions it can impose on the availability of the data. The insertion of security can cause earlier depletion of energy and storage resources, causing unavailability of data. Similarly, if security of any one node (especially in central point network management) is compromised or any DoS attack is launched, data becomes inaccessible.

Availability of data becomes an important security requirement because of the mentioned arguments. The security protocol should consume less energy and storage, which can be achieved by the reuse of code and making sure that there is a minimum increase in communication due to the functioning of security protocols.

Processing within the networking and en-route filtering can be used to subsidize the effects of malicious attacks and other issues that may arise because of an increase in communication due to utilization of security scheme. There is also a need to avoid a central management scheme in sensor networks as they can affect the availability of data due to single point failures. These steps will also make the network robust against attacks.

Self-Organization

As mentioned in previous sections, one of the characteristics of a WSN is their composition and distribution. A typical WSN may have hundreds of nodes performing different operations, installed at various locations. Ad hoc networks are also sensor networks, with the same flexibility and extensibility. These otherwise attractive properties of a WSN pose a serious threat to the overall security situation of the network, raising the importance of a self-organized and robust structure of network.

For using a public key cryptography-based scheme, an efficient design is needed that takes into account all the situations for sharing the key and is capable of trust management among different nodes. Keys can be redistributed between the nodes and base stations to provide key management. Schemes can use symmetric cryptography that apply key pre-distribution methods.

Secure Localization

A WSN makes use of geographical-based information for identification of nodes, or for accessing whether the sensors belong to the network or not. Some attacks work by analyzing the location of the nodes. An adversary may probe the headers of the packets and protocol layer data for this purpose. This makes the secure localization an important feature that must be catered to during our implementation of a security protocol.

Time Synchronization

Most sensor network applications rely on some form of time synchronization. In order to conserve power, an individual sensor's radio may be turned off for periods of time. Furthermore, sensors may wish to compute the end-to-end delay of a packet as it travels between two pair-wise sensors. A more collaborative sensor network may require group synchronization for tracking applications, etc.

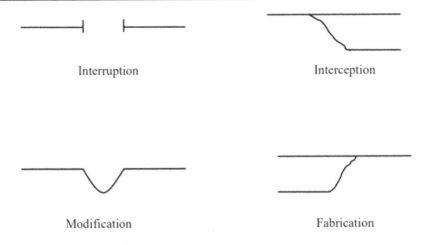

Interruption   Interception

Modification   Fabrication

FIGURE 2.1   Four classes of system security threats classified by Pfleeger.

SECURITY CLASSES

Pfleeger (2009) has identified four classes of security in computing systems. We integrate these four threat classes in sensor networks. In computing systems, the major assets are hardware, software and data. While in sensor networks, our goal is to protect the network itself, the nodes and communication among the sensor nodes. The four classes of threats that exploit the vulnerability of our security goals are illustrated in Figure 2.1.

In an interruption, a communication link in sensor networks becomes lost or unavailable. Examples of this sort of threat are node capture, message corruption, addition of malicious code, etc. An interception means a sensor network has been compromised by an adversary where the attacker gains unauthorized access to sensor node or data in it. An example of this type of attack is node capture attacks. Modification means the unauthorized party not only accesses the data but tampers with it; for example, modifying the data packets being transmitted, causing a DoS attack such as flooding the network with bogus data. In fabrication, an adversary injects false data and compromises the trustworthiness of information.

ATTACKS ON SENSOR NETWORKS

WSNs are vulnerable to security attacks due to the broadcast nature of the transmission medium. Furthermore, WSNs have an additional vulnerability because nodes are often

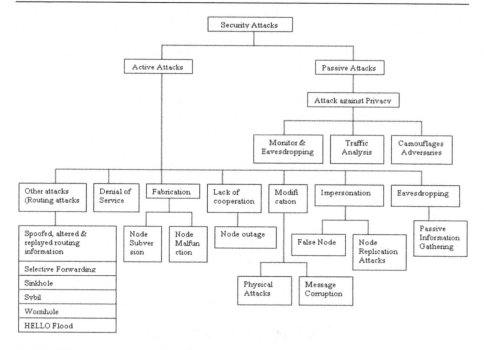

FIGURE 2.2   Classification of security attacks under general categories.

placed in a hostile or dangerous environment where they are not physically protected. Basically, attacks are classified as active attacks and passive attacks. Figure 2.2 shows the classification of attacks under general categories and Figure 2.3 shows the attack classification on a WSN.

Passive Information Gathering

The monitoring and listening of the communication channel by unauthorized attackers is known as a passive attack. The attacks against privacy are passive in nature.

Attacks Against Privacy

The main privacy problem is not that sensor networks enable the collection of information. In fact, much information from sensor networks could probably be collected through direct site surveillance. Rather, sensor networks intensify the privacy problem because they make large volumes of information easily available through remote access. Hence, adversaries need not be physically present to maintain surveillance. They can gather information at low risk in an anonymous manner.

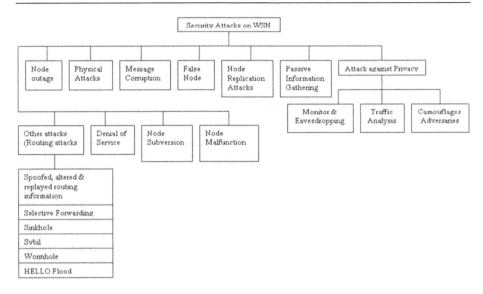

FIGURE 2.3 Classification of security attacks on a WSN.

Some of the more common passive information-gathering attacks (Undercoffer et al., 2002) against sensor privacy are discussed.

Monitor and Eavesdropping

This is the most common attack to privacy. By snooping the data, the adversary could easily discover the communication contents. When the traffic conveys the control information about the sensor network configuration, which contains potentially more detailed information than accessible through the location server, the eavesdropping can act effectively against the privacy protection.

Traffic Analysis

Even when the messages transferred are encrypted, it still leaves a high possibility analysis of the communication patterns. Sensor activities can potentially reveal enough information to enable an adversary to cause malicious harm to the sensor network.

Camouflage Adversaries

One can insert their node or compromise the nodes to hide in the sensor network. After that, these nodes can copy as a normal node to attract the packets, then misroute the packets, conducting the privacy analysis.

Active Attacks

The unauthorized attackers monitor, listen to and modify the data stream in the communication channel, known as an active attack. The following attacks are active in nature:

1. Routing Attacks in Sensor Networks
2. DoS Attacks
3. Node Subversion
4. Node Malfunction
5. Node Outage
6. Physical Attacks
7. False Node
8. Node Replication Attacks

Routing Attacks

The attacks which act on the network layer are called routing attacks. The following are the attacks that happen while routing the messages.

Spoofed, Altered and Replayed Routing Information
An unprotected ad hoc routing is vulnerable to these types of attacks, as every node acts as a router, and can therefore directly affect routing information.

- Create routing loops
- Extend or shorten service routes
- Generate false error messages
- Increase end-to-end latency (Karlof & Wagner, 2003)

Selective Forwarding
A malicious node can selectively drop only certain packets; especially effective if combined with an attack that gathers traffic via the node. In sensor networks, it is assumed that nodes faithfully forward received messages, but some compromised nodes might refuse to forward packets. However, neighbors might start using another route (Karlof & Wagner, 2003).

Sinkhole Attack
Attracting traffic to a specific node is called a sinkhole attack. In this attack, the adversary's goal is to attract nearly all the traffic from a particular area through a compromised node. A sinkhole attack typically works by making a compromised node look especially attractive to surrounding nodes (Karlof & Wagner, 2003).

Sybil Attacks
A single node duplicates itself and is presented in multiple locations. The Sybil attack targets fault-tolerant schemes such as distributed storage, multipath routing and topology maintenance. In a Sybil attack, a single node presents multiple identities to

other nodes in the network. Authentication and encryption techniques can prevent an outsider to launch a Sybil attack on the sensor network (Karlof & Wagner, 2003).

Wormhole Attacks
In the wormhole attack, an attacker records packets (or bits) at one location in the network, tunnels them to another location and retransmits them into the network (Karlof & Wagner, 2003).

HELLO Flood Attacks
An attacker sends or replays a routing protocol's HELLO packet from one node to another with more energy. This attack uses HELLO packets as a weapon to convince the sensors in WSN. In this type of attack, an attacker with a high radio transmission range and processing power sends HELLO packets to a number of sensor nodes that are isolated in a large area within a WSN. The sensors are thus influenced that the adversary is their neighbor. As a result, while sending the information to the base station, the victim nodes try to go through the attacker as they know that it is their neighbor and are ultimately spoofed by the attacker (Karlof & Wagner, 2003).

Denial of Service
DoS is produced by the unintentional failure of nodes or malicious action. A DoS attack is meant not only for the adversary's attempt to subvert, disrupt or destroy a network, but also for any event that diminishes a network's capability to provide a service. In WSNs, several types of DoS attacks in different layers might be performed. At the physical layer, the DoS attacks could be jamming and tampering; at the link layer, collision, exhaustion and unfairness; at the network layer, neglect and greed, homing, misdirection, black holes; and at the transport layer, this attack could be performed by malicious flooding and de-synchronization. The mechanisms to prevent DoS attacks include payment for network resources, pushback, strong authentication and identification of traffic (Pathan et al., 2006).

Node Subversion

The capture of a node may reveal its information, including disclosure of keys, and thus compromise the whole sensor network. A particular sensor might be captured and information (key) stored on it might be obtained by an adversary (Pathan et al., 2006).

Node Malfunction

A malfunctioning node will generate inaccurate data that could expose the integrity of the sensor network, especially if it is a data-aggregating node such as a cluster leader (Pathan et al., 2006).

Node Outage

Node outage is the situation that occurs when a node stops its function. In the case where a cluster leader stops functioning, the sensor network protocols should be robust enough to mitigate the effects of node outages by providing an alternate route (Pathan et al., 2006).

Physical Attacks

Sensor networks typically operate in hostile outdoor environments. In such environments, the small form factor of the sensors, coupled with the unattended and distributed nature of their deployment, make them highly susceptible to physical attacks, i.e., threats due to physical node destructions. Unlike many other attacks mentioned previously, physical attacks destroy sensors permanently, so the losses are irreversible. For instance, attackers can extract cryptographic secrets, tamper with the associated circuitry, modify programming in the sensors or replace them with malicious sensors under the control of the attacker.

False Node

A false node involves the addition of a node by an adversary and causes the injection of malicious data. An intruder might add a node to the system that feeds false data or prevents the passage of true data. Insertion of a malicious node is one of the most dangerous attacks that can occur. Malicious code injected in the network could spread to all nodes, potentially destroying the whole network, or even worse, taking over the network on behalf of an adversary (Zia & Zomaya, 2006).

Node Replication Attacks

Conceptually, a node replication attack is quite simple; an attacker seeks to add a node to an existing sensor network by copying the node ID of an existing sensor node. A node replicated in this approach can severely disrupt a sensor network's performance. Packets can be corrupted or even misrouted. This can result in a disconnected network, false sensor readings, etc. If an attacker can gain physical access to the entire network he/she can copy cryptographic keys to the replicated sensor nodes. By inserting the replicated nodes at specific network points, the attacker could easily manipulate a specific segment of the network, perhaps by disconnecting it altogether (Perrig et al., 2004).

LAYERING-BASED SECURITY APPROACH

Layering-based security is a network security approach that uses several components to protect operations with multiple levels of security measure. The purpose of a layering-based security approach is to make sure that every individual defense component has a backup to counter any flaws or gaps in other defenses of security.

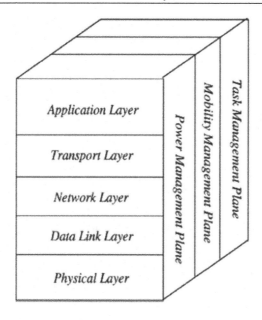

FIGURE 2.4   A simplified protocol stack.

Individual layers in a multi-layered security approach focus on a specific area where malware could attack. These layers work together to tighten security and have a better chance of stopping intruders from breaching networks than using a single security solution. A simplified protocol stack for a WSN is summarized in Figure 2.4.

Physical Layer

The physical layer emphasizes the transmission media between sending and receiving nodes, the data rate, signal strength and frequency types. Ideally, FHSS (frequency hopping spread spectrum) is used in sensor networks.

Jamming is a common attack on the physical layer of a wireless network. Jamming provides a fixed connection with the radio frequency being used by the nodes of the network. Jamming can interrupt the network impressive if a single frequency is used throughout the network. In this way, jamming can cause excessive energy consumption at a node by injecting impertinent packets. The receivers' nodes will as well consume energy by getting those packets. The physical layer also suffers from another attack, which is tampering. In this attack, nodes are vulnerable to tampering or physical harm. Table 2.2 describes physical layer threats and countermeasures in a WSN (Modares et al., 2011).

TABLE 2.2   Physical layer threats and countermeasures in a WSN

PHYSICAL LAYER THREATS	COUNTERMEASURES
Interference	Channel hopping and blacklisting
Jamming	Channel hopping and blacklisting
Sybil	Physical protection of devices
Tampering	Protection and changing of key

Data Link Layer

A data link layer does the error detection and correction and encoding of data. The link layer is vulnerable to jamming and DoS attacks. TinySec (Singla & Sachdeva, 2013) has introduced link layer encryption that depends on a key management scheme. However, an attacker having better energy efficiency can still rage an attack. Protocols like LMAC have better anti-jamming properties that are a viable countermeasure at this layer. Table 2.3 describes data link layer threats and countermeasures in a WSN.

Network Layer

A network layer is responsible for routing messages from node to node, node to cluster leader, cluster leaders to cluster leaders, cluster leaders to the base station and vice versa. Routing protocols in sensor networks are of two types:

1. ID-based protocols, in which packets are routed to the destination based on the IDs specified in the packets.
2. Data-centric protocols (Li et al., 2010), in which packets contain attributes that specify the type of data being provided.

Law and Havinga (2005) have described Karlof and Wagner's (2003) routing attacks in sensor networks as follows:

- Packets are dropped completely, or selectively.
- The network is flooded with global broadcasts.
- Some sensor nodes in the network are misguided into believing that nodes are either multiple hops away or that do not exist at all in the neighbors.
- A significant proportion of the traffic is tunneled from one place in the network to another distant place of the network, depriving other parts of the network that under normal circumstances would have received the traffic themselves.
- Sometimes traffic is lured to a particular node or a small group of nodes, depriving other parts of the network that normally would have received the traffic themselves.
- Security of routing protocols depends on the location of nodes and the encryption techniques.

Table 2.4 describes network layer threats and countermeasures in a WSN.

TABLE 2.3   Data link layer threats and countermeasures in a WSN

DATA LINK LAYER THREATS	COUNTERMEASURE
Collision	CRC and time diversity
Exhaustion	Protection of network ID and other information that is required to join device
Spoofing	Use different path for re-sending the message
Sybil	Regularly changing of key
De-synchronization	Using different neighbors for time synchronization
Traffic analysis	Sending dummy packet in quiet hours and regular monitoring WSN network
Eavesdropping	Key protects DLPDU from eavesdropper

TABLE 2.4   Network layer threats and countermeasures in a WSN

NETWORK LAYER THREAT	COUNTERMEASURE
Eavesdropping	Session keys protect NPDU from eavesdropper.
DoS	Protection of network-specific data link network ID, etc. Physical protection and inspection of network.
Selective Forwarding	Regular network monitoring using source routing.
Sybil	Resetting of device and changing of session keys.
Traffic Analysis	Sending of dummy packet in quiet hours and regular monitoring WSN network.
Wormhole	Physical monitoring of field devices and regular monitoring of network using source routing. Monitoring system may use packet leach techniques.

Transport Layer

The transport layer is not a safe layer from attack, as in the case of flooding. Flooding can be something as simple as sending many connection requests to a vulnerable node (Modares et al., 2011). In this case, the sender must be allocated to manage the connection request. Thus, node resources will be exhausted, rendering the node useless.

APPLICATION LAYER

Data is collected and managed at the application layer; therefore, it is important to ensure the reliability of data. Wagner (2004) has presented a resilient aggregation scheme, which is applicable to a cluster-based network where a cluster leader acts as an aggregator in sensor networks. However, this technique is applicable if the aggregating node is in the range with all the source nodes and there is no intervening aggregator between the aggregator and source nodes. In a hierarchical clustering approach, the communication channel between the aggregator and the base station has potentially limited bandwidth because the cluster leader as an aggregator itself is a sensor node (Law & Havinga, 2005; Wagner, 2004). To prove the validity of the aggregation, cluster leaders use the cryptographic techniques to ensure data reliability.

CONCLUSION

This chapter presents a detailed study on the security of a WSN. Firstly, this chapter covers the constraints of WSNs, security requirements in these networks and various possible attacks and the corresponding countermeasures. Then a holistic view of the security issues is presented. After this, security in sensor networks is discussed and its related issues. Security is an important requirement and is complicated enough to be set up in a different field of a WSN. Also, attacks and layered-based attacks on WSNs and their possible countermeasures were discussed. Many security issues and their countermeasures in WSNs remain open.

REFERENCES

Akyildiz, I. F., Su, W., Sankarasubramaniam, Y., & Cayirci, E. (2002). A survey on sensor networks. *IEEE Communications Magazine*, *40*(8), 102–114.

Boyle, D., & Newe, T. (2008). Securing wireless sensor networks: Security architectures. *Journal of Networks*, *3*(1), 65–77.

Carman, D. W., Kruus, P. S., & Matt, B. J. (2000). Constraints and approaches for distributed sensor network security (final). *DARPA Project Report,(Cryptographic Technologies Group, Trusted Information System, NAI Labs)*, *1*(1), 1–39.

Deng, J., Han, R., & Mishra, S. (2006). INSENS: Intrusion-tolerant routing for wireless sensor networks. *Computer Communications*, *29*(2), 216–230.

Estrin, D., Govindan, R., Heidemann, J., & Kumar, S. (1999). Next century challenges: Scalable coordination in sensor networks. In *Proceedings of the 5th Annual ACM/IEEE International Conference on Mobile Computing and Networking* (pp. 263–270).

Ganeriwal, S., Balzano, L. K., & Srivastava, M. B. (2008). Reputation-based framework for high integrity sensor networks. *ACM Transactions on Sensor Networks (TOSN)*, *4*(3), 1–37.

Hartung, C., Balasalle, J., & Han, R. (2005). *Node compromise in sensor networks: The need for secure systems*. Department of Computer Science University of Colorado at Boulder.

Hill, J., Szewczyk, R., Woo, A., Hollar, S., Culler, D., & Pister, K. (2000). System architecture directions for networked sensors. *ACM Sigplan Notices*, *35*(11), 93–104.

Hu, L., & Evans, D. (2003). Secure aggregation for wireless networks. In *2003 Symposium on Applications and the Internet Workshops, 2003. Proceedings* (pp. 384–391).

Hu, L., & Evans, D. (2004). Using Directional Antennas to Prevent Wormhole Attacks. *NDSS*, *4*, 241–245.

Karlof, C., & Wagner, D. (2003). Secure routing in wireless sensor networks: Attacks and countermeasures. *Ad Hoc Networks, 1*(2–3), 293–315.

Karp, B., & Kung, H.-T. (2000). GPSR: Greedy perimeter stateless routing for wireless networks. In *Proceedings of the 6th Annual International Conference on Mobile Computing and Networking* (pp. 243–254).

Law, Y. W., & Havinga, P. J. M. (2005). How to secure a wireless sensor network. In *2005 International Conference on Intelligent Sensors, Sensor Networks and Information Processing* (pp. 89–95).

Li, Y.-X., Qin, L., & Liang, Q. (2010). Research on wireless sensor network security. In *2010 International Conference on Computational Intelligence and Security* (pp. 493–496).

Liang, Z., & Shi, W. (2005). Enforcing cooperative resource sharing in untrusted P2P computing environments. *Mobile Networks and Applications, 10*(6), 971–983.

Liang, Z., & Shi, W. (2008). Analysis of ratings on trust inference in open environments. *Performance Evaluation, 65*(2), 99–128.

Modares, H., Salleh, R., & Moravejosharieh, A. (2011). Overview of security issues in wireless sensor networks. In *2011 Third International Conference on Computational Intelligence, Modelling & Simulation* (pp. 308–311).

Papadimitratos, P., & Haas, Z. (2002). Secure routing for mobile ad hoc networks. In *Communication Networks and Distributed Systems Modeling and Simulation Conference (CNDS 2002), CONF.*

Pathan, A.-S. K., Lee, H.-W., & Hong, C. S. (2006). Security in wireless sensor networks: issues and challenges. *2006 8th International Conference Advanced Communication Technology, 2*, 6 pp.

Perrig, A., Stankovic, J., & Wagner, D. (2004). Security in wireless sensor networks. *Communications of the ACM, 47*(6), 53–57.

Perrig, A., Szewczyk, R., Tygar, J. D., Wen, V., & Culler, D. E. (2002). SPINS: Security protocols for sensor networks. *Wireless Networks, 8*(5), 521–534.

Pfleeger, C. P. (2009). *Security in computing.* India: Pearson Education.

Sharma, S. (2009). *Energy-efficient secure routing in wireless sensor networks.*

Singla, A., & Sachdeva, R. (2013). Review on security issues and attacks in wireless sensor networks. *International Journal of Advanced Research in Computer Science and Software Engineering, 3*(4), 529–534.

Slijepcevic, S., Potkonjak, M., Tsiatsis, V., Zimbeck, S., & Srivastava, M. B. (2002). On communication security in wireless ad-hoc sensor networks. In *Proceedings. Eleventh IEEE International Workshops on Enabling Technologies: Infrastructure for Collaborative Enterprises* (pp. 139–144).

Stankovic, J. A., Abdelzaher, T. E., Lu, C., Sha, L., & Hou, J. C. (2003). Real-time communication and coordination in embedded sensor networks. *Proceedings of the IEEE, 91*(7), 1002–1022.

Tanachaiwiwat, S., Dave, P., Bhindwale, R., & Helmy, A. (2003). Poster abstract secure locations: routing on trust and isolating compromised sensors in location-aware sensor networks. In *Proceedings of the 1st International Conference on Embedded Networked Sensor Systems* (pp. 324–325).

Undercoffer, J., Avancha, S., Joshi, A., & Pinkston, J. (2002). Security for sensor networks. *CADIP Research Symposium*, 25–26.

Wagner, D. (2004). Resilient aggregation in sensor networks. In *Proceedings of the 2nd ACM Workshop on Security of Ad Hoc and Sensor Networks* (pp. 78–87).

Zia, T., & Zomaya, A. (2006). Security issues in wireless sensor networks. *2006 International Conference on Systems and Networks Communications (ICSNC'06)*, 40.

QoS as a Means of Providing WSN Security

3

INTRODUCTION

Quality of Service (QoS) aims at providing better networking services over current technologies such as ATM, Ethernet and others. The Internet uses the best-effort model, as it provides no guarantees on when packets will be delivered. And it does not differentiate between network streams. The main three parameters for QoS are latency (delay), jitter and loss. Delay is the total amount of time a network spends to deliver a frame of data from source to destination. Jitter in turn is the delay between two consecutive packets in that frame, while loss determines the maximum amount of packets loss the stream can tolerate to provide good quality. Each parameter has been investigated thoroughly and many solutions are proposed such as forward error correction and interleaving (Kurose, 2005). Other QoS parameters include reliability, network availability and bandwidth.

Providing hard guarantees as in Integrated Services (IntServ) or soft guarantees as in Differentiated Services (DiffServ) are the two main approaches to QoS on the Internet. IntServ (Braden et al., 1994) establishes a virtual dedicated link between source and destination. The Resource Reservation Protocol (RSVP) signaling protocol responsible for checking the network desired bandwidth and delay requirements. IntServ provides per-flow reservation; therefore, every node needs to maintain state information about every flow. As a result, IntServ suffers from a scalability problem. DiffServ (Nichols et al., 1998) offers different levels of service classes; it employs a Differentiated Services Code Point (DSCP-6 bits) field in the IP's Type of Service (ToS) byte to assign a different class to each flow. In turn, each network node treats every flow differently, which is known as the per-hop behavior (PHB). Therefore, state information about every flow is not needed along the network path. A third model of QoS on the Internet is known as adaptive applications that adapt to network congestion based on QoS feedback by adjusting the streaming speed. Bolot and Turletti (1994)

DOI: 10.1201/9781003257608-3

proposed a set of feedback mechanisms for use in adaptation of the output rate of video coders according to the state of the network.

Extending QoS to wireless networks presents new challenges due to radio channel characteristics, mobility management (Garcıa-Macıas et al., 2003), higher loss, battery power constraints and low bandwidth (Mahadevan & Sivalingam, 1999). However, most current QoS protocols can be implemented in WLAN with some modifications because the last hop is the only wireless stage in these networks. In wireless networks like ad hoc wireless networks or the new emerging wireless sensor networks that are totally wireless, a new set of QoS parameters, mechanisms and protocols are needed.

Wireless sensor networks (WSNs) are composed of many tiny, low-cost, low-power and scattered devices called sensor nodes. Each node integrates a processor, memory, transceiver and power source in one small device that has the ability to observe, process and send data about observed phenomenon to its neighboring nodes destined to a central processing unit sometimes referred to as a sink. A sensor node should have the ability to process as much information locally as possible instead of just disseminating raw data to save energy, because radio frequency (RF) communication is the key energy consumer (Estrin et al., 2001). Usually the main source of energy in a sensor node is a battery; so the lifetime for any node depends on the life of the battery itself. For these reasons, many Media Access Control (MAC) protocols have been proposed to bring radio communication on and off periodically instead of just listening to the channel all the time, e.g., SMAC (Willig & Karl, 2005). Energy conservation is one of the main obstacles to any proposed protocol in sensor networks, while maintaining high QoS measurements is the main goal in traditional networks (Akyildiz et al., 2002).

Sensor nodes are densely and randomly deployed. This can provide better accuracy and more energy savings since nodes can use short-range communication. However, if not managed properly, data redundancy and collisions may occur. For example, in a forest hundreds of nodes are programmed to inform a central sink if the temperature exceeds 45°C. When the event occurs, many nodes may disseminate at once the same information to the sink, resulting in data redundancy and implosion at the sink. To solve this problem while maintaining a degree of reliability, data aggregation techniques combine and summarize the data coming from different sources into one data stream (Madden et al., 2002).

Routing in sensor networks is different from routing in a traditional network because each sensor does not necessarily have a global unique ID. Selecting the next hop node becomes harder. More details about routing will be discussed in another chapter.

Wireless sensor networks inherit almost all the challenges from regular wireless local area networks (WLANs) and mobile ad hoc networks (MANETs) in addition to the following (Estrin et al., 2001Akyildiz et al., 2002):

- A sensor node suffers from very limited power source, not like PDAs or laptops which usually are recharged.
- A sensor network topology faces frequent changes due to external forces like animals, tanks or humans; or internal reasons like power or software failure.

- A sensor node does not have a global ID, which makes most of the current network protocols inapplicable to a WSN.
- Sensor networks mainly operate without any human intervention and they should be self-configurable.
- Sensor nodes are densely deployed which increase redundancy and collisions.
- Sensors have the ability to know the nature of information they are currying, unlike traditional network where intermediate nodes only forward packets of data.
- Sensor nodes normally use the broadcast communication model, while traditional networks use point-to-point communication.

For all the above reasons, implementing QoS in sensor networks differ from regular QoS implementations in other types of networks. The next section discusses the QoS in WSNs in general, followed by some challenges in deploying normal QoS mechanisms in wireless sensor networks.

QUALITY OF SERVICES IN WIRELESS SENSOR NETWORKS

Regular wired networks mainly send data between nodes without the knowledge of the nature of the carried data (data transparency). They mainly use an end-to-end communication model; therefore, parameters like delay, bandwidth, jitter and loss can provide acceptable QoS if managed properly. In a WSN these parameters are not fully applicable because sensor nodes mostly communicate using a non-end-to-end model; each node communicates only with neighboring nodes. That means no connection needs to be established between the source and destination at the beginning of the transmitting process. Another problem arises from the fact that intermediate sensor nodes have the ability to generate data as well, besides routing. The most challenging problem is energy, and all these factors arise new QoS parameters like coverage, exposure, energy cost and network lifetime.

The problem of coverage could happen when no sensor could observe and inform the sink about an event. This may happen because of noisy channels, deployment location or network management (Chen & Varshney, 2004). Exposure is related to coverage that provides measures of how an object can be observed by a sensor over a period of time. Energy cost defines the process of finding the best route to a destination according to energy conservation. Network lifetime is the total time of a WSN until it is not able to satisfy a user's needs.

Implementing the two QoS models of Internet on a WSN would not be practical. IntServ mainly depends on reserving the bandwidth between source and destination while saving state information on each intermediate node. This can be impractical in enhanced sensor network (ESN) for three main reasons: the complexity to achieve such service; second, limited memory capability in each sensor node that can't save per-flow state information; and last because the route usually is not known between source and destination at the beginning of the transmission process. DiffServ faces another problem besides complexity, that the core ideas behind DiffServ is queuing and prioritizing packets based on service priority level. Queuing requires a large memory, which normally a sensor node doesn't have.

Reliability, as a measure of QoS, has the ability to detect and repair packet losses in a WSN, as well as it should provide reliable methods for transporting data from sink to node and vice versa; therefore, reliability protocols are categorized into two groups: event-to-sink and sink-to-event.

Event-to-sink transport usually carries information about observed phenomena; in most cases it might be critical data needs to be reliably communicated to the sink. Several protocols has been proposed such as Reliable Multi-Segment Transport (RMST) (Sohrabi et al., 2000) and Event-to-Sink Reliable Transport (ESRT) (Reason & Rabaey, 2004). Sink-to-sensor usually carries queries or updates control information. A protocol such as Pump Slowly Fetch Quickly (PSFQ) (Stann & Heidemann, 2003) is proposed for reliable transfer of tasks and reprogramming the WSN nodes.

QoS Concept and Security Effect

As defined in Crawley et al. (1998), quality of service is "a set of service requirements to be met by the network while transporting a flow". Here, a flow is "a packet stream from source to a destination (unicast or multicast) with an associated Quality of Service (QoS)". In other words, QoS is a measurable level of service delivered to network users, which can be characterized by packet loss probability, available bandwidth, end-to-end delay, etc. Such QoS can be provided by network service providers in terms of some agreement (Service Level Agreement, or SLA) between network users and service providers. For example, users can require that for some traffic flows, the network should choose a path with minimum 2 mbs bandwidth.

Security services are to provide information secrecy, data integrity and resource availability for users. Information secrecy means to prevent the improper disclosure of information in the communications, while data integrity is to prevent improper mod-ification of data and resource availability is considered to preventing improper denial of services (Karlof & Wagner, 2003).

All of these attacks are aiming at one or more of the preventions revealed in Klenk and Weber (n.d.). Although security concerns in mobile traditional networks apply to sensor networks, the solutions are not the same.

Security is an overhead to the existing network QoS measurements; therefore, it has a strong influence on QoS of a network as well as providing (RAS). QoS metrics such as authentication delay, mobility, cost, call-dropping probability and throughput of communication due to authentication overhead has to be affected. Typically au-thentication delay causes a pause for data transmission which decreases the throughput. Moreover, length of keys and complexity of algorithms used have an

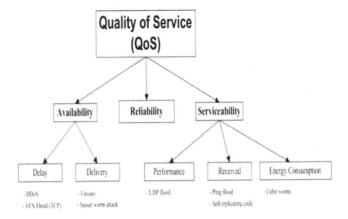

FIGURE 3.1 Integration of security analysis with QoS.

adverse effect. Also, the size of packets transmitted is increased to include security parameters that affect the payload of messages.

Identifying the possible threats that may face sensor networks will help in designing secure WSNs, as these threats are the ones hindering QoS. However, in the case of WSNs, longer keys would have a disastrous effect on the QoS of the network; therefore, it is important to classify security levels based on information secrecy, data integrity and resource availability. These aspects can be designed into the system with variations of security strength classes.

Integration of security analysis with QoS design needs to meet both security and satisfy certain QoS requirements simultaneously from a long view. Different from most of the existing works that deal with a WSN strategy to achieve QoS, we extend QoS support to the model by introducing a number of active security requirements distributed in a gradient fashion based on their logical connection to the QoS requirements in Figure 3.1.

QoS Challenges in Sensor Networks

Different from an IP network, a sensor network naturally supports multiple service types, and thus provides different QoS. The service types range from CBR (Constant Bit Rate), which guarantees bandwidth, delay and delay jitter, to UBR (Unspecified Bit Rate), which virtually provides no guarantees (just like today's "best-effort" IP network). While sensor networks inherit most of the QoS issues from the general wireless networks, their characteristics pose unique challenges. The following is an outline of design considerations for handling QoS traffic in wireless sensor networks.

Bandwidth limitation: A typical issue for general wireless networks is securing the bandwidth needed for achieving the required QoS. Bandwidth limitation is going to be a more pressing issue for wireless sensor networks. Traffic in sensor networks can be burst with a mixture of real-time and non-real-time traffic. Dedicating available bandwidth solely to QoS traffic will not be acceptable. A trade-off in image/video quality may be necessary to accommodate non-real-time traffic. In addition, simultaneously using multiple independent routes will sometimes be needed to split the traffic and allow for meeting the QoS requirements. Setting up independent routes for the same flow can be very complex and challenging in sensor networks due to energy constraints, limited computational resources and potential increase in collisions among the transmission of sensors.

Removal of redundancy: Sensor networks are characterized with high redundancy in the generated data. For unconstrained traffic, elimination of redundant data messages is somewhat easy since simple aggregation functions would suffice. However, conducting data aggregation for QoS traffic is much more complex. A comparison of images and video streams is not computationally trivial and can consume significant energy resources. A combination of system and sensor level rules would be necessary to make aggregation of QoS data computationally feasible. For example, data aggregation of imaging data can be selectively performed for traffic generated by sensors pointing to same direction since the images may be very similar. Another factor of consideration is the amount of QoS traffic at a particular moment. For low traffic, it may be more efficient to cease data aggregation since the overhead would become dominant. Despite the complexity of data aggregation of imaging and video data, it can be very rewarding from a network performance point of view given the size of the data and the frequency of the transmission.

Energy and delay trade-off: Since the transmission power of a radio is proportional to the distance squared or even higher order in noisy environments or in the nonflat terrain, the use of multi-hop routing is almost a standard in wireless sensor networks. Although the increase in the number of hops dramatically reduces the energy consumed for data collection, the accumulative packet delay magnifies. Since packet queuing delay dominates its propagation delay, the increase in the number of hops can not only slow down packet delivery but also complicate the analysis and the handling of delay-constrained traffic. Therefore, it is expected that QoS routing of sensor data would have to sacrifice energy efficiency to meet delivery requirements. In addition, redundant routing of data may be unavoidable to cope with the typical high error rate in wireless communication, further complicating the trade-off between energy consumption and delay of packet delivery.

Buffer size limitation: Sensor nodes are usually constrained in processing and storage capabilities. Multi-hop routing relies on intermediate relaying nodes for storing incoming packets for forwarding to the next hop. While a small buffer size can conceivably suffice, buffering of multiple packets has some advantages in wireless sensor networks. First, the transition of the radio circuitry between transmission and reception modes consumes considerable energy and thus it is advantageous to receive many packets prior to forwarding them. In addition, data aggregation and fusion involve multiple packets. Multi-hop routing of QoS data would typically require long sessions and buffering of even larger data, especially when the delay jitter is of interest. The buffer size limitation will increase the delay variation that packets incur while traveling on different routes and even on the same route. Such an issue will complicate medium access scheduling and make it difficult to meet QoS requirements.

Support of multiple traffic types: Inclusion of a heterogeneous set of sensors raises multiple technical issues related to data routing. For instance, some applications might require a diverse mixture of sensors for monitoring temperature, pressure and humidity of the surrounding environment; detecting motion via acoustic signatures; and capturing the image or video tracking of moving objects. These special sensors are either deployed independently or the functionality can be included on the normal sensors to be used on demand. Readings generated from these sensors can be at different rates, subject to diverse QoS constraints and following multiple data delivery models, as explained earlier. Therefore, such a heterogeneous environment makes data routing more challenging.

QoS Metrics in WSN Layers

QoS provisioning in individual layers depends on layer capability. Therefore, each layer has layer specific parameters that are used for performance evaluation and QoS assessment. In Table 3.1, QoS parameters are assigned to each layer in a WSN, as described in Y. Wang et al. (2006). Since different combinations of proposed parameters could define different QoS levels, WSNs could be categorized and could provide predictable performance.

Application-Specific QoS Parameters

Due to the large number of applications and widespread use of WSNs, QoS provisioning requirements are diversified. However, as described in Chen and Varshney (2004), primary application-specific QoS parameters are:

TABLE 3.1 QoS parameters in WSN layers

WSN LAYER	QOS PARAMETERS
Application layer	System lifetime; response time; data novelty; detection probability; data reliability; data resolution
Transport layer	Reliability; bandwidth; latency; cost
Network layer	Path latency; routing maintenance; congestion probability; routing robustness; energy efficiency
Connectivity maintenance layer	Network diameter; network capacity; average path cost; connectivity robustness; connectivity maintenance
Coverage maintenance layer	Coverage percentage; coverage reliability; coverage robustness; coverage maintenance
MAC layer	Communication range; throughput; transmission reliability; energy efficiency
Physical layer	Depend on capabilities of sensor components (sensing, data processing and communication component)

- Coverage: Determined by the specific requirements during the deployment of sensors.
- Exposure: Determines how well an object can be observed over a period of time.
- Measurement errors: Determined by the measurement precision of sensors.
- Optimum number of active sensors.

Network-Specific QoS Parameters

From the network perspective, it is important to effectively utilize network resources, while concurrently delivering QoS-constrained data from sensors. Since numerous applications have common requirements, they are divided into three data delivery models, as described in Chen and Varshney (2004):

- Event-driven model: Most applications in this model are interactive, do not tolerate delays, are determined by the task and not end-to-end applications. Furthermore, the data obtained from the sensors mostly contain much redundancy, though data generated by a single sensor may be of very low intensity. The response action must be quick and reliable.
- Query-driven model: Most applications in this model are interactive, query-specific delay tolerant, mission critical and not end-to-end applications. Queries could be sent on demand and also used to manage and reconfigure sensor nodes. Data is pulled by the sink.
- Continuous model: Data from the sensors are continuously sent to the sink at a predetermined rate. When transferring video, image or audio data in real time, the following conditions must be satisfied:
  - Delay must be constrained.
  - Certain bandwidth requirements must be fulfilled.
  - Packet loss can be tolerant but only to a certain extent.
  - Applications must not be end-to-end.

When transferring non-real-time data, delay and packet losses are tolerated.

Since different applications have various requirements, in some networks it is necessary to use a combination of the above models, the hybrid model. As a result of the fact that most applications in WSNs are not end-to-end applications, new collective QoS parameters can be defined:

- Collective latency: Difference in time between generation of first packet and arrival of the last packet to the sink (for one event).
- Collective packet loss: Number of loss packets during information delivery (for one event).
- Collective bandwidth: Bandwidth that the reporting of the event requires.
- Information throughput: At the sink from a set of correlated sensors.

RELATED STUDIES

Most approaches in wireless sensor networks are to extend the network lifetime while meeting network performance requirements in terms of minimizing the energy consumption. To highlight the novelties of the proposed method for maximizing the lifetime of sensor networks, the results of the proposed model shall be briefly discussed in comparison with two existing models: the upper bounds of the lifetime and the node density control for maximizing lifetime algorithms. The node density control algorithm (Esseghir & Bouabdallah, 2008) proposes a new model for minimizing energy consumption that depends on the distribution model of the sensor node in the network to explore the relationship of lifetime and the density distribution manner of the sensor node onto the events area. However, all of the nodes should use the same transmission range, which causes exhaustion in the energy of the nodes. The proposed model analyzes the network lifetime with the node density control approach by deriving the optimum transmission ranges of the nodes. In the upper bound algorithm (Bhardwaj et al., 2001), a new strategy for collaborative information for a routing protocol is proposed. This strategy constructs a realistic network topology model to simulate the gathering and processing of information to investigate the optimal lifetime for some levels of deployment control. In this specific topology, there are several different multi-paths that data packets which originate at a specific source node can use to send to the sink node. Therefore, these multi-paths also include paths with which the node does not necessarily communicate directly through a single hop. Instead, the node can transmit the data packet directly to another node, which is two hops or a multihop away, by spending more energy. Thus, the total number of paths from the source node to the sink grows exponentially as the number of sensor nodes in the network topology increases. However, implementing such a strategy is difficult because it is necessary to determine the exact locations of all of the nodes in the network topology and then to coordinate all of the nodes so that different collaborative strategies are sustained over different periods. The proposed scheme finds the optimal number of hops without taking into consideration all of the possible multihop paths. Only two modes of communication are used: single hopping and multi-hopping with an optimum transmission radius. Our scheme is very easy to implement and does not require any exact knowledge of the node locations.

One of the many multi-constrained QoS routing challenges is developing a new routing metric. An abundance of routing metrics have been developed for ad hoc networks and are usually applied in WSNs. The hop count was one of the earliest routing metrics used, while expected transmission count (ETX) is the most favored routing metric because of its accuracy in estimating the link quality. An extension of ETX, the expected transmission time (ETT), can be viewed as a new metric that considers the influence of the packet size as well as the link quality. Weighted cumulative ETT (WCETT) is designed to account for the diversity of the channels in wireless communication technology, where the nodes use multiple radios at the same time (Akyildiz & Wang, 2009). Several improvements to these routing protocols to achieve different requirements of wireless networks are found in literature. In Yang et al. (2005), the authors analyze the performance of the existing routing metrics to investigate how the network performance requirements, such as the delay and throughput, are met. Improved ETT (iETT) is proposed in Biaz et al. (2008) as a new routing metric based on ETT to investigate the whole impact of the individual high-loss channel rate on the performance of path routing; the authors also consider the MAC layer overheads in calculating the data transmission. A cross-layer of co-operative diversity communication for decision routing is proposed in He and Li (2012), which studies cooperative communication for the routing protocol to derive a new routing metric that exploits the link quality of each potential relay and considers every individual cooperative transmission scheme. An optimal path from the source to the sink is then selected using the new optimal link metric. Most of the previous existing routing metrics focused on only a single service metric such as energy or reliability in a single path.

In spite of the availability of several routing protocols in WSNs, the design of new routing metrics for multi-hop communication is still an open research area for many reasons. A few studies consider multiple QoS constraints in multi-path routing strategies in sensor networks because the complete and accurate state information is not available as a result of the periodic changes in the link quality and the traffic engineering. However, the hop count and link quality are most frequently used in routing metrics to discover and utilize the improvement in the performance of the routing protocols in the WSNs. In Lan et al. (2008), a new QoS routing protocol is applied to multimedia WSNs, called the real-time and energy-aware routing (REAR), is proposed. This protocol chooses delay as a QoS-measurement parameter to construct a cost function for evaluating the energy efficiency. The proposed protocol uses an advanced Dijkstra algorithm to evaluate the structure of the multi-path mechanism and to choose the neighbor distance between nodes i and j amid all of the paths for sending real data. To reduce the queue delay for a real-time event packet while monitoring events that occur, a classifier queue model F (Queue j) is used for each node to address real-time and ordinary data and to balance the network life cycle and save on energy consumption. The protocol suffers from overhead complexity in creating the multi-path routing algorithm because the state of the information that is associated with each path is incomplete and inaccurate from the changing traffic and link quality.

In Mahapatra et al. (2006) and Ahmed and Fisal (2008), a novel real-time approach with a load-distributed routing protocol (RTLD) is proposed. It computes the optimal forwarding hop based on three metrics: the link packet reception rate (PRR), the residual power of the sensor battery and the packet velocity per single hop. The proposed routing protocol is composed of four functional components: power management, neighborhood management, location management and routing management. In routing management, there are three subfunctional forwarding processes: metric calculations, mechanism forwarding and routing problem handling. Power consumption management determines both the transceiver power and the transmission power states of the node by using the MICAz sensor node to develop the RTLD. Uncertainty in the dynamic network topology and traffic changing caused this protocol to elaborate the energy consumption profile for diverse levels of duty cycles of the sensor network, which is used to derive the trade-off between the energy conservation and the QoS.

The ReInForM protocol, as described in Deb et al. (2003) employs probabilistic flooding to deliver the information awareness packet and service at desired priority levels of reliability at a proportional cost for sensor networks. This protocol operates through the proposed dynamic and randomized multi-path forwarding mechanism to forward multiple copies of the same information packet in multi-path routing according to the decision of the source, to route the packets toward the sink. The routing mechanism is based on local knowledge of network conditions, such as channel error, hops counting to sink and out-degree. Information on the network conditions is stored on the head of the header of the packets without requiring any data caching at any sensor node, while using the dynamic packet state (DPS) method, which causes an increase in the probability of information delivery. This protocol is not designed specifically for real-time or multimedia traffic; therefore, it does not consider the delay deadlines of the packet when selecting the multiple paths. A chosen path might not be able to meet the deadline; yet it will duplicate the packets that might cause a high cost of energy consumption and the occupation of useful channel bandwidth utilization without improving the system performance.

In Yang et al. (2010), the network coding-reliable multi-path routing (NC-RMR) protocol for WSNs is presented. The NC-RMR protocol employs the computational method of paths and next-hop node selection as in the ReInForM protocol, but it is different from ReInForM. The first difference is in avoiding the redundancy of copies of packets; NC-RMR applies the network coding mechanism in delivering packets through a multi-path from source to sink. Second, to increase the level of reliability, the NC-RMR protocol employs a hop-to-hop mechanism to establish a disjoint and braided multi-path routing protocol. The successful delivery packet probability is expressed as $p_k = (1 - e)^k$, where k is defined as the number of successful hops toward the sink. The computation of reliability is performed using the Bernoulli distribution, specifically, $\sum_{i=0}^{m} C_M^i \times (1 - p_k)^{M-i} \times p_k^i$. The NC-RMR protocol includes a load balance that is implemented by the braided multi-path and optimal next hop-to-hop node selection. The disadvantage of this proposed scheme is the suggestion that node-disjoint multi-path routing conserves energy, but the selection of the path could have more hops to reach the destination. Additionally, the system might not have the ability to adapt quickly for a time-varying link quality condition. Conversely, NC-RMR saves 67% of the overhead in terms of the maintenance and complexity, which makes it capable of a 50% higher resilience to node failure.

Unlike an end-to-end (E2E) QoS scheme that influences the performance, another soft QoS mapped into links on a path is provided based on local link state information of wireless ad hoc and sensor networks; for example, critical bandwidth ratio. Stochastic integer programming addresses the E2E soft QoS problem in a rigorous way. Consequently, a model that is based on probability exploration to provide E2E soft-QoS parameters under multiple constraints for a multi-path-routing protocol (MCMP) is proposed in Huang and Fang (2008). The authors suggest that a distributable manner is the main requirement to achieve a high level of E2E soft-QoS of the selection path. The partition is obtained from the hop requirements for both the additive delay and the multiplicative reliability, which is formulated as $L_i^d = (BoundedDelay - Delaynode_i)/Hopcount$, where the Hopcount is a counter of the hops from the source to the sink, Delaynode$_i$ is the value of the delay involved for processing data at node i and BoundedDelay is the definition of the total delay from the source to the sink. Reliability formation is formed as $L_i^d = \sqrt[Hopcount]{Re_i}$, where Re_i is defined as the reliability requirements that are assigned to the path through node i. In Huang and Fang (2008), both the delay and the reliability constraints are provided, and in Bagula and Mazandu (2008), a third constraint is added, namely, the energy constraints. Thus, the energy, delay and reliability become competitive constraints in WSNs, which generate a trade-off between the single-path and multi-path routing deployments, where minimizing both the delay and energy constraints and the maximizing reliability are at stake. Although the proposed model addresses the issues of multi-constrained QoS in WSNs through a combination of the resource of multi-path for traffic flow, it does not consider accounting for the predictability of the network for topology to minimizing the energy consumption and the delay, respectively. Our proposed model considers the predictability of the network topology to search the multi-path and choose one of them.

Bagula and Mazandu (2008) extend the model proposed in Huang and Fang (2008) into a new model that is called energy constrained multi-path (ECMP), which is generated by building on geospatial energy propagation to formulate QoS routing in WSNs. This model is expressed as $w(S_i, S_{i+1}) = \varepsilon_1 + \varepsilon_2 \times \|x_{si} - x_{si+1}\|^n$, where $S_i, S_{i+1} \in$ Link for $i = 1, 2, \ldots p$ is an ordered pair of two sensor nodes in the path and $\varepsilon_1 = \varepsilon_{11} + \varepsilon_{12}$, where $\varepsilon 11$ is defined as the energy per bit consumed in the transmission mode by S_i and ε_{12} is defined as the energy per bit consumed in the receiving mode by S_i. The location $\|x_{si} - x_{si+1}\|$ of each pair of sensor nodes is defined as the Euclidean distance. The concept of geospatial energy propagation depends on the Pythagorean theorem, which shows whether the distance between the two sensor nodes is larger than another link. The Pythagorean theorem finds that the energy transmission between two sensor nodes is shared with the source; thus, the choice of other links that connect a sensor with higher-energy transmission to forward the packets leads to energy efficiency. The MCMP model proposes an arbitrary selection link more accurately with a random choice if it is the optimal selection for minimizing the energy consumption. Thus, the ECMP model attempts to find a subset from a set of sensor nodes that have a lower expected energy transmission, while meeting the QoS requirements by delivering packets to the sink. The ECMP model searches for the subset of multi-paths from the source to the sink that satisfy the requirements of the data source for the QoS and the total energy of transmission. The concept of this protocol is inspired by geospatial energy propagation, which depends on the Pythagorean theorem and leads to the overhead message control problem. Unlike our proposed mathematical framework, which is borrowed from mixed integer programming (MIP) and is based on the LR method, we define critical parameters to control the adaptive switching of hop-by-hop QoS routing protocols in WSNs. At the same time, the ECMP model uses the optimization method borrowed from the zero-one mathematical framework (Schulz, 1977).

A novel cross-layer cooperative communication has been studied. The transparency behavior between the physical layer (PHY) and MAC is proposed in Chehri and Mouftah (2012) to improve the overall network performance by exchanging information between these protocol layers. The author aimed to develop a cross-layer protocol for an efficient routing algorithm by including joint energy consumption and green routing at the network layer, using an optimization scheme based on adaptive modulation at the PHY and using suitable power saving with a sleep mode mechanism at the MAC. The proposed routing algorithm selects the optimal multi-hop path based on the battery energy level by the apativate modulation and dynamic power transmission of each sensor node.

RELIABILITY, AVAILABILITY AND SERVICEABILITY (RAS)

As WSNs are expected to be adopted in many industrial, health care and military applications, their RASs are becoming critical. In recent years, the diverse potential applications for WSNs have been touted by researchers and the general press (Pottie & Kaiser, 2000). In many WSN systems, to provide sufficient RAS can often be absorbed in the network cost. Nevertheless, as noticed earlier (Estrin et al., 2001), network designers face "two fundamentally conflicting goals: to minimize the total cost of the network and to provide redundancy as a protection against major service interruptions".

For availability and serviceability, remote testing and diagnostics is needed to pinpoint and repair (or bypass) the failed components that might be physically unreachable. Severe limitations in the cost and the transmitted energy within WSNs negatively impact the reliability of the nodes and the integrity of transmitted data. The application itself will greatly influence how system resources (namely, energy and bandwidth) must be allocated between communication and computation requirements to achieve requisite system performance. The following presentation demonstrates how different application wireless sensor nodes can influence the resource usability.

Power states are states of particular devices; as such, they are generally not visible to the user. For example, some devices may be in the off state even though the system as a whole is in the working state.

These states are defined very generically in this section to enable applications adopted in our approach. Many devices do not have all four power states defined. Devices may be capable of several different low-power modes, but if there is no user-perceptible difference between the modes only the lowest power mode will be used. We define four power states according to advanced configuration power interface (ACPI) (X. Wang, Gu, et al., 2005):

- Ready – (or busy) is when the system or device is fully powered up and ready for use.
- Idle – is an intermediate system dependent state that attempts to conserve power. The CPU enters the idle state when no device activity has occurred

within a machine defined time period. The machine won't return to the busy state until a device raises a hardware interrupt or the machine accesses a controlled device.

- Suspend – is the lowest level of power consumptions available in which memory preserves all data and operational parameters. The device won't perform any computations until it resumes normal activity, which it does when signalled by an external event such as a button press, timer alarm or receipt of request.
- Off – the device is powered down and inactive. Operational and data parameters might or might not be preserved.

Figure 3.2 shows the general current ranges for each operating state as well as the power distribution for a PDA class of devices. Cliff Brake affirms that the CPU accounts for approximately 30% of power and the screen 42% when backlit; these percentages vary slightly with each PDA class (X. Wang, Chellappan, et al., 2005). In an idle state, the CPU loses nearly all current and the backlight is turned off, equating to an approximate 64% power reduction.

This can be deceiving, however. In an idle state, if the wireless local area network (LAN) card picks up a network request and transmits an acknowledgment, the CPU will consume power at a higher level. Worse yet, once on, the card might pick up multiple requests and, unless the user has altered the CPU's communication protocol, it

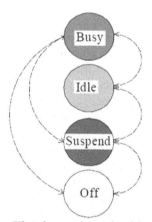 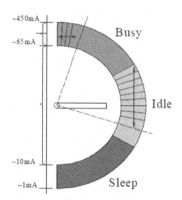

The dynamic and wide range of power in between states provide means of determining thresholds of a normal power levels and activities in each states.

High Current (mA) ranges sustained over certain periods of time in different power stat provide a means of detecting abnormal behavior and attack

FIGURE 3.2 State power distribution (adapted from a Dell Axim) and battery-based intrusion detections (B-BID) power drain rate thresholds. The longer a threshold is held high in the busy and idle states, the greater the likelihood that an anomalous activity is present.

will try to send multiple acknowledgments for each request. In addition, the power required to transmit is greater than it is to receive by approximately 1.5:1 (Chan et al., 2003; Desmedt & Jajodia, 1997).

The justification of idle state resource consumption can only be identified through worst or best scenarios as follows:

$$E = N\left(1 + \frac{r}{t}\right)^T \qquad (3.1)$$

The inputs are the total number of nodes (N), threshold (r), the time taken (t) and total time (T). One of the purposes of a model such as this is to make predictions and try "What If?" scenarios. You can change the inputs and recalculate the model and you'll get a new answer. You might even want to plot a graph of the expected results (E) vs. time (T). In some cases, you may have a fixed results rate, but what do you do if the results rate is allowed to change? For this simple equation, you might only care to know a worst/best-case scenario, where you calculate the expected value based upon the lowest and highest results rates that you might expect.

While examining WSN nodes and proposing the necessary QoS required for increasing both the availability and serviceability of the system, our approach is service oriented and was particularly motivated by recent proposals to define QoS for a WSN. In one definition, QoS measures application reliability with a goal of energy efficiency (Perillo & Heinzelman, 2003). An alternative definition equates QoS to spatial resolution (Iyer & Kleinrock, 2003). This latter work also presented a QoS control strategy based on a Gur game paradigm in which base stations broadcast feedback to the network's sensors. QoS control is required for the assumption that the number of sensors deployed exceeds the minimum needed to provide the requisite service.

This work presents two new techniques to maintain QoS under a variety of network constraints. We first adapt the proposed Gur game strategy to operate in energy-poor environments and then propose a new, extremely low-energy control strategy based on individual feedback in a random access communication system. In particular, our work is applicable to networks that are deployed in remote, harsh environs (e.g., space applications). Such networks are constrained by (1) high die-off rates of nodes and (2) inability to be replenished. The performance of the algorithms is demonstrated throughout using numerical examples as follows in Equations (3.2) and (3.3):

$$Reliability = 1 - \frac{t}{mean\_time\_between\_failure} \qquad (3.2)$$

$$Availability = \frac{mean\_time\_between\_failure}{mean\_time\_between\_failure + mean\_time\_to\_repair} \qquad (3.3)$$

$$M\% = \frac{m \times 100\%}{n}$$

$$Serviceability = 1 - expx - \left(\frac{t}{mean\_time\_to\_repair} \right) \tag{3.4}$$

where m is a number of failed nodes within WSN, n is number of nodes within WSN and $M\%$ is possible percentage of failed nodes within given WSN.

CALCULATING PROBABILITY OF NODE AVAILABILITY IN A WSN

The availability of several implementations is derived from Equation (3.3) for mean time between failure (MTBF) and mean time to repair (MTTR). Due to the power issue and the unpredictable wireless network characteristics, it is possible that applications running on the sensor nodes might fail. Thus, techniques to improve the availability of sensor nodes are necessary. Estimated MTBF in our sensor nodes is based on the individually calculated failure rates for each component and the circuit board. Next, for the redundant system versions, if the failure rates (λ) of each redundant element are the same, then the MTBF of the redundant system with n parallel independent elements (i) (Arora et al., 2005) are taken as:

$$mean\_time\_between\_failure = \sum_{i=1}^{n} \frac{1}{i\lambda} \tag{3.5}$$

The MTTR can be estimated by the sum of two values, referred to as mean time to detect (MTTD) the failures and the time to repair (TTR) (MTTR = MTTD + TTR). Notice that this part might be severely affected by the network connections.

Consider the technique (Chiang et al., 2004) where the consumer starts the reparation mechanism by activating the local functional test. Once it completes, the test result is sent back to the consumer for analysis. If a failure occurs, the consumer will send the repair message to the sensor node and initialize the backup component. Acknowledgment is sent back to the consumer once the reparation is completed. If the message latency from the consumer to the target node is d seconds and the test time is c seconds, then we calculate MTTR as Equation (3.6):

$$mean\_time\_to\_repair: 4d + c \tag{3.6}$$

For the sensor node without the test interface module (Chiang et al., 2004), the consumer sends the measured data request command to the suspected sensor node. In order to check the data integrity, the same request command will also be sent to at least two other nearby sensor nodes. The consumer compares the three collected streams of data and pinpoints the failed node. Once the failure is confirmed, the consumer will notify the surrounding sensor node to take over the applications of the failed node. Once the failure is confirmed, the consumer will notify the surrounding sensor node to take over the applications of the failed node. Again, if the message latency from the consumer to the target node is d seconds, then MTTR is:

$$mean\_time\_to\_repair \sim 8d \tag{3.7}$$

To estimate realistic MTTR numbers, we use a study (Y.-H. Yang & Feng, 2003) where, for WSNs, a thermostat application with 64 sensor nodes is simulated. Due to the power and protocol requirements, the average latency of related messages is 1,522s. By applying this to our MTTR estimations, the test time c is much smaller and can be neglected.

The reliability of a system is defined as the probability of system survival of Equation (3.8) in a period of time. Therefore, using the Poisson probability (Eddous & Stansfield, 1997) implemented for WSNs, we have as well an estimate of the probability of a "failed" situation for the whole WSN in given time interval, e.g. for one day (24 hours) to demonstrate the reliability of our presented approach.

$$probability\,(r) = \frac{m^r \times e^{-m}}{r!} \tag{3.8}$$

where $probability(r)$ is a probability of a failure system working with "r" failed nodes within a WSN for given time interval, $r \geq 0$, m is an average number of failed nodes within a WSN and $e = 2.718$; for example, on average there are three failed nodes in a WSN for 24 hours. Then we calculate the probabilities of failure system working as:

$$probability\,(\text{``r''} fails\_for\_24\_hours) = \frac{3^r \times e^{-3}}{r!}$$

$$probability\,(\text{``0''} fails\_for\_24\_hours) = P(0) = \frac{3^0 \times e^{-3}}{0!} = 0.0498$$

$$probability\,(\text{``1''} fails\_for\_24\_hours) = P(1) = \frac{3^1 \times e^{-3}}{1!} = 0.1494$$

$$probability\,(\text{``4''} fails\_for\_24\_hours) = P(4) = \frac{3^4 \times e^{-3}}{4!} = 0.1680$$

From this example, we can see that with a progressive increase of fail nodes quantity of a WSN, the risk of unstable work also increases.

EXPERIMENTS AND EVALUATIONS

The discussion in this section will be about achieving two primary factors of dependability in WSN applications: availability and reliability. In the classical definition, a system is highly available if the fraction of its downtime is very small, either because failures are rare, or because it can restart very quickly after a failure (Mbowe & Oreku, 2014).

The performance of the proposed approach is demonstrated throughout using numerical examples. The reliability of a system is defined as the probability of system survival in a period of time. Since it depends mainly on the operating conditions and operating time, the metrics of mean time between failure (MTBF) is used. For time period of duration t, the MTBF is related to the reliability as follows(Chiang et al., 2004):

$$mean\_time\_between\_failure \tag{3.9}$$

The availability of a system is closely related to the reliability, since it is defined as the probability that the system is operating correctly at a given time. Dependence availability and reliability on the MTBF is presented in Figure 3.3.

Calculating availability is related to the MTBF and mean time to repair (MTTR) by the following relation(Chiang et al., 2004):

$$Availability = \frac{mean\_time\_between\_failure}{mean\_time\_between\_failure + mean\_time\_to\_repair} \tag{3.10}$$

Considering the availability of each node in isolation, from Equation (3.10), the MTTR should be minimized, while the MTBF should be maximized. While the MTBF is given by manufacturing practices and components used, the value of the MTTR can be controlled by both individual node and network design:

$$M\% = \frac{m \times 100\%}{n} \tag{3.11}$$

where m is a number of failed nodes within WSN, n is a number of nodes within WSN and $M\%$ is possible percentage of failed nodes within a given WSN. The serviceability of a system is defined as the probability that a failed system will restore to the correct operation. Serviceability is closely related to the repair rate and the MTTR (Chiang et al., 2004):

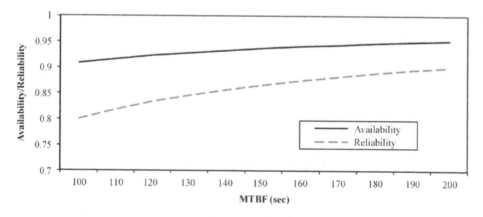

FIGURE 3.3 Dependence availability and reliability on the MTBF.

$$Serviceability = 1 - expx - \left(\frac{t}{mean\_time\_to\_repair} \right) \tag{3.12}$$

A fundamental service in sensor networks is the determination of time and location of events in the real world. This task is complicated by various challenging characteristics of sensor networks, such as their large scale, high network dynamics, restricted resources and restricted energy. We use Hawk sensor nodes for determination time of data transmitting in fulfilling the QoS under these constraints. We illustrate the practical feasibility to our approaches by concrete applications of real sensor nodes (Hawk Sensor Nodes) to our experiments and the results of availability and reliability of sensor nodes to reveal QoS from our experiment can be seen in Figure 3.3.

In any system one must consider the reliability of its components when ascertaining overall system performance. Thus, our question was whether the proposed strategy performed adequately for various levels of sensor reliability. Equation (3.2) does not include any information regarding expected sensor life and thus assumes static network resources, which is clearly not the case in WSNs. For example, sensors may fail at regular intervals due to low reliability, due to cost-driven design choices, environmentally caused effects (especially in harsh environments), loss of energy, etc.

We measured the processing throughput, i.e., the number of data-transmitted events that each phase is able to process per second and time taken to transmit these data within selected sensor nodes, as can be seen in a graph presentation in Figure 3.4.

We plot the node availability vs. average latency, which lumps together the characteristics of the channel, the number of retransmission retries on the failure, as well as the node-dependent features such as retransmission time-outs in Figure 3.5.

In Figure 3.6, we examine WSN nodes to transmit the data in evaluating (RAS). Two sensor nodes with 32 bytes were used for estimating the connection time with a different transmitting rate. With 0.0625 t/s, we were able to connect 32 packets. To ask one sensor node to transmit the data, we need two data packets (one for asking, another one for receiving the answer). To estimate time to connection we have to transmit only two packets. The number of packets = file size/packet size. Time = number of packets/ data transmitting rate. This can be used to propose the necessary infrastructure required

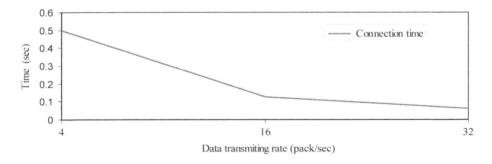

FIGURE 3.4 Connection time for 4/16/32 pack/sec.

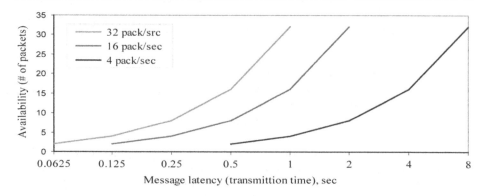

FIGURE 3.5   Availability of a node in a WSN.

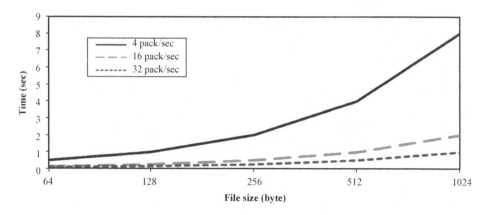

FIGURE 3.6   Transmitting time in a different number of packets to access (RAS).

for increasing both the availability and serviceability of the system, in spite of the absence of a reliable transport layer. Hence, this can be used to analyze and detect delay, delivery, performance or energy consumptions.

CONCLUSION

Implementations of QoS in WSNs is still in the early stages; great efforts need to be invested. Difficulties in a WSN mainly come from resource constraints, besides lack of standardizations. This chapter analyzed the major work in this field, trying to en-compass current research efforts in a straightforward approach. After reviewing the past research work, we conclude that achieving similar QoS performance of traditional networks in a WSN is unachievable; there is a continuous trade-off between limited sensor resources like power, memory or computational capabilities and QoS support. However, we are not expecting to utilize a WSN to process a huge amount of data like the Internet. WSNs mainly will be used to process less network traffic and deal with fewer numbers of users at any time. Therefore, high support of QoS for all types of network streams is not required; besides, there is no need for high-quality video or audio streams in a WSN.

Additionally, this chapter covers the security of wireless sensor networks considered through QoS. Using QoS components (RAS), we found that security can be achieved in a sense that, while trying to get QoS it's easy to detect, malicious action when certain parts of applications are not attained, i.e., when requesting service and its availability is not fulfilled, then this should be taken as an unusual sign or an attack is happening. We evaluated models to show how QoS can be linked to secure WSNs and, using sensor nodes, we have assessed the need of the system to indicate unusual activities that may cause a failure to reach QoS; ultimately, this can provide notifications of malicious action in the long run.

One primordial issue is to satisfy application QoS requirements while providing a high-level abstraction that addresses wireless sensor network security. Notice that although we consider primarily testing in the lab, the proposed solutions can easily be applied to testing in a factory with large size sensor network applications. With the proposed approach, such tests can be easily parallelized by applying a wireless broadcast to many nodes at once. As a result, the proposed approach can be used in a variety of testing scenarios.

Security issues in utilizing wireless sensor applications have been discussed with data integrity aspects. A secure model is proposed with flow of security classes providing different levels of security using QoS. However, our finding found that effects of security metrics place a lot of burden on the QoS of the overall system; thus, decreasing performance.

REFERENCES

Ahmed, A. A., & Fisal, N. (2008). A real-time routing protocol with load distribution in wireless sensor networks. *Computer Communications*, *31*(14), 3190–3203.

Akyildiz, I. F., Su, W., Sankarasubramaniam, Y., & Cayirci, E. (2002). Wireless sensor networks: A survey. *Computer Networks*, *38*(4), 393–422.

Akyildiz, I. F., & Wang, X. (2009). *Wireless mesh networks (Vol. 3)*. John Wiley & Sons.

Arora, A., Ramnath, R., Ertin, E., Sinha, P., Bapat, S., Naik, V., Kulathumani, V., Zhang, H., Cao, H., & Sridharan, M. (2005). Exscal: Elements of an extreme scale wireless sensor network. *11th IEEE International Conference on Embedded and Real-Time Computing Systems and Applications (RTCSA'05)*, 102–108.

Bagula, A. B., & Mazandu, K. G. (2008). Energy constrained multi-path routing in wireless sensor networks. *International Conference on Ubiquitous Intelligence and Computing*, 453–467.

Bhardwaj, M., Garnett, T., & Chandrakasan, A. P. (2001). Upper bounds on the lifetime of sensor networks. *ICC 2001. IEEE International Conference on Communications. Conference Record (Cat. No. 01CH37240)*, *3*, 785–790.

Biaz, S., Qi, B., & Ji, Y. (2008). Improving expected transmission time metric in multi-rate multi-hop networks. *2008 5th IEEE Consumer Communications and Networking Conference*, 533–537.

Bolot, J.-C., & Turletti, T. (1994). A rate control mechanism for packet video in the Internet. *Proceedings of INFOCOM'94 Conference on Computer Communications*, 1216–1223.

Braden, R., Clark, D., & Shenker, S. (1994). *RFC1633: Integrated services in the internet architecture: An overview*. RFC Editor.

Chan, H., Perrig, A., & Song, D. (2003). Random key predistribution schemes for sensor networks. *2003 Symposium on Security and Privacy, 2003*, 197–213.

Chehri, A., & Mouftah, H. T. (2012). Energy efficiency adaptation for multihop routing in wireless sensor networks. *Journal of Computer Networks and Communications, 2012*.

Chen, D., & Varshney, P. K. (2004). QoS Support in Wireless Sensor Networks: A Survey. *International Conference on Wireless Networks, 233*, 1–7.

Chiang, M. W., Zilic, Z., Radecka, K., & Chenard, J.-S. (2004). Architectures of increased availability wireless sensor network nodes. *2004 International Conferce on Test*, 1232–1241.

Crawley, E., Nair, R., Rajagopalan, B., & Sandick, H. (1998). *A Framework for QoS-based Routing in the Internet*.

Deb, B., Bhatnagar, S., & Nath, B. (2003). ReInForM: Reliable information forwarding using multiple paths in sensor networks. *28th Annual IEEE International Conference on Local Computer Networks, 2003. LCN'03. Proceedings*, 406–415.

Desmedt, Y., & Jajodia, S. (1997). *Redistributing secret shares to new access structures and its applications*. Citeseer.

Eddous, M., & Stansfield, R. (1997). Methods of decision making. *UNITY, Audit*.

Esseghir, M., & Bouabdallah, N. (2008). Node density control for maximizing wireless sensor network lifetime. *International Journal of Network Management, 18*(2), 159–170.

Estrin, D., Girod, L., Pottie, G., & Srivastava, M. (2001). Instrumenting the world with wireless sensor networks. *2001 IEEE International Conference on Acoustics, Speech, and Signal Processing. Proceedings (Cat. No. 01CH37221)*, *4*, 2033–2036.

Garcıa-Macıas, J. A., Rousseau, F., Berger-Sabbatel, G., Toumi, L., & Duda, A. (2003). Quality of service and mobility for the wireless internet. *Wireless Networks, 9*(4), 341–352.

He, X., & Li, F. Y. (2012). Metric-based cooperative routing in multihop Ad Hoc networks. *Journal of Computer Networks and Communications, 2012*.

Huang, X., & Fang, Y. (2008). Multiconstrained QoS multi-path routing in wireless sensor networks. *Wireless Networks, 14*(4), 465–478.

Iyer, R., & Kleinrock, L. (2003). QoS control for sensor networks. *IEEE International Conference on Communications, 2003. ICC'03, 1*, 517–521.

Karlof, C., & Wagner, D. (2003). Secure routing in wireless sensor networks: Attacks and countermeasures. *Ad Hoc Networks, 1*(2–3), 293–315.

Klenk, F. K. S. S. A., & Weber, A. G. M. (n.d.). Securing ad hoc routing protocols. In *Proceedings of the 30th EUROMICRO conference (EUROMICRO 2004))* (pp. 514–519).

Kurose, J. F. (2005). *Computer networking: A top-down approach featuring the internet, 3/E*. Pearson Education India.

Lan, Y., Wenjing, W., & Fuxiang, G. (2008). A real-time and energy aware QoS routing protocol for multimedia wireless sensor networks. *2008 7th World Congress on Intelligent Control and Automation*, 3321–3326.

Madden, S., Franklin, M. J., Hellerstein, J. M., & Hong, W. (2002). TAG: A tiny aggregation service for ad-hoc sensor networks. *ACM SIGOPS Operating Systems Review*, *36*(SI), 131–146.

Mahadevan, I., & Sivalingam, K. M. (1999). Quality of service architectures for wireless networks: IntServ and DiffServ models. *Proceedings Fourth International Symposium on Parallel Architectures, Algorithms, and Networks (I-SPAN'99)*, 420–425.

Mahapatra, A., Anand, K., & Agrawal, D. P. (2006). QoS and energy aware routing for real-time traffic in wireless sensor networks. *Computer Communications*, *29*(4), 437–445.

Mbowe, J. E., & Oreku, G. S. (2014). Quality of service in wireless sensor networks. *Wireless Sensor Network, 2014*.

Nichols, K., Blake, S., Baker, F., & Black, D. (1998). *RFC2474: Definition of the differentiated services field (DS field) in the IPv4 and IPv6 headers*. RFC Editor.

Perillo, M., & Heinzelman, W. B. (2003). Providing application QoS through intelligent sensor management. *Proceedings of the First IEEE International Workshop on Sensor Network Protocols and Applications, 2003*, 93–101.

Pottie, G. J., & Kaiser, W. J. (2000). Wireless integrated network sensors. *Communications of the ACM*, *43*(5), 51–58.

Reason, J. M., & Rabaey, J. M. (2004). A study of energy consumption and reliability in a multihop sensor network. *ACM SIGMOBILE Mobile Computing and Communications Review*, *8*(1), 84–97.

Schulz, G. (1977). Taha, HA, Integer Programming Theory, Applications and Computations, New York-San Francisco-London. Academic Press. 1975. XII, 380 S., $19.50. *ZaMM*, *57*(9), 562–563.

Sohrabi, K., Gao, J., Ailawadhi, V., & Pottie, G. J. (2000). Protocols for self-organization of a wireless sensor network. *IEEE Personal Communications*, *7*(5), 16–27.

Stann, F., & Heidemann, J. (2003). RMST: Reliable data transport in sensor networks. *Proceedings of the First IEEE International Workshop on Sensor Network Protocols and Applications, 2003*, 102–112.

Wang, X., Chellappan, S., Gu, W., Yu, W., & Xuan, D. (2005). Search-based physical attacks in sensor networks. *Proceedings. 14th International Conference on Computer Communications and Networks, 2005. ICCCN 2005*, 489–496.

Wang, X., Gu, W., Schosek, K., Chellappan, S., & Xuan, D. (2005). Sensor network configuration under physical attacks. *International Conference on Networking and Mobile Computing*, 23–32.

Wang, Y., Liu, X., & Yin, J. (2006). Requirements of quality of service in wireless sensor network. *International Conference on Networking, International Conference on Systems and International Conference on Mobile Communications and Learning Technologies (ICNICONSMCL'06)*, 116.

Willig, A., & Karl, H. (2005). Data transport reliability in wireless sensor networks. a survey of issues and solutions. *PIK-Praxis Der Informationsverarbeitung Und Kommunikation*, *28*(2), 86–92.

Yang, Y., Wang, J., & Kravets, R. (2005). Designing routing metrics for mesh networks. *IEEE Workshop on Wireless Mesh Networks (WiMesh)*, 1–9.

Yang, Y., Zhong, C., Sun, Y., & Yang, J. (2010). Network coding based reliable disjoint and braided multi-path routing for sensor networks. *Journal of Network and Computer Applications*, *33*(4), 422–432.

Yang, Y.-H., & Feng, Y.-C. (2003). Survey of reliability and availability evaluation of complex system using Monte Carlo techniques. *Systems Engineering-Theory & Practice*, *2*, 80–85.

The Security Framework for Wireless Sensor Networks

4

INTRODUCTION

Wireless sensor networks (WSNs) refer to a heterogeneous system combining tiny sensors and actuators with general-purpose computing elements. These tiny sensors have some limitations in power supplies, bandwidth, memory size and energy (Akyildiz et al., 2002a; Loveric & Sieffert, 2007). Thus, the resource-limited nature of sensor networks poses great challenges for security (Akyildiz et al., 2002b). Furthermore, these sensor networks have attracted much attention and are highly recognized for their utility in a wide range of applications. For example, in the military, WSNs have been used for some applications such as sensing techniques for military commands, control, communications, computing, intelligence, surveillance, reconnaissance and targeting systems. In healthcare, sensor nodes can also be used for monitoring patients and assisting disabled patients. In addition, there are lots of applications for WSNs including commercial applications for managing inventory, monitoring product quality and monitoring disaster areas (Datema, 2005; Undercoffer et al., 2002).

Because of the resource-constrained nature of WSNs, users need to consider the best and the most suitable security mechanism against adversaries in WSNs (Walters et al., 2007). Generally, there are some serious limitations with current security mechanisms. For understanding these limitations, it is essential to realize differences between a WSN and general ad hoc networks (Sakarindr & Ansari, 2007; Zhou & Haas, 1999). The most important differences between sensor networks and ad hoc networks are as follows:

DOI: 10.1201/9781003257608-4

- The number of sensor nodes in a sensor network can be significantly higher than the nodes in an ad hoc network.
- Sensor nodes are densely deployed.
- Sensor nodes are prone to failures.
- The topology of a sensor network varies constantly.
- Sensor nodes basically use a broadcast communication. In contrast, most ad-hoc networks are based on point-to-point communications.
- Sensor nodes are limited in power, computational capacities, and memory.
- Sensor nodes may not have global identification (ID) because of the large amount of overhead and large number of sensors.

SECURITY REQUIREMENTS IN WSNS

A WSN is a special type of network. It shares some commonalities with a typical computer network, but also exhibits many characteristics that are unique to it. The security services in a WSN should protect the information communicated over the network and the resources from attacks and misbehavior of nodes. The most important security requirements in WSN are listed below:

1. **Data confidentiality**
   The security mechanism should ensure that no message in the network is understood by anyone except the intended recipient. In a WSN, the issue of confidentiality should address the following requirements (Carman et al., 2000; Perrig et al., 2002): (i) a sensor node should not allow its readings to be accessed by its neighbors unless they are authorized to do so, (ii) key distribution mechanism should be extremely robust, (iii) public information such as sensor identities and public keys of the nodes should also be encrypted in certain cases to protect against traffic analysis attacks.

2. **Data integrity**
   The mechanism should ensure that no message can be altered by an entity as it traverses from the sender to the recipient.

3. **Availability**
   This requirements ensures that the services of a WSN should be available even in presence of internal or external attacks such as a denial of service attack (DoS). Different approaches have been proposed by researchers to achieve this goal. While some mechanisms make use of additional communication among nodes, others propose the use of a central access control system to ensure successful delivery of every message to its recipient.

4. **Data freshness**
   Data freshness implies that the data is recent and ensures that no adversary can replay old messages. This requirement is especially important when the

WSN nodes use shared keys for message communication, where a potential adversary can launch a replay attack using the old key as the new key is being refreshed and propagated to all the nodes in the WSN. A nonce or time-specific counter may be added to each packet to check the freshness of the packet.

5. **Self-organization**

   Each node in a WSN should be self-organizing and self-healing. This feature of a WSN also poses a great challenge to security. The dynamic nature of a WSN makes it sometimes impossible to deploy any pre-installed shared key mechanism among the nodes and the base station (Eschenauer & Gligor, 2002). A number of key pre-distribution schemes have been proposed in the context of symmetric encryption (Eschenauer & Gligor, 2002; Hwang & Kim, 2004; Liu et al., 2005). However, for application of public-key cryptographic techniques an efficient mechanism for key distribution is very much essential. It is desirable that the nodes in a WSN self-organize among themselves not only for multi-hop routing but also to carry out key management and developing trust relations.

6. **Secure localization**

   In many situations, it becomes necessary to accurately and automatically locate each sensor node in a WSN. For example, a WSN designed to locate faults requires accurate locations of sensor nodes to identify the faults. A potential adversary can easily manipulate and provide false location information by reporting false signal strength, replaying messages, etc. if the location information is not secured properly. The authors (Capkun & Hubaux, 2006) have described a technique called verifiable multi-lateration (VM). In multi-lateration, the position of a device is accurately computed from a series of known reference points. The authors have used authenticated ranging and distance bounding to ensure accurate location of a node. Because of the use of distance bounding, an attacking node can only increase its claimed distance from a reference point. However, to ensure location consistency, the attacker would also have to prove that its distance from another reference point is shorter. As it is not possible for the attacker to prove this, it is possible to detect the attacker. Lazos and Poovendran (2005) have described a scheme called secure range-independent localization (SeRLoC). The scheme is a decentralized range-independent localization scheme. It is assumed that the locators are trustworthy and cannot be compromised by any attacker. A sensor computes its location by listening to the beacon information sent by each locator that includes the locator's location information. The beacon messages are encrypted using a shared global symmetric key that is pre-distributed in the sensor nodes. Using the information from all the beacons that a sensor node receives, it computes its approximate location based on the coordinates of the locators. The sensor node then computes an overlapping antenna region using a majority vote scheme. The final location of the sensor node is determined by computing the center of gravity of the overlapping antenna region.

7. **Time synchronization**

   Most of the applications in sensor networks require time synchronization. Any security mechanism for a WSN should also be time-synchronized. A collaborative WSN may require synchronization among a group of sensors. In Ganeriwal et al. (2005), a set of secure synchronization protocols have been proposed.

8. **Authentication**

   It ensures that the communicating node is the one that it claims to be. An adversary can not only modify data packets but also can change a packet stream by injecting fabricated packets. It is, therefore, essential for a receiver to have a mechanism to verify that the received packets have indeed come from the actual sender node. In case of communication between two nodes, data authentication can be achieved through a message authentication code (MAC) computed from the shared secret key. A number of authentication schemes for WSNs have been proposed by researchers, most of which are for secure routing.

WIRELESS SENSOR NETWORKS' SECURITY FRAMEWORK

In this section, defense mechanisms for combatting various types of attacks on WSNs will be discussed. Due to the limitations and difficulties that persist in the WSN discussed in the previous section, the security of WSNs is much more complicated. Correspondingly, there are many solutions for the security issues. Based on the research interests of the security of WSNs, four major components are as follows: (1) secure triple-key management scheme, (2) secure routing mechanism, (3) secure localization mechanism and (4) malicious node detection and prevention technique. Secure routing and secure localization mechanisms are protected by secure triple-key management scheme to ensure communication secrecy and authenticity. If the proposed key management scheme is compromised, then we can detect the malicious node using our malicious node detection mechanism. Figure 4.1 illustrates the WSN security frameworks. The following section describes the four components of the framework.

The Secure Triple-Key Management Scheme

Key management is critical to meet the security goals of confidentiality, integrity and authentication to prevent the sensor Nnetworks from being compromised by an adversary. Due to the ad hoc nature and resource limitations of sensor networks, providing a right key management is challenging. Traditional key management schemes based on trusted third parties, like a certification authority (CA), are impractical due to unknown

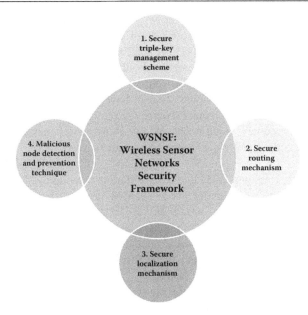

FIGURE 4.1   Wireless sensor network security framework.

topology prior to deployment. A trusted CA is required to be present at all times to support public key revocation and renewal (Hu et al., 2004). Trusting on a single CA for key management is more vulnerable; a compromised CA will risk the security of an entire sensor network (Hu et al., 2004). Decompose the key management problem into the following:

- **Key pre-distribution:** installation of keys in each sensor node prior to distribution – Neighbor discovery: discovering the neighbor node.
- **End-to-end path key establishment:** end-to-end communication with those nodes which are not directly connected.
- **Isolating aberrant nodes:** identifying and isolating damaged nodes.
- **Key-establishment latency:** reducing the latency resulted from communication and power consumption.

The fundamental problem we realize in WSN security is to initialize the secure communication between sensor nodes by setting up secret keys between communicating nodes. In general, we call this key establishment. There are three types of key establishment techniques (Du et al., 2004, 2005): trusted-server scheme, self-enforcing scheme and key pre-distribution scheme. The trusted server scheme depends on a trusted server e.g., Kerberos (Neuman & Ts'o, 1994). The self-enforcing scheme depends on asymmetric cryptography using public keys. However, limited computation resources in sensor nodes make this scheme less desirable. A simple solution is to store a master secret key in all the nodes and obtain a new pair-wise key. In this case, capture of one node will compromise the whole network. Storing the master key in tamper-resistant sensor nodes increases the cost and energy consumption of sensors. Another key pre-distribution scheme (Du et al., 2005) is to let each sensor carry N − 1 secret pair-wise keys, each of which is known only to this sensor and one of the other N − 1 sensors (N is the total number of sensors). Extending the network makes this technique impossible as existing nodes will not have the new nodes keys.

Our secure triple-key management scheme (Zia & Zomaya, 2006) consists of three keys: two pre-deployed keys in all nodes and one in-network generated cluster key for a cluster to address the hierarchical nature of sensor network.

- K_n (network key): generated by the base station, pre-deployed in each sensor node and shared by the entire sensor network. Nodes use this key to encrypt the data and pass onto the next hop.
- K_s (sensor key): generated by the base station, pre-deployed in each sensor node and shared by the entire sensor network. The base station uses this key to decrypt and process the data and the cluster leader uses this key to decrypt the data and send to the base station.
- K_c (cluster key): generated by the cluster leader and shared by the nodes in that particular cluster. Nodes from a cluster use this key to decrypt the data and forward to the cluster leader. Nodes will use this key only when they are serving the purpose as a cluster leader; otherwise, nodes will not need to decrypt the message received from other nodes thus saving the energy and processing power.

Triple key serves the purpose of confidentiality and authentication. The section below describes how this scheme works:

Base Station to Node Key Calculation

The base station uses K_n to encrypt and broadcast data. When a sensor node receives the message, it decrypts it by using its K_s. This process is as follows: base station encrypts its own ID, a current time stamp TS and its K_n as a private key. The base station generates a random seed S and assumes itself at level 0. The packet contains the following fields:

Kn	MAC	ID	TS	message	Level 0

The sensor node decrypts the message received from the base station using K_s. Here, MAC is message authentication code for a message (m).

Nodes to Cluster Leader Key Calculation

When a node sends a message to a cluster leader, it constructs the message as follows:

{IDsn, Kn, TS, MAC, (message)}

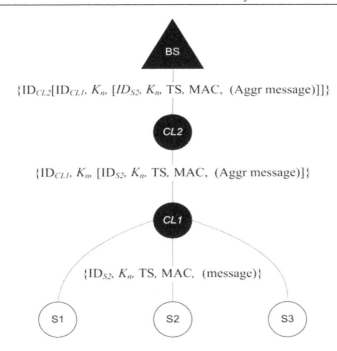

FIGURE 4.2   Key calculation from Sensor Node S2 to Cluster Leader CL1, Cluster Leader CL1 to Cluster Leader CL2 and Cluster Leader CL2 to the Base Station BS.

The cluster leader checks the ID from the packet. If the ID in the packet matches the ID it holds, it verifies the authentication and integrity of the packet through MAC. Otherwise, the packet is dropped by the cluster leader. The node builds the message using the fields below:

Kn	MAC	ID	TS	message	Level 2

Figure 4.2 illustrates the key calculation process from nodes to cluster leaders and to the base station.

Cluster Leader to Next Hop Cluster Leader Key Calculation

The cluster leader aggregates the messages received from its nodes and forwards it to the next-level cluster leader or, if the cluster leader is one hop away from the base station, it directly sends the message to the base station. The receiving cluster leader checks its routing table and constructs the following packet to be sent to the next-level cluster leader or to the base station. The cluster leader adds its own ID CLn, its network and cluster key in incoming packet, and rebuilds the packet as:

ID, KCLn, [IDsn, Kn, TS, MAC, (Aggr message)]}

Kn	MAC	ID	TS	message	Level 1

Here, ID is the ID of the receiving cluster leader that wraps the message and sends it to the next hop cluster leader or to the base station if directly connected. The next hop cluster leader receives the packet and checks the ID. If the ID embedded in the packet is same as it holds, it updates the ID for the next hop and broadcast it, or else the packet is discarded. An Aggr message refers to the message aggregated by the cluster leader.

Cluster Leader to Base Station Key Calculation

The base station receives the packet from its directly connected cluster leader; it checks the ID of sending cluster leader and verifies the authentication and integrity of the packet through MAC. The cluster leader directly connected with the base station adds its own ID along with the packet received from the sending cluster leader. The packet contains the following information:

IDCL2[IDCL1, Kn, [IDs2, Kn, TS, MAC, (Aggr message)]]}

Analysis of Secure Triple-Key Management Scheme

To analyze performance and overhead of the proposed Secure Triple-Key Scheme (STKS), it was compared with two well-known security schemes: TinySec (Karlof et al., 2004) and MiniSec (Luk et al., 2007). The packet format comparison in Table 4.1 and overhead comparison in Table 4.2 shows that the STKS does not have any additional overhead.

Also, STKS overcomes the weaknesses of TinySec. As per our analysis, TinySec is confusing because of its three different states: (1) no TinySec (CRC), (2) TinySec-Auth and (3) TinySec-AE. Also, TinySec assumes a message length of 8 bytes or more and does not address smaller messages. TinySec fails to provide secure

TABLE 4.1   Packet format in TinySec-Auth, TinySec-AE, MiniSec and STKS

Dest (2)	AM (1)	Len (1)	Data (29)	MAC (4)				
(a) Tiny-Sec-Auth (Authentication only): +8b								
Dest (2)	AM (1)	Len (1)	AM (1)	Src (2)	Ctr (2)	Data (29)	MAC (4)	
(b) Tiny-Sec-AE (Authentication and Encryption): +12b								
Len (1)	PCF (2)	DSN (1)	DstPAN (2)	Dest (2)	AM (1)	Src (2)	Data (29)	MAC (4)
(c) MiniSec U or B: +15b								
ID (3)	Keys (3)	TS (1)	Data (29)	MAC (4)				
(d) STKS: +11b								

TABLE 4.2 Comparison of overhead in TinySec and WSNF

	APPLICATION DATA	PACKET OVERHAND	TOTAL SIZE	TIME TO TRANSMIT	INCREASE OVER TINYOS STACK	LATENCY OVERHEAD	ENERGY OVERHEAD
TinySec-Auth	29	8	37	26.6	1.50%	1.70%	3%
TinySec-AE	29	12	41	28.8	8%	7.30%	10%
STKS	29	11	40	28.3	6.30%	5.90%	8.20%

localization or a secure routing mechanism while STKS address these weaknesses. Furthermore, TinySec does not provide security against insider attacks when a node is captured or compromised, whereas STKS detects the malicious nodes and disperses the information about the presence of such malicious nodes to their neighbors. Although MiniSec provides a good level, its overhead is far greater than TinySec and STKS.

Figure 4.3(a),(b) shows a comparative study of the security overhead in TinySec, MiniSec and STKS. It can be observed that the overhead for STKS is lower than those of the other three security schemes, as can be seen from the experimental results and evaluation of other components of the proposed framework. Low overheads allow the effective use of RC5 and CBC to achieve a high degree of security in sensor networks.

Secure Routing

In our secure routing mechanism, all the nodes have a unique ID#. Once the network is deployed, the base station builds a table containing ID#s of all the nodes in the network. After the self-organizing process, the base station knows the topology of the network. Nodes use our secure triple-key management scheme to collect the data and pass onto the cluster leader, which aggregates the data and sends it to the base station. We adapt the energy-efficient secure data transmission algorithms by Çam et al. (2003) and modify it with our secure triple-key management scheme to make it resilient against attacks in WSNs. Two algorithms (1) sensor node and (2) base station are presented below for secure data transfer from node to base station and base station to node communication:

The node algorithm performs the following functions:

- Sensor nodes use the K_n to encrypt and transmit the data
- Transmission of encrypted data from nodes to cluster leader
- Appending ID# to data and then forwarding it to a higher level of cluster leaders
- The cluster leader uses K_c to decrypt and then uses its K_n to encrypt and send the data to next level of cluster leaders, eventually reaching the base station

The base station algorithm is responsible of the following tasks:

- Broadcasting of K_s and K_n by the base station
- Decryption and authentication of data by the base station

Node Algorithm

1. Step 1: If sensor node i wants to send data to its cluster leader, go to step 2, else exit the algorithm.
2. Step 2: Sensor node i requests the cluster leader to send K_c.

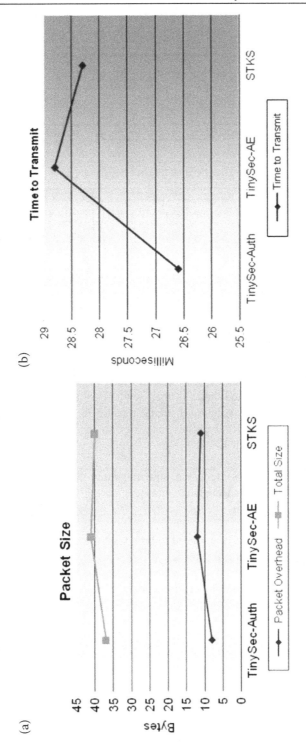

FIGURE 4.3 TinySec vs STKS. (a) Packet comparison; (b) time to transmit a packet.

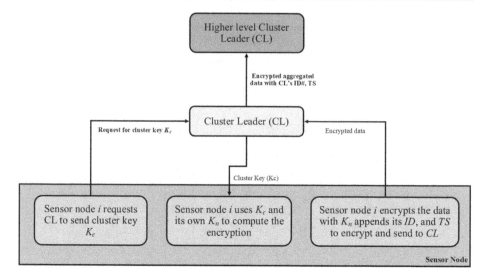

FIGURE 4.4   Sensor node i to cluster leader and base station communication.

3. Step 3: Sensor node i uses K_c and its own K_n to compute the encryption key K_{i,c_n}.
4. Step 4: Sensor node i encrypts the data with K_{i,c_n} and appends its ID# and the T_S to the encrypted data and then sends them to the cluster leader.
5. Step 5: Cluster leader receives the data, appends its own ID# and then sends them to the higher-level cluster leader or to the base station if directly connected. Go to step 1.

Figure 4.4 demonstrates this algorithm and illustrates the communication between sensor node i and the cluster leader.

Base Station Algorithm

1. Step 1: Check if there is any need to broadcast the message. If so, broadcast the message encrypting it with K_n.
2. Step 2: If there is no need to broadcast the message then check if there is any incoming message from the cluster leaders. If there is no data being sent to the base station, go to step 1.
3. Step 3: If there is any data coming to the base station then decrypt the data using K_s, ID# of the node and T_S within the data.
4. Step 4: Check if the decryption key K_s has decrypted the data perfectly. This leads to check the credibility of the T_S and the ID#. If the decrypted data is not perfect discard the data and go to step 6.
5. Step 5: Process the decrypted data and obtain the message sent by sensor nodes

6. Step 6: Decide whether to request all sensor nodes for retransmission of data. If not necessary, then go back to step 1.
7. Step 7: If a request is necessary, send the request to the sensor nodes to retransmit the data. When this session is finished go back to step 1.

This routing technique using our triple-key management scheme provides a strong resilience towards spoofed routing information attacks, selective forwarding, sinkhole attacks, Sybil attacks, wormholes and HELLO flood attacks presented in Karlof and Wagner (2003).

Secure Localization

Determining the location of nodes is very important for many sensitive applications. Due to the deployment nature of sensor networks, security is a major concern. This section is divided into two parts: (1) determining the node location and (2) securing the node location.

Determining the Node Location

A basic feature of a location system is the ability to determine the location of a node and verify its distance from the neighboring nodes (Sastry et al., 2003). In our secure localization mechanism, each node determines its position by calculating its distance from its neighbors using four well-known methods in triangulation: lateration, attenuation, propagation and angulations. Figure 4.5 illustrates the triangulation process to determine the node location. Each node determines its position by calculating its distance from its neighbors.

Triangulation process:

$$\frac{\sin A}{X} = \frac{\sin B}{Y} = \frac{\sin C}{Z} \quad (sines\ laws)$$

$$\left. \begin{array}{l} A^2 = B^2 + C^2 - 2BC \cos X \\ B^2 = A^2 + C^2 - 2AC \cos Y \\ C^2 = A^2 + B^2 - 2AB \cos Z \end{array} \right\} \quad (coses\ laws)$$

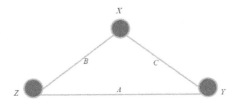

FIGURE 4.5 Triangulations.

Node location in triangulation is calculated by using trigonometry laws of sines and cosines as follows:

- **Lateration**

  We assume that when the nodes are deployed they know their location through an atomic multileteration process (Savvides et al., 2001). In this process, the node estimates its location if it is in the range of three other nodes. When a base station sends a beacon to form the network topology, the nodes reply with their position in the network. Each node determines its position by calculating its distance from its neighbors.

- **Attenuation**

  In the attenuation triangulation model, the signal strength decreases as the distance between two nodes increases. We assume a dense network where nodes are deployed in close distances. In a hierarchical clustered model, the parent nodes are aware of their child nodes' locations.

- **Propagation**

  Node A sends a message to node B and node B calculates the time difference $t2 - t1$ between two nodes. $t1$ is the time recorded when a message leaves node A and $t2$ is when a message arrives at node B.

- **Angulations**

  Angulations use angles to determine the distance between nodes using directional antennas. In a 2-D position, two angles and one distance measurement is used, while in a 3-D position two angles, one length and one azimuth measurement is used.

Securing the Node Location: An Analysis

Nodes change their position when they move in a dynamic network or if an adversary has compromised the node. In the event of a compromise, a node is considered a malicious node. The localization process described here is protected by the secure triple-key management scheme.

The base station broadcasts a beacon message to the sensor network; this message is encrypted by K_n. If the receiving node is a cluster leader, it decrypts the message using K_s and encrypts it again with its K_n and forwards it to the nodes in its cluster. Every node in that cluster use its K_c to decrypt the message, adds its location and replies back to the cluster leader with its location encrypted with K_n. The cluster leader receives the locations from all nodes in the cluster and encrypts it with K_n and sends it to the base station. The base station uses its K_s to decrypt the message and becomes aware of the nodes' location in the entire network. The process of base station to cluster leader and nodes and vice versa is described in the following steps:

1. Step 1: To establish the secure communication, the base station builds a packet that contains IDBS, K_n, TS, MAC, S (message).

2. Step 2: The cluster leader builds a packet containing the following information: IDCL, K_n, TS, MAC, S (message).
3. Step 3: The nodes to cluster leader packet consists of IDsn, K_n, TS, MAC, S (message).
4. Step 4: The cluster leader aggregates the messages received from the nodes in its cluster and forwards it to the base station using the packet: IDCL, K_n, TS, MAC, S (Aggr message).

Malicious Node Detection Mechanism

This section describes the fourth and last component of the framework. In our malicious node detection mechanism, we consider the dynamic and scalable nature of sensor networks where sensor nodes are replaced after reaching energy exhaustion. The message sending node observes the packet receiving node; hence, becoming a monitor to watch the behavior of the receiving node. Due to the broadcast nature of WSNs, the monitoring node watches if the receiving node is sending the packet intact or alters the packet contents other than adding its header information.

A malicious node is a compromised node where an adversary has somehow been able to break the encryption (Khalil et al., 2005) and has gotten access to the secure keys and routing protocols of the sensor network. The malicious node detection mechanism is protected by our underlying security framework that is based on a set of three secure keys (TKS). This section demonstrates how a malicious node is detected if, in a less likely event, of a secure triple-key management scheme compromise.

In the proposed malicious node detection technique, we use a monitoring mechanism. In this mechanism, when node A sends a message to node B, it converts itself to a monitoring mode we refer to here as Am. Due to the broadcast nature of WSNs, Am monitors the behavior of node B after sending the message. When node B transmits the message to the next node, Am hears that and compares it with the message it has sent to node B; hence, establishing the original and actual message. If the message transmitted by node B is original, then node Am ignores it and continues with its own tasks but if there is a difference between the original and actual messages greater than a predefined threshold, the message is considered suspicious and node B is now considered a suspicious node Bs. In our experimental evaluation, we used a value of three as a threshold to determine an anomaly.

Each node builds a node suspicious table containing the reputation of nodes in the cluster. Entries in this table contain the node ID and the number of suspicious and unsuspicious entries. Nodes update this table every time they identify a suspicious activity by increasing the suspicious count by one for that particular node. In Table 4.3

TABLE 4.3 Node suspicious table

NODE ID	SUSPICIOUS ENTRIES	UNSUSPICIOUS ENTRIES
ID	NS > 1	NU > 1

below, ID is the unique ID of the sensor node, NS denotes node suspicious and NU is the node unsuspicious entries.

All the nodes locally build a node suspicious table. Every time A^m identifies a suspicious entry, it adds into its node suspicious table and disseminates this information among its neighbors and all the nodes listening to this message update their node suspicious table. This broadcast message also acts as an inquiry. Nodes listening to this message reply with their opinion about B_s. In Figure 4.6, nodes C and D are neighboring nodes of A_m and B_s. They listen to the transmission from B_s and respond with a suspicious entry if the suspicious count for B_s in its node suspicious table is greater than its unsuspicious count; otherwise, it responds with unsuspicious (Figure 4.7).

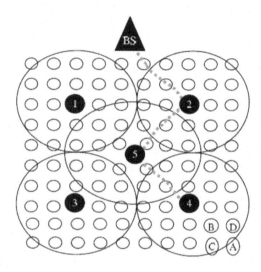

FIGURE 4.6   Node A^m (monitoring node) and B_s (suspicious node) and nodes C and D neighboring nodes.

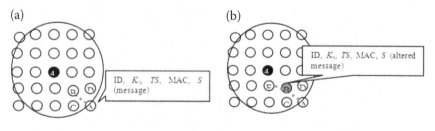

(a)

ID, K_n, TS, MAC, S (message)

Message sent by Node A
ID, K_n, TS, MAC, S (message)

(b)

ID, K_n, TS, MAC, S (altered message)

Message altered by Node B
ID, K_n, TS, MAC, S (altered message)

FIGURE 4.7   (a) Shows a message sent by node A, secured with our network key K_n and in (b), an altered message is shown from node B.

An ID is the node's unique identifier, K_n is the network key, TS is an encrypted time stamp, MAC is the message authentication code generated using K_n for message m and S is the randomly generated seed value by the base station.

Node A_m collects the replies from neighbors and updates its node suspicious table; it increases its own suspicious entry for B_s by one and the unsuspicious entries accordingly.

Once the suspicious entries reach a threshold, node A_m broadcasts that node B_s is a suspicious node and all the neighboring nodes update their node suspicious tables that a malicious node is present in the cluster. When the presence of a suspicious node message reaches a cluster leader, it isolates B_s by erasing B_s ID from its nodes table and discards any message coming from B_s. The cluster leader broadcasts the message that node B_s has been isolated; therefore, any message originated from B_s is discarded by its neighboring nodes and hence isolating node B_s from the network.

THREAT MODEL

Threats in sensor networks can be classified as external and internal. External threats occur from outside the sensor network and may amount to mere passive eavesdropping on data transmissions, but can extend to injecting bogus data into the network to consume network resources and rage denial of service (DoS) attacks. Internal threats stem from compromised nodes running malicious data or from attackers who have stolen the cryptographical contents from legitimate nodes. The proposed framework addresses both internal and external threats.

Roosta et al. (2006) have categorized attackers as mote-class attackers and laptop-class attackers. A mote-class attacker has access to a few motes with the same capabilities as other motes in the network. A laptop-class attacker has access to more powerful devices, such as laptops. This gives the adversary an advantage over the sensor network since it can launch more serious attacks.

An insider attack vs. an outsider attack: An outside attacker has no special access to the sensor network, such as passive eavesdropping, whereas an inside attacker has access to the encryption keys or other codes used by the network. Thus, an inside attacker could, for example, be a compromised node that is a legitimate part of the sensor network.

A passive attacker vs. an active attacker: Passive attackers are only interested in collecting sensitive data from the sensor network, which compromises the privacy and confidentiality requirements. In contrast, the active attackers' goal is to disrupt the function of the network and degrade its performance. For example, the attacker might inject faulty data into the network by pretending to be a legitimate node.

The next classification of attacks is based on network layers: attacks at the physical layer, at the data link layer and at the network layer. A physical layer attacker mainly exhausts the resources available by transmitting the radio signals on a wireless channel. A data link layer attacker violates the predefined protocols of the link layer. This kind of attack also leads to a denial of service attack. A network layer attacker

TABLE 4.4   Threats in various layers under WSN (Jain et al., 2012)

LAYERS	ATTACKS
Physical	1. Denial of Service (DoS)
	2. Tempering
Data Link	1. Jamming
	2. Collision
Network	1. Sybil Attack
	2. Wormhole Attack
	3. Sinkhole Attack
	4. Flooding
Application	1. Desynchronization
	2. Aggregation-Based Attacks

threatens the sensor applications and services. In this, localization and aggregation are used to prevent from this attack (Table 4.4).

TRUST MODEL

Generally, the security of WSNs can be achieved by cryptographic mechanisms. These mechanisms are very powerful against outsider attacks. However, they are not efficient at dealing with insider attacks. When a node in a sensor network is compromised, cryptographic keys of this node will also be compromised. Consequently, the node cannot be identified as legitimate or not by only using cryptographic solutions. Furthermore, they fail in identifying misbehavior of selfish nodes and faulty nodes. To solve these issues, trust-based models have been proposed.

Trust is defined as a subjective view of the reliability of other entities or functions, including authenticity of data, connectivity of path, processing capability of node and availability of service, etc. The trust model is used to evaluate the trustworthiness of nodes, based on a proper set of trust metrics. They have strong capabilities to identify the malicious entities and offer a prediction of one's future behavior. Trust is not only used for achieving the general security of WSNs but also used in many applications like routing, data aggregation, access control and intrusion detection (Kumar et al., 2012). However, trust systems are vulnerable to some specific attacks such as bad mouthing, white washing, on-off and conflicting behavior attacks. These attacks need special consideration and countermeasures.

The trust model consists of three components: data trust, behavior trust and historical trust. Real-time data, regional data and historical data are considered in the calculation of data trust. This ensures that the data trust is coherent and reduces the possibility of false positives. Behavior trust is based on the statistical value of abnormal behavior. Historical trust is given initially and then updated according to the comprehensive trust. In the model, some thresholds are set. According to the trust value and the threshold value, we can update each trust value.

The trust model proposed in this section can be thought of as a simple form of anomaly detection. The basis of detection depends on the degree of trust between perceived objects and decision objects. The computation and storage of trust value are all located on the decision objects. The perceived objects of WSNs are only involved in the data collection and forwarding. Therefore, the reliability of the trust value is guaranteed.

Trust Evaluation Model

The trust evaluation model is mainly used in the perception layer of WSNs. The perception layer of WSNs can be subdivided into the sensor node, relay node and sink node. The different types of nodes have different behaviors and data. In this paper, we only give the evaluation to the sensor and relay nodes. The sink node directly communicates with the gateway, so its security is relatively easy to guarantee. In the data transmission phase, the sensor nodes collect data and transmit it to the relay nodes (the cluster head). The relay nodes carry out data fusion and transfer data to the sink. The trust value of the sensor nodes is calculated in the cluster heads. The trust value of the cluster head is calculated in the sink head.

In this model, the trust evaluation is made up of three parts: behavior trust, data trust and historical trust. Behavior trust consists of two parts: direct behavior trust and historical behavior trust. Data trust is composed of direct data trust, regional relative trust and historical data trust. The initial value of historical trust is given and is updated according to the value of comprehensive trust and the threshold value. The trust evaluation model is shown in Figure 4.8.

Trust Evaluation of the Sensor Node

Data Trust of the Sensor Node
In order to obtain accurate information, a large number of sensor nodes are usually deployed in the monitoring area. This reduces the precision requirements of individual sensor nodes. In addition, a large number of redundant nodes also give the system strong fault tolerance and can increase the coverage range of the monitoring area and reduce the cave or blind. This feature also gives the opportunity to use monitoring data in conducting trust evaluation. In this paper, data trust is composed of direct data trust, regional relative trust and historical data trust.

Direct Data Trust
In this model, the relay node is responsible for preserving the historical sensor data. The monitoring indicators are assumed to be continuous, and do not have the characteristics of jump. Since the monitoring indicators are assumed to be continuous, the difference between real-time monitoring data and historical data should theoretically be within a certain range. If the difference between the real-time monitoring data and the historical data is too large, it represents abnormal nodes. So, direct data trust can be

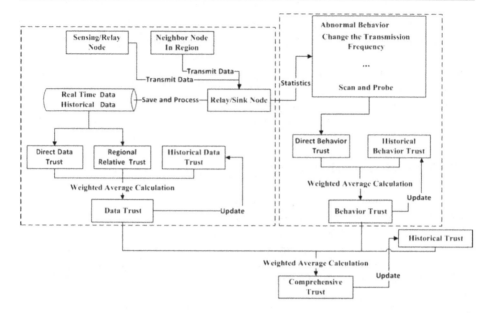

FIGURE 4.8   The trust evaluation model.

calculated by using the real-time monitoring value and the historical data of sensor nodes. The historical data is the average of data in the recent period of time. The real-time monitoring data of the i-th sensor node is recorded as r_{Data_i}, and the historical value is recorded as h_{Data_i}. The direct data trust of the i-th sensor node is recorded as $_{data}^{ddt}T_i$. The $_{data}^{ddt}T_i$ can be calculated by Equation (4.1):

$$_{data}^{ddt}T_i = MAX \times \left(\left(\left(|r_{Data_i} - h_{Data_i}| - ddt_K \right) > 0? \; 0: \; ||r_{Data_i} - h_{Data_i}| - ddt_K|/ddt_K \right) \right) \qquad (4.1)$$

where *MAX* is a maximum value and it is set by experience or experts. The value of ddt_K is the threshold and it is defined as the upper bound of the absolute value of the difference between the real-time monitoring value and the historical value, set by experience or experts. The initial value of $_{data}^{ddt}T_i$ is set to *MAX* and $_{data}^{ddt}T_i \in [0, MAX]$.

For example, set $r_{Data_i} = 28.8$, $h_{Data_i} = 26$, $ddt_K = 5$, $MAX = 100$, then $_{data}^{ddt}T_i = \lfloor 100 \times (((|28.7 - 26| - 5) > 0? \; 0: \; |28.7 - 26| - 5|)/5) \rfloor = \lfloor 100 \times ((-2.3 > 0? \; 0: \; 2.3)/5) \rfloor = \lfloor 100 \times (2.3/5) \rfloor = \lfloor 46 \rfloor = 46$.

Regional Relative Trust
A region is a set of sensor nodes that are in communication with the same relay node. Within a certain region, the difference of the real-time data of the same monitoring index should be within a certain range. Based on this, we give the regional relative trust. In order to compute simplicity, we use the weighted average of real-time monitoring values – which comes from the other trusted nodes in the region – to participate in the computation. The regional relative trust of the i-th sensor node is

calculated by the real-time monitoring data of the i-th sensor node and the average value of the real-time monitoring data of other sensor nodes in the region. Assuming that the i-th sensor node has n neighbors in the trust list and the data trust of neighbor nodes is greater than or equal to Th_{susp}^{data}, the average of real-time monitoring data is recorded as n_{AVER_i}, and it can be calculated by Equation (4.2), wherein j is a natural number.

$$n_{AVER_i} = \sum_{j=1}^{n} r_{Data_j}/n \qquad (4.2)$$

$$dif_i^{rrt} = \begin{cases} rrt_K, \ n_{AVER_i} = 0 \\ (|r_{Data_i} - n_{AVER_i}| - rrt_K) > 0? \ 0: \ ||r_{Data_i} - n_{AVER_i}| - rrt_K|, \ n_{AVER_i} \neq 0 \end{cases}$$

The regional relative trust of the i-th sensor node is recorded as $_{data}^{rrt}T_i$, and it can be calculated by Equation (4.3):

$$_{data}^{rrt}T_i = MAX \times (dif_i^{rrt}/rrt_K) \qquad (4.3)$$

where MAX is equal to the previous values. The value of rrt_K is the threshold, and it is defined as the upper bound of the absolute value of the difference between the real-time monitoring value and the average mean of n neighbors, set by experience or experts. The initial value of $_{data}^{rrt}T_i$ is set to MAX and $_{data}^{rrt}T_i \in [0, MAX]$.

Data Trust of the Sensor Node
The value of data trust is obtained by the weighted average calculation using direct data trust, regional relative trust and historical data trust. The direct data trust and regional relative trust can be calculated by Equations (4.1) and (4.3), respectively. The initial value of the historical data trust is set manually, and then updated according to the data trust value. The data trust of the i-th sensor node is recorded as $data\ T_i$. The historical data trust of the i-th sensor node is recorded as $_{data}^{hdt}T_i$. The calculation method is shown in Equation (4.4):

$$data\ T_i = [\alpha \times {}_{data}^{ddt}T_i + \beta \times {}_{data}^{rrt}T_i + \gamma \times {}_{data}^{hdt}T_i] \qquad (4.4)$$

where α, β, γ are weighting coefficients and $0 < \alpha$, β, $\gamma < 1$, $\alpha + \beta + \gamma = 1$. The user, the experts and the experience can set its value.

Historical Data Trust
The initial value of historical data trust is set to MAX and updated according to the data trust. The two thresholds are given respectively: suspected abnormal threshold (recorded as Thdatasusp) and abnormal threshold (recorded as Thdataabn). The calculation method is shown in Equation (4.5):

$$
{}^{hdt}_{data}T_i = \begin{cases} data\ T_i,\ data\ T_i < Th^{data}_{susp} \\ data\ T_i - |data\ T_i < Th^{data}_{susp}|,\ Th^{data}_{susp} < data\ T_i < Th^{data}_{abn} \\ data\ T_i - \tau_{data} \times |data\ T_i < Th^{data}_{abn}|,\ data\ T_i \geq Th^{data}_{abn} \end{cases} \tag{4.5}
$$

In this equation, τ_{data} ($\tau_{data} \geq 1$) is the penalty coefficient. It can adjust the intensity of punishment.

Behavior Trust of the Sensor Node
We judge the state of nodes by collecting the behavior characteristics of nodes. The malicious behaviors of the sensor node mainly include distorted information, injected information, changing of the transmission frequency, scanning, probing, etc. The malicious behavior in tampering with data can be attributed to the data trust evaluation. In this, we only consider changing the transmission frequency, scanning and probing. Behavior trust is divided into direct behavior trust and historical behavior trust.

Direct Behavior Trust
The transmission frequency of sensor data is usually fixed, and so the transmission frequency becomes one of the important indicators for detecting the node behavior. The standard transmission frequency of the sensor nodes is set to M. The actual transmission frequency of the i-th sensor node is denoted as mi. When the network is stable, the relay node of each sensor node is stable. The behavior of sensor nodes to scan and detect other relay nodes is usually considered abnormal. The number of the i-th sensor node scanning and probing is recorded as t_i. The direct behavior trust of the i-th sensor node is recorded as ${}^{dbt}_{behavior}T_i$. The calculation method is shown in Equation (4.6):

$$
dif^{rrt}_i = t_i > TH_{sp}\ ?\ 0:\ |t_i > TH_{sp}|
$$

$$
{}^{dbt}_{behavior}T_i = \varepsilon_1 \times \lfloor MAX \times ((m_i < (M - \delta)\&\&m_i < (M - \delta))?\ 1:\ 0)
$$
$$
+ \varepsilon_2 \times \lfloor MAX \times (dif^{rrt}_i / TH_{sp}) \rfloor \rfloor \tag{4.6}
$$

where MAX is equal to the previous values, ε_1 and ε_2 are weighting coefficients and $0 < \varepsilon_1,\ \varepsilon_2 < 1,\ \varepsilon_1 + \varepsilon_2 = 1$. The user, experts and experience can set the value. The value of δ is a fault tolerance factor, and TH_{sp} is the threshold value, which is used to represent the upper bound of the number of scanning and probing.

Behavior Trust of the Sensor Node
The value of behavior trust is obtained by the weighted average calculation, using direct behavior trust and historical behavior trust. The direct behavior trust can be calculated by Equation (4.6). The initial value of the history behavior trust is set manually and then updated according to behavior trust. The behavior trust of the i-th sensor node is recorded as ${}_{behavior}T_i$. The historical behavior trust of the i-th sensor node is recorded as ${}^{hbt}_{behavior}T_i$. The calculation method is shown in Equation (4.7):

$$_{behavior}T_i = \lambda_1 \times {}_{behavior}^{dbt}T_i + \lambda_2 \times {}_{behavior}^{hbt}T_i \tag{4.7}$$

where λ_1, λ_2 are weighting coefficients, and $0 < \lambda_1, \lambda_2 < 1$, $\lambda_1 + \lambda_2 = 1$. The user, experts and experience can set the value.

Historical Behavior Trust
The initial value of historical behavior trust is set to *MAX* and updated according to behavior trust. The two thresholds are given, respectively: suspected abnormal threshold (recorded as $Th_{susp}^{behavior}$) and abnormal threshold (recorded as $Th_{abn}^{behavior}$). The calculation method is shown in Equation (4.8):

$$_{behavior}^{hbt}T_i = \begin{cases} _{behavior}T_i, \ {}_{behavior}T_i < Th_{susp}^{behavior} \\ _{behavior}T_i - |_{behavior}T_i - Th_{susp}^{behavior}|, \ Th_{susp}^{behavior} < {}_{behavior}T_i < Th_{abn}^{behavior} \\ _{behavior}T_{ii} - \tau_{behavior} \times |_{behavior}T_i - Th_{abn}^{behavior}|, \ {}_{behavior}T_i \geq Th_{abn}^{behavior} \end{cases} \tag{4.8}$$

In this equation, $\tau_{behavior}$ ($\tau_{behavior} \geq 1$) is the penalty coefficient. It can adjust the intensity of punishment.

Comprehensive Trust of the Sensor Node
The value of the comprehensive trust is given by the weighted average calculation, using data trust, behavior trust and historical trust. Data trust and behavior trust can be calculated by Equations (4.4) and (4.7), respectively. The initial value of the history trust is set manually and updated according to the comprehensive trust value. The comprehensive trust of the *i*-th sensor node is recorded as T_i. The historical trust of the *i*-th sensor node is recorded as Tihistory. The calculation method is shown in Equation (4.9):

$$T_i = [\phi_1 \times {}_{data}T_i + \phi_2 \times {}_{behavior}T_i + \phi_3 \times {}_{history}T_i] \tag{4.9}$$

where ϕ_1, ϕ_2, ϕ_3 are weighting coefficients, and $0 < \phi_1, \phi_2, \phi_3 < 1$, $\phi_1 + \phi_2 + \phi_3 = 1$. The user, experts and experience can set the value.

Historical Trust of the Sensor Node
The historical trust of the sensor nodes is similar to that of the historical data trust and the historical behavior trust. Its initial value is set to *MAX*. The calculation method is shown in Equation (4.10):

$$_{history}T_i = \begin{cases} T_i, \ T_i < Th_{susp} \\ T_i - |T_i - Th_{susp}|, \ Th_{susp} < T_i < Th_{abn} \\ T_i - \tau \times |T_i - Th_{abn}|, \ T_i \geq Th_{abn} \end{cases} \tag{4.10}$$

In this equation, $\tau\,(\tau \geq 1)$ is the penalty coefficient. It can adjust the intensity of punishment. The values of Th_{susp} and Th_{abn} are the threshold values.

Trust Evaluation of the Relay Node

The relay node is responsible for the trust evaluation of sensor nodes, data forwarding and data fusion. The sink node executes the trust evaluation of the relay node, and it also includes data trust, behavior trust and historical trust. The value of the comprehensive trust is also obtained by the weighted calculation of data trust, behavior trust and historical trust.

Data Trust

The calculation process of trust in relay nodes is similar to that of sensor nodes. The difference is mainly focused on the data and the definition of region. The data are the fused data in the relay node. The region is a collection of all relay nodes that are limited within a certain range (e.g., a circle with a radius R), or are in communication with the same sink node. Therefore, the calculation process of the relay node is not introduced in detail.

Trust List

In this paper, a trust list is introduced in order to guarantee the reliability of the data involved in fusion. Each sensor node needs to be authenticated in the access network, so the initial value of the trust list contains all the sensor nodes. In the subsequent operation, the trust list is updated according to the comprehensive trust of each sensor node. The update process is shown in Figure 4.9.

Figure 4.9 shows the update process for the trust list and historical trust. According to Equation (4.10), the following judgment and calculation will be performed.

If the comprehensive trust is lower than the suspected threshold, then the history trust is equal to the comprehensive trust.

If the comprehensive trust is higher than the suspected threshold, then the anomaly threshold is compared. If it is lower than the anomaly threshold, then the penalty operation is performed to update the historical trust.

If the comprehensive trust is lower than the anomaly threshold, the sensor node is considered to be credible. So, after the historical trust is updated and the trust list is checked, if the sensor node does not exist, it is added to the trust list.

If the comprehensive trust is higher than the anomaly threshold, the penalty factor is introduced to calculate and update historical trust, and then the sensor node is removed from the trust list.

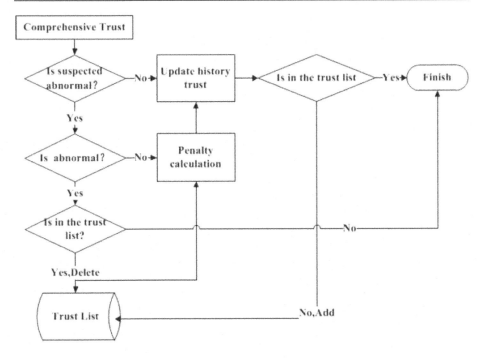

FIGURE 4.9   Update of the trust list.

CONCLUSION

One of the basic goals for WSNs is to collect information from the physical world. Using WSNs has lots of advantages including: (1) avoiding unnecessary wiring, (2) accommodating new devices at any time, (3) providing flexibility to go through partitions and (4) having enhanced mobility and reducing the cost of implementation compared to wired networks. In contrast, disadvantages can include: (1) possible loss of signal, (2) signals not readily accessing the networks and (3) the nodes in WSNs being battery-powered.

One of the major challenges facing WSNs today is the security. Security in sensor networks has been an increasingly important issue for academia, industry individuals and groups working in this fast-growing research area. This chapter includes many security solutions or mechanisms based on threat and trust management security methods that are suggested to achieve the security services while considering the limitations of the WSNs. The trust evaluation model in this chapter not only makes full use of sensor data, but it also includes behavior data and historical data that can help to detect the state of the node according to the data trust. However, there is no security mechanism that can provide complete security. Designing a secure WSN requires proper mapping of security solutions or mechanisms with different security parameters.

REFERENCES

Akyildiz, I. F., Su, W., Sankarasubramaniam, Y., & Cayirci, E. (2002a). A survey on sensor networks. *IEEE Communications Magazine, 40*(8), 102–114.

Akyildiz, I. F., Su, W., Sankarasubramaniam, Y., & Cayirci, E. (2002b). Wireless sensor networks: A survey. *Computer Networks, 38*(4), 393–422.

Çam, H., Ozdemir, S., Muthuavinashiappan, D., & Nair, P. (2003). Energy efficient security protocol for wireless sensor networks. *2003 IEEE 58th Vehicular Technology Conference. VTC 2003-Fall (IEEE Cat. No. 03CH37484), 5,* 2981–2984.

Capkun, S., & Hubaux, J.-P. (2006). Secure positioning in wireless networks. *IEEE Journal on Selected Areas in Communications, 24*(2), 221–232.

Carman, D. W., Kruus, P. S., & Matt, B. J. (2000). Constraints and approaches for distributed sensor network security (final). *DARPA Project Report (Cryptographic Technologies Group, Trusted Information System, NAI Labs), 1*(1), 1–39.

Datema, S. (2005). *A case study of wireless sensor network attacks.* Delft University of Technology.

Du, W., Deng, J., Han, Y. S., Chen, S., & Varshney, P. K. (2004). A key management scheme for wireless sensor networks using deployment knowledge. *IEEE INFOCOM 2004, 1.*

Du, W., Deng, J., Han, Y. S., Varshney, P. K., Katz, J., & Khalili, A. (2005). A pairwise key predistribution scheme for wireless sensor networks. *ACM Transactions on Information and System Security (TISSEC), 8*(2), 228–258.

Eschenauer, L., & Gligor, V. D. (2002). A key-management scheme for distributed sensor networks. *Proceedings of the 9th ACM Conference on Computer and Communications Security,* 41–47.

Ganeriwal, S., Čapkun, S., Han, C.-C., & Srivastava, M. B. (2005). Secure time synchronization service for sensor networks. *Proceedings of the 4th ACM Workshop on Wireless Security,* 97–106.

Hu, F., Ziobro, J., Tillett, J., & Sharma, N. K. (2004). *Secure wireless sensor networks: Problems and solutions.* Rochester, New York, USA: Rochester Institute of Technology.

Hwang, J., & Kim, Y. (2004). Revisiting random key pre-distribution schemes for wireless sensor networks. *Proceedings of the 2nd ACM Workshop on Security of Ad Hoc and Sensor Networks,* 43–52.

Jain, A., Kant, K., & Tripathy, M. R. (2012). Security solutions for wireless sensor networks. *2012 Second International Conference on Advanced Computing & Communication Technologies,* 430–433.

Karlof, C., Sastry, N., & Wagner, D. (2004). TinySec: A link layer security architecture for wireless sensor networks. *Proceedings of the 2nd International Conference on Embedded Networked Sensor Systems,* 162–175.

Karlof, C., & Wagner, D. (2003). Secure routing in wireless sensor networks: Attacks and countermeasures. *Ad Hoc Networks, 1*(2–3), 293–315.

Khalil, I., Bagchi, S., & Nina-Rotaru, C. (2005). DICAS: Detection, diagnosis and isolation of control attacks in sensor networks. *First International Conference on Security and Privacy for Emerging Areas in Communications Networks (SECURECOMM'05),* 89–100.

Lazos, L., & Poovendran, R. (2005). SeRLoc: Robust localization for wireless sensor networks. *ACM Transactions on Sensor Networks (TOSN), 1*(1), 73–100.

Liu, D., Ning, P., & Li, R. (2005). Establishing pairwise keys in distributed sensor networks. *ACM Transactions on Information and System Security (TISSEC), 8*(1), 41–77.

Loveric, S., & Sieffert, M. (2007). *Survey on Security Challenges as Related to Wireless Sensor Networks*. Technical Report, University of Binghamton.

Luk, M., Mezzour, G., Perrig, A., & Gligor, V. (2007). MiniSec: A secure sensor network communication architecture. *2007 6th International Symposium on Information Processing in Sensor Networks*, 479–488.

Neuman, B. C., & Ts'o, T. (1994). Kerberos: An authentication service for computer networks. *IEEE Communications Magazine, 32*(9), 33–38.

Perrig, A., Szewczyk, R., Tygar, J. D., Wen, V., & Culler, D. E. (2002). SPINS: Security protocols for sensor networks. *Wireless Networks, 8*(5), 521–534.

Roosta, T., Shieh, S., & Sastry, S. (2006). Taxonomy of security attacks in sensor networks and countermeasures. *The First IEEE International Conference on System Integration and Reliability Improvements, 25*, 94.

Sakarindr, P., & Ansari, N. (2007). Security services in group communications over wireless infrastructure, mobile ad hoc, and wireless sensor networks. *IEEE Wireless Communications, 14*(5), 8–20.

Sastry, N., Shankar, U., & Wagner, D. (2003). Secure verification of location claims. *Proceedings of the 2nd ACM Workshop on Wireless Security*, 1–10.

Savvides, A., Han, C.-C., & Strivastava, M. B. (2001). Dynamic fine-grained localization in ad-hoc networks of sensors. *Proceedings of the 7th Annual International Conference on Mobile Computing and Networking*, 166–179.

Undercoffer, J., Avancha, S., Joshi, A., & Pinkston, J. (2002). Security for sensor networks. *CADIP Research Symposium*, 25–26.

Walters, J. P., Liang, Z., Shi, W., & Chaudhary, V. (2007). Wireless sensor network security: A survey. *Security in Distributed, Grid, Mobile, and Pervasive Computing, 1*(367), 6.

Zhou, L., & Haas, Z. J. (1999). Securing ad hoc networks. *IEEE Network, 13*(6), 24–30.

Zia, T., & Zomaya, A. (2006). A secure triple-key management scheme for wireless sensor networks. *Proceedings IEEE INFOCOM 2006. 25TH IEEE International Conference on Computer Communications*, 1–2.

Secure Key Management Scheme (SKMS)

5

INTRODUCTION

Recent advances in electronic and computer technologies have paved the way for the proliferation of wireless sensor networks (WSNs). As we have already discussed, the sensor networks usually consist of a large number of ultra-small autonomous devices. Each device, called a sensor node, is battery powered and equipped with integrated sensors, data processing capabilities and short-range radio communications. In typical application scenarios, sensor nodes are spread randomly over the deployment region under scrutiny and collect sensor data. Examples of sensor network projects include SmartDust (Kahn et al., 1999) and WINS (Pottie & Kaiser, 2000).

Sensor networks are being deployed for a wide variety of applications (Akyildiz et al., 2002), including military sensing and tracking, environment monitoring, patient monitoring and tracking, smart environments, etc. When sensor networks are deployed in a hostile environment, security becomes extremely important, as they are prone to different types of malicious attacks. For example, an adversary can easily listen to the traffic, impersonate one of the network nodes or intentionally provide misleading information to other nodes. This requires sophisticated security solutions that are challenging because of the wireless node connectivity, low-power sensors and unattended operation of the tiny sensors may become open to various threats. During a physical node capture, an attacker may compromise a node to get its stored keys. When a node is compromised, it may lead to a compromise of other non-compromised nodes. WSN security, thus, depends on the effective key distribution that should be resistant to attacks. Hence, characterization of the potential attacks that may occur in the WSN becomes very important for a secure network protocol. To set up a secure communication among the tiny sensors, a secret shared key with other neighboring nodes has to be established. A key management scheme (KMS) is very important to provide integrity, confidentiality and authentication of data traffic. KMS is the process to compute the keys, maintain key establishment and the monitoring continuing keying relationships between authorized users (Zhang & Varadharajan, 2010). The resistance of a key management scheme sometimes may decrease with an increase in the number of captured nodes, resulting in degraded security of the overall network. It is very important as well as critical to provide a robust underlying key distribution to safeguard the network operation with various potential threats. It can only be achieved when the designer has a clear understanding of the potential vulnerabilities that may be exploited by the adversary (Simplício Jr et al., 2010; Xiao et al., 2007). Node capture is a great concern in sensor networks as exposure of secret cryptographic keys may destroy a large proportion of links in a network (Camtepe & Yener, 2005; Lee et al., 2007; Nabavi & Mousavi, 2018; Sun & He, 2006). When a node is physically captured by the adversary, its keying material gets exposed. It can be used to further attack the network (Bhushan & Sahoo, 2018). The adversary is assumed to have the capability to compromise any node and intercept any wireless communication. In most WSNs, there is lack of control with no prior deployment information of sensor nodes (Blundo et al., 1992; Du et al., 2005). Sometimes the nodes are not able to communicate due to physical distance being greater than communication range, node failures, adversarial attack, etc. An open research problem is how to bootstrap secure communications among sensor nodes, i.e., how to set up secret keys among communicating nodes.

KEY MANAGEMENT IN A WIRELESS SENSOR NETWORK

Key management includes the processes of key setup, the initial distribution of keys and key revocation (removal of the compromised key). To provide security, communication should be encrypted and authenticated. The open problem is how to bootstrap secure communications between sensor nodes, i.e., how to set up secret keys between communicating nodes. This problem is known as the key agreement problem. There are three types of general key agreement schemes: trusted-server scheme, self-enforcing scheme and key pre-distribution scheme. The trusted-server scheme depends on a trusted server for key agreement between nodes, e.g., Kerberos. This type of scheme is not suitable for sensor networks because there is no trusted infrastructure in sensor networks. The self-enforcing scheme depends on asymmetric cryptography, such as key agreement using public key certificates. However, limited computation and energy resources of sensor nodes often make it undesirable to use public key algorithms, such as the Diffie-Hellman key agreement or RSA. The third type of key agreement scheme is key pre-distribution, where key information is distributed among all sensor nodes prior to deployment. If we know which nodes will be in the same neighborhood before deployment, keys can be decided a priori. However, most sensor network deployments are random; thus, such a priori knowledge does not exist. There exist a number of key pre-distribution schemes that do not rely on a priori deployment knowledge. A naive solution is to let all the nodes carry a master secret key. Any pair of nodes can use this global master secret key to achieve key agreement and obtain a new pair-wise key. This scheme does not exhibit desirable network resilience: if one node is compromised, the security of the entire sensor network will be compromised. Some existing studies suggest storing the master key in tamper-resistant hardware to reduce the risk, but this increases the cost and energy consumption of each sensor. Furthermore, tamper-resistant hardware might not always be safe. Another key pre-distribution scheme is to let each sensor carry all secret pair-wise keys, each of which is known only to this sensor and one of the other sensors. The resilience of this scheme is perfect because a compromised node does not affect the security of other nodes; however, this scheme is impractical for sensors with an extremely limited amount of memory because network size could be large. Moreover, adding new nodes to a preexisting sensor network is difficult because the existing nodes do not have the new nodes' keys to date; the only practical options for the distribution of keys to sensor nodes of large-scale distributed sensor networks whose physical topology is unknown prior to deployment would have to rely on key pre-distribution. Keys would have to be installed in sensor nodes to accommodate secure connectivity between nodes. Security services such as authentication and key management are critical to secure the communication between sensors in hostile environments. As one of the most fundamental security services, pair-wise key establishment enables the sensor nodes to communicate securely with each other using cryptographic techniques. Many security-critical applications that depend on key management processes demand a high level of fault tolerance when a node is compromised. Another important thing is the size of key and amount of computation needed for that key while doing its operation. Thus, we have to make a trade-off between security and the available resources while designing an efficient key management scheme to achieve better security.

KEY MANAGEMENT SCHEMES

Key management schemes (KMS) are the collections of processes and mechanisms that support secure communication between two valid parties. It is of prime concern for WSN security. Numerous KMSs have been developed for a WSN. One of the earliest schemes is an EG scheme where keys are randomly stored to sensor nodes from a huge pool of pre-distributed keys by key distribution server (KDS) (Eschenauer & Gligor, 2002). Two neighboring nodes can communicate only when they share one common key identifier in the key ring. This scheme was further improved by authors in Chan et al. (2003) in which instead of one key, the nodes have to share q key identifiers. This scheme has better security potency compared to the basic scheme. In this scheme, if two nodes are unable to create a common key in the discovery of a shared key, then these nodes form the path key with intermediate nodes of the path. A multipath key reinforcement scheme is also introduced in Chan et al. (2003), in which the common key is periodically updated to ensure that the key is not used by any other node. A deployment-based KMS is presented by Du et al. (2004) by in which the number of keys assigned to a sensor node directly depends on its deployment location. The neighboring nodes are supposed to carry more common key rings compared to non-neighboring nodes. It is assumed that neighboring nodes communicate more than non-neighboring nodes. Use of pre-deployment knowledge is necessary for this kind of KMS. Li et al. (2006) presented a path key establishment scheme that is robust on demand, for the nodes that do not have common keys. In this scheme, secure proxies are discovered and then the path key is transmitted. It shows a high level of security against the node capture. Ling and Znati (2007) presented a set of disjoint paths for symmetric key negotiation between two end nodes. The shortcoming of the scheme that the path key is revealed to each intermediate node is addressed in this paper. A method to discover secure proxies is also discussed in Liu et al. (2005). An end-to-end key establishment is given by Talawar and Hansdah (2015), using the trust that is initially established between the nodes. It is shown that the protocol is scalable as it establishes the key on demand and only required keys are established. An energy-aware secure route selection is given in Hayajneh et al. (2014) to expand the lifetime of the network. A key establishment scheme, PIKE, is proposed with reduced communication and memory overhead with good security (Chan & Perrig, 2005). Newell et al. (2014) discussed the main factors that influence the design of KMS and provide a trade-off between links established, overhead incurred in communication and resistance to node capture. A multi-path scheme is proposed that is based on en-coding scheme. A friend-based scheme is presented by Gupta et al. (2006), in which friend nodes are discovered by source nodes to send the path key to destination nodes. This scheme has lower communication overhead and better resilience against node capture compared to a proxy-based scheme. A cooperative secret delivery of a new link key is given in Deng and Han (2013). Some of the path key is based on disjoint paths is presented in Zhang et al. (2016) and Ghafoor et al. (2016). Location-based KMS is introduced by Liu and Ning (2003). Node capture strategies are discussed in Lin et al. (2016, 2015, 2013). An application-based KMS is defined in Yu et al. (2011). A hash chained pre-distribution is introduced by Bechkit et al. (2013). An on-demand path key establishment is given in Li et al. (2005). All path keys are known to S, and D is ensured in this scheme with high probability. Stavrou and Pitsillides (2010) have presented a survey of secure multi-path routing protocols and categorize them on the basis of security-related operational objectives. A new threat model is also given in this paper. A hop-by-hop authentication scheme is presented by Sheu and Cheng (2007) to prevent byzantine attacks and saves energy. An efficient disjoint path key establishment is given in Zhang and Gao (2013) by Zhang et al. An efficient disjoint path key establishment is introduced in Zhang and Gao (2013). Pandey et al. (2016) presents a symmetric key pre-distribution–based secure authentication where computational burden is decreased by eliminating extra processing. In Rai and Tewari (2012), the authors proposed an authentication-based secure route discovery and maintenance framework for mobile nodes. It has also reduced overhead.

Most of the path key establishment schemes consider the same probability of attack for all nodes. But this may not hold for some critical applications like battlefield sur-veillance where the attacker attacks the nodes with different probability. Attack modeling can be effectively used to improve the network designer capacity to protect against such attacks ahead of the occurrence in the network. The attack modeling of a node capture may also be applied to know the attacking activities of the adversary and, hence, the complete attacking process can be more efficiently expressed and used. There is a need to develop a path key establishment based on an efficient attack model to improve its performance.

All key management schemes can be categorized in to two types i.e., pre-distribution key management schemes where key information is distributed among all sensor nodes prior to deployment and in situ key management schemes that do not require keying information prior to deployment. This pre-distribution can be divided into several categories based on Key Pool, Random Pair Wise Key, Key Space, Group, Grid, Deployment Knowledge, Polynomial, Matrix Based, Tree, Combinatorial Design, Hyper Cube, Id, Energy, Location, etc. Besides these categories of key pre-distribution, there are several other probabilistic key pre-distribution schemes in place.

PRE-DISTRIBUTION KEY MANAGEMENT SCHEMES

All key pre-distribution schemes must cope with the unpredictability of the network topology prior to deployment. Thus, a key pre-distribution scheme requires extra keying information to be pre-loaded in order to achieve desirable key-sharing probability between neighboring sensors. As a side effect, part of the keying information may not be utilized during the network lifetime. Further, this uncertainty can degrade the scalability of key pre-distribution schemes.

Key Pool-Based Pre-Distribution Key Management Schemes

In these schemes, a large key pool is computed offline and each sensor is preloaded with keys selected randomly without replacement from the key pool. These keys form a sensor's key ring. A pair of sensors can establish a secure communication channel as long as their key rings have at least one key in common. If there is no common key, a path key needs to be established with the help of an intermediary node that shares a key with each node in the pair. In 2002, Laurent Eschenauer and Virgil D. Gligor of Maryland University proposed a probabilistic key pre-distribution scheme (Eschenauer & Gligor, 2002). The main idea was to let each sensor node randomly pick a set of keys from a key pool before deployment so any two sensor nodes have a certain probability of sharing at least one common key. This scheme has three important features, i.e., key distribution, revocation and re-keying. This approach is scalable and flexible and is superior to the traditional key pre-distribution schemes. This scheme is assumed as the basic scheme in a research field of key management of wireless sensor network security. In 2003, Haowen Chan, Adrian Perrig and Dawn Song of Carnegie Mellon University further extended the idea of basic scheme and developed q-composite key pre-distribution scheme (Chan et al., 2003). The q-composite key pre-distribution scheme also uses a key pool but requires two sensors compute a pair-wise key from at least q pre-distributed keys they share. By increasing the amount of key overlap required for key setup, the resilience of the network against node capture was increased. As the amount of required key overlap increases, it becomes exponentially harder for an attacker within a given key set to break the link. In 2007, Ashok Kumar Das and Indranil Sengupta of the Indian Institute of Technology, Kharagpur, India, proposed a key establishment scheme suitable for mobile sensor networks for establishing keys between sensor nodes in an environment where the sensor nodes are highly mobile. They proposed it for mobile sensor networks with the help of additional auxiliary sensor nodes. This scheme supports efficiently adding new nodes after initial deployment and also works for any deployment topology. The main idea behind this scheme is to deploy a small number of additional high-end nodes along with a large number of low-end sensor nodes in the network, so that high-end sensors can help in pair-wise key establishment procedures between sensor nodes. This scheme provides very high network connectivity as well as high resilience against a node capture attack than the existing schemes and is highly applicable for mobile sensor networks. It also supports dynamic node addition after initial deployment. In 2010, Jianmin Zhang and Yu Ding of Henan Institute of Engineering, China, developed a new key management scheme (Zhang & Ding, 2010) using sub-key pool to enlarge the size of key pool. The novelty of this approach is that before network deployment they use each key in the pool to generate a sub-key pool using hash function. With more keys in the key pool, the security level against nodes capture has improved. In that year, Wenqi Yu of the Henan Institute of Engineering, China, presented an improved key management scheme for wireless sensor networks(Yu, 2010). In this proposed scheme, the hash value of all keys is put in the key pool to form a new key pool. Keys in the key pool are called the original keys and the hash value of the original keys is called derivative keys. With the one-way hash function, the proposed scheme can make attackers get less key information from the compromised sensor nodes.

Pair-Wise Key-Based Pre-Distribution Key Management Schemes

Random pair-wise key scheme perfectly preserves the secrecy of the rest of the network when any node is captured, and enables node-to-node authentication and quorum-based revocation. In 2003, Haowen Chan, Adrian Perrig and Dawn Song of Carnegie Mellon University proposed the random pair-wise scheme (Chan et al., 2003). In the predeployment phase, a total of several unique node identities are generated. The key is stored in both nodes' key rings along with the ID of the other node that also knows the key. This scheme has a feature to revoke the entire key ring of any sensor node, when that sensor node is compromised. Distributed node revocation is possible by having neighboring nodes broadcast "public votes" against a detected misbehaving node. If any node observes more than some threshold number of public votes against some node, then it breaks off all communication with that node. The random pair-wise scheme possesses perfect resilience against node capture attacks as well as support for node-based revocation and resistance to node replication. In 2009, Stephen Anokye, Thabo Semong, Qiaoliang Li and Qiang Hu of Hunan University, China, made improvements on the random pair-wise scheme by Chang, Perrig and Song (Anokye et al., 2009). This scheme significantly reduces the memory and computational overheads and it has better connectivity. In that year, Hung-Min Sun, Yue-Hsun Lin,Cheng-Ta Yang and Mu-En Wu proposed a novel pair-wise key establishment scheme (Sun et al., 2009). It has several advantages i.e., it eliminates the path-key phase, the memory demand in this scheme is less, it enhances the security against node capturing attacks, it is flexible and it achieves fully connectivity without increasing storage requirement of sensors. In 2010 Sujun Li, Siqing Yang, Suying Zhu and Fuqiang Yan of the Hunan Institute of Humanities, Science and Technology, China, proposed a pair-wise key establishment scheme (Li et al., 2010). In this scheme, keys stored in a node that include two parts: the greater part are transformed by the hash function and the rest come from the global key pool directly.

Key Space-Based Pre-Distribution Key Management Schemes

Sensors pre-load multiple pieces of keying information, each of which belongs to a particular key space. Two sensors can compute a shared key if they have keying information from the same key space. However, the process involves expensive modular multiplications. In 2003, Donggang Liu and Peng Ning of North Carolina State University presented an instantiation of the key space-based key management scheme (Liu et al., 2005). This scheme consists of the following three components in the general framework: sub-set assignment, polynomial share discovery and path discovery. In this scheme, sensors can be added dynamically without having to contact the previously deployed sensors. This scheme allows the network to grow. In that year, Wenliang Du, Jing Deng, Yunghsiang S.Han and Pramod K. Varshney proposed a pair-wise key pre-distribution scheme (Du et al., 2005). This has been built upon Blom's key pre-distribution scheme and combines the random key pre-distributions method with it. This key pre-distribution scheme consists of three phases: key pre-distribution phase, key agreement phase and computation of memory usage etc. This scheme has several important properties, i.e., it is scalable and flexible. It is substantially more resilient against node capture.

Group-Based Probabilistic Pre-Distribution Key Management Schemes

Scalability issues and the group-based schemes are proposed. Sensors are grouped based on IDs, and nodes with the same deployment group or the same cross-group are pre-loaded with pair-wise keys. Group-based schemes release the strong topology assumption that it adopts. The trade-off for this flexibility exists in the form of higher communication overhead when two neighboring sensors try to establish a path key. In 2005, Zhen Yu and Yong Guan of Iowa State University proposed a group-based key pre-distribution scheme using sensor deployment knowledge (Yu & Guan, 2005). In this scheme, a sensor field is partitioned into hexagonal grids. Sensor nodes are divided into groups. The scheme consists of a series of slightly different methods depending on how to distribute secret information among neighboring groups and how much information to be stored in each node. This scheme achieves a higher degree of connectivity of the sensor network with a lower memory requirement and offers a stronger resilience against node capture attacks. In 2006, Li Hui, Chen Kefei, Zheng Yanfei and Wen Mi of Shanghai Jiao Tong University, China, presented an efficient key management scheme (Hui et al., 2006) for resource-limited sensor networks. The idea behind this scheme is to use secret sharing to distribute a group key and manage group member as well as a group header. This key management scheme is fully localized and do not need a base station or other third party to be involved, which can save energy consumption in communication. In that year, Biswajit Panja, Sanjay Madria and Bharat Bhargava described a group key management protocol for hierarchical sensor networks (Panja et al., 2006) where each sensor node generates a partial key dynamically using a function. The function takes partial keys of its children as arguments. The group key management protocol supports the establishment of two types of group keys; one for the nodes within a group and the other among a group of cluster heads. The protocol handles freshness of the group key dynamically, and eliminates the involvement of a trusted third party. This scheme is able to compute the partial keys and the group key within a minor period. The energy consumption for generating the partial keys and the group key is very small compared to the total available energy. In 2007, Guorui Li, Jingsha He and Yingfang Fu of Beijing University of Technology, China, proposed a group-based dynamic key management scheme (Li et al., 2007) in wireless sensor networks. In this scheme, there is no requirement for such infrastructure as base stations and cluster heads and the dynamic key update feature ensures the security of the network without tampering the compromised sensor nodes. Nahar Sultana, Ki Moon Choi and Eui-Nam Huh of Kyung Hee University proposed a group key management protocol also in 2007 (Huh & Sultana, 2007) by introducing identity-based infrastructure for secure communication in mobile wireless sensor networks. To ensure scalability and dynamic reconfigurability, the system takes a cluster-based approach by which group members are broken into clusters and leaders of clusters securely communicate with each other to agree on a group key in response to membership change and member mobility events. This protocol has high probability to be resilient for secure communication among mobile nodes. In 2008, Ashok Kumar Das and Inranil Sengupta of Indian Institute of Technology, Kharagpur, proposed a deterministic group-based key pre-distribution scheme (Das & Sengupta, 2007). This scheme guarantees that a direct key is always established between any two neighbor sensors in any deployment group. In this approach, it is efficient to replace a compromised group head node in a cluster by a new fresh group head node without affecting the existing sensor nodes in that cluster. This scheme has better performance in order to add fresh cluster head nodes as well as sensor nodes into an existing network and it possesses significantly better resilience against node capture and provides unconditional security against node capture. It is easy to deploy sensor nodes in a deployment group randomly by using this scheme. In that year, Linchun Li, Jianhua Li, Yue Wu and Ping Yi of Shanghai Jiao Tong University, China, proposed a group key management scheme for wireless sensor networks (Li et al., 2008) in terms of the unreliable wireless channel and unsafe environment. This scheme implements node revocation through a broadcast polynomial to counteract the node compromise attack to provide a reliable communication. This scheme can efficiently revoke the compromised sensor nodes, implicitly authenticate the updated group keys and tolerate the key-update message loss under the unreliable wireless communication channel. Yugeng Sun, Juwei Zhang, Hao Ji and Ting Yang proposed a novel distributed key management scheme in 2008 (Sun et al., 2008), focusing on the management of encryption keys in clustered sensor networks. In this scheme, the sensor nodes are divided into some group, inner group pair-wise keys are set up by a group key and inter-group pair-wise keys. This scheme has some appealing properties, i.e., it's key connectivity is high, is perfectly resilient against node compromise and needs less memory to store the keys. Shu Yun Lim, Meng-Hui Lim, Sang Gon Lee and Hoon Jae Lee proposed a new hybrid group key management scheme (Lim et al., 2008) for hierarchical self-organizing wireless sensor network architecture also in 2008. By using this approach, multi-level security can be achieved to secure groups of sensors at different levels. They place the cryptographic burden where the resources are less constrained: at the forwarding nodes and the access points. In this scheme, access points and forwarding nodes initially perform a key agreement protocol and each sensor node in a cluster later on establishes a group key with the forwarding node using a key transport scheme dynamically after deployment. The key management scheme enables low-level sensor nodes to set up a cryptographic group key requiring only an initial secret and its static private key, regardless of the network size. More promisingly, it is able to implement these encryption primitives in an efficient way without sacrificing their strength. Ting Yuan, Jianqing Ma and Shiyong Zhang of Fudan University, China, proposed a random key management scheme in 2008 (Yuan et al., 2008), which organizes sensor nodes into groups and uses multiple key pools to achieve higher security in large-scale sensor networks. This scheme divides the lifetime of the involved sensor network into a bounded number of deployment phases. All the sensor nodes to be deployed are organized into groups and are deployed within specific deployment phases. The key pre-distribution and the group deployment introduced by this scheme relieve the side effect incurred by node capture attacks while ensuring a high intra-group and inter-group connectivity. This scheme is shown to be better resilient against node capture. In 2009, YingZhi Zeng, Yan Xia and JinShu SU proposed a group key management scheme (Zeng et al., 2009) for a wireless sensor network. This is an original scheme to the wireless sensor network for creating loop keys and their maintenance and renewing. It is feasible, efficient and secure for key establishment and maintenance in wireless sensor networks. This scheme is more balanced, cost saving, efficient and safe. In 2010, Guorui Li, Ying Wang and Jingsha He (Guorui Li et al., 2010) proposed a Refined Key Link Tree (RKLT) scheme that incorporates a dirty key path into the key link tree-based group key management scheme. By delaying key update operations in dirty key paths, the number of duplicate key update messages for auxiliary nodes can be reduced, which also brings down the energy cost. This scheme requires fewer re-keying messages.

Kun Zhang and Cuirong Wang of Northeastern University at Qinhuangdao, China, proposed a new group key management scheme (Yuan Yang et al., 2010) also in 2010. With grouping design and identity authentication of the nodes, this scheme improves the security connectivity and supports more large-scale networks. At the same time, the scheme reduces the node's memory overhead. This scheme suits a wireless sensor network application that has an upper security request.

Grid-Based Pre-Distribution Key Management Schemes

In 2005, Haowen Chan and Adrian Perrig of Carnegie Mellon University described Peer Intermediaries for Key Establishment (PIKE) (Chan & Perrig, 2005). It achieves a trade-off in both communications per node and memory per node. This scheme establishes keys between any two nodes regardless of network topology or node density. This makes it applicable to a wider range of deployment scenarios than random key pre-distribution. This scheme enjoys a uniform communication pattern for key establishment, which is hard to disturb for an attacker. The distributed nature of this scheme also does not provide a single point of failure to attack. It has the advantage that key establishment is not probabilistic, so any two nodes are guaranteed to be able to establish a key. In that year, Mohammed Golam Sadi, Dong Seong Kim and Jong Sou Park of Hankuk Aviation University presented an efficient framework (Sadi et al., 2005) for establishing pair-wise keys. The concept and analysis of this scheme explains its better improved resilience to node capture than the existing schemes along with a very high probability to establish pair-wise keys between nodes in an efficient way. In 2006, R. Kalindi, R. Kannan, S. S. Iyengar and A. Durresi of Louisiana State University, USA, proposed a sub-grid based key pre-distribution scheme (Kalindi et al., 2006) for distributed sensor networks. This scheme uses multiple mappings of keys to nodes. In each mapping, every node gets a distinct set of keys, which it shares with different nodes. The key assignment is done such that, there will be keys in common between nodes in different sub-grids. After randomly being deployed, the nodes discover common keys and authenticate and communicate securely. This scheme is able to achieve better security. In 2008, Nguyen Xuan Quy, Vishnu Kumar, Yunjung Park, Eunmi Choi and Dugki Min presented a grid-based scheme (Quy et al., 2008). This scheme exploits new deployment knowledge and communication signal range of sensors. With such knowledge, each node only needs to carry a smaller number of keys while archiving a higher connectivity. This scheme also opens a new way for long peer-to-peer communication, where the increasing signal range does not lead to much of an increase in the number of keys for each sensor.

Deployment Knowledge-Based Pre-Distribution Key Management Schemes

Wenliang Du, Jing Deng, Yunghsiang S. Han, Shigang Chen and Pramod K. Varshney developed a random key pre-distribution scheme (Du et al., 2004) using deployment knowledge in 2004. The goal of this scheme is to allow sensor nodes to find a common secret key with each of their neighbors after deployment. This scheme has several important contributions, i.e., node deployment knowledge has been modeled in a wireless sensor network, and a key pre-distribution scheme has been developed based on this model and it has shown that key pre-distribution with deployment knowledge can substantially improve a network's connectivity and resilience against node capture, and reduce the amount of memory required. In 2007, Chun-Fai Law, Ka-Shun Hung and Yu-Kwong Kwok of The University of Hong Kong, China, proposed a key pre-distribution scheme (Law et al., 2007) based on adaptability to post-deployment contexts that exploits neighboring keys from connected neighbors to reach unconnected nodes and has several salient features, such as high connectivity, high resilience and efficient memory usage. In 2008, Zhen Yu and Yong Guan, Member, IEEE proposed a novel key management scheme (W. Du et al., 2004) using deployment knowledge. In this scheme, a target field is divided into hexagon grids and sensor nodes are divided into the same number of groups as that of grids, where each group is deployed into a unique grid. By using deployment knowledge, they drastically reduce the number of potential groups from which a node's neighbors may come. Thus, a pairwise key can be generated efficiently for any two-neighbor nodes. This scheme achieves a higher connectivity with a much lower memory requirement and a shorter transmission range. In 2009, Paul Loree, Kendall Nygard and Xiaojiang Du presented an efficient post-deployment key management scheme (Loree et al., 2009) designed for heterogeneous sensor networks. The scheme does not assume any prior knowledge about sensor deployment and location. It takes advantage of a few powerful high-end sensor nodes and achieves efficient and effective key establishment in a sensor network. This scheme has small communication, storage and computation overhead and achieves strong resilience against the node compromise attack. In 2010, Juwei Zhang and Liwen Zhang of Henan University of Science & Technology, China, proposed a routing-driven distributed key management scheme based on deployment knowledge (RDDKM) (Du et al., 2007), which only establishes shared keys for neighbor sensors that communicate with each other. In this scheme, the sensor nodes are divided into some group, intra-group pair-wise keys are set up only between the nodes that need to communicate with each other and inter-group pair-wise keys are established between cluster head sensors. This scheme has some appealing properties, i.e., its key connectivity is high, is perfectly resilient against node compromise, needless memory to store the keys and cost less energy.

Polynomial-Based Probabilistic Pre-Distribution Key Management Schemes

Ngo Trong Canh, Tran Van Phuong, Young-Koo Lee, Sungyoung Lee and Heejo Lee presented a new key pre-distribution scheme using bivariate polynomial combining with expected deployment knowledge (Canh et al., 2007) in 2007. This approach has an advantage in terms of resilience against nodes that are compromised. The pair-wise keys in the setup phase are computed from the sharing key spaces between each two nodes. In 2008, Hu Tong-sen, Chen Deng and Tian Xian-zhong of Zhejiang University of Technology, China, proposed an enhanced polynomial-based key establishment scheme (EPKES) (Tong-sen et al., 2008) for a wireless sensor network. This scheme improves the security level of a WSN. This scheme is scalable and flexible. New nodes can be very easily added, and session keys can be directly established with the existing nodes when needed. This scheme has good key connectivity, scalability, direct key establishment, resilience to nodes capture and storage consumption. Hua-Yi Lin, DeJun Pan, Xin-Xiang Zhao and Zhi-Ren Qiu proposed a pre-deployment key management scheme (Lin et al., 2008) that requires a few memory capacities and CPU computations to address secure data transmissions in wireless sensor networks in 2008. The proposed scheme exploits threshold key management mechanisms by the Lagrange Interpolation polynomial, generating a key set for sensor nodes, and uses symmetric and irreversible cryptography schemes to encrypt transmitted data by the generated keys with a message authentication code (MAC). The sensor nodes merely have to aggregate and encrypt received data without complicated cryptography operations. The proposed approach can achieve rapid and efficient secure data transmissions with low communications, and is proper to be implemented on large-scale sensor networks. In 2010, Min Li, Jun Long, Jianping Yin, Yongan Wu and JieRen Cheng of National University of Defense Technology, China, proposed an efficient key management scheme (Li et al., 2010) based on dynamic generation of polynomials for heterogeneous sensor networks that fully utilized the heterogeneity of sensor nodes. The scheme can support large-scale heterogeneous sensor network because the polynomials that are used to compute the cluster keys are dynamically generated after deployment. Moreover, the renewal of keys is simple and convenient. The prominent feature of this scheme is that it didn't need a key pool like traditional key management schemes. Polynomials are generated dynamically after deployment.

Matrix-Based Pre-Distribution Key Management Schemes

Ting Yuan, Shiyong Zhang and Yiping Zhong of Fudan University, China, proposed a matrix-based random key pre-distribution scheme (Yuan et al., 2007) in 2007, which uses simple linear algebraic operations to derive common keys. In this scheme, they choose multiple key maps from the key map pool to assign initial keys to nodes. They do not have to exchange key indices in order for any pair of nodes to discover their common key set used for composing their session key. In 2008, Ni Chen, Jian Bo Yao and Gang Jun Wen of the University of Electronic Science and Technology of China proposed an improved LU matrix key-distribution scheme (Zheng et al., 2008) for wireless sensor networks based on the LU matrix, the hash function and the clustered structure. This scheme can keep the key connectivity with the network topology changes, delete and update key information with the network topology changes to avoid key information and reduce communication, computation and key storage overhead.

Tree-Based Pre-Distribution Key Management Schemes

A. S. Poornima and B. B. Amberker proposed a tree-based key management scheme for heterogeneous sensor networks in 2008 (Poornima & Amberker, 2008). This scheme handles various events like node addition, node compromise and key refresh at regular intervals and supports revocation of the compromised nodes and the energy-efficient re-keying. In that year, Yi-Ying Zhang, Wen-Cheng Yang, Kee-Bum Kim and Myong-Soon Park of Korea University, Korea, presented an AVL tree-based dynamic key management to enhance network security and survivability (Zhang et al., 2008). This approach can efficiently protect the network against attacks of eavesdropping or captured nodes compromise and is adopted to address challenging security issues of runtime wireless sensor networks. Even if the adversaries crack the sensor network keys, the entire network still remains safety under the timely protection of the re-key mechanism. Also in 2008, H. M. N. Dilum Bandara, Anura P. Jayasumana and Indrajit Ray of Colorado State University, USA, presented a secure cluster tree formation algorithm (Bandara et al., 2008). This scheme is independent of key pre-distribution and network topology, does not require a priori neighborhood information or location awareness and retains most of the desirable cluster and cluster tree characteristics while building the secure cluster tree. In 2010, Chih-Yu Lin of Asia University, Taiwan, proposed a quad tree-based location management scheme to overcome the limitations of traditional tree-based key pre-distribution schemes (Lin, 2010). The quad tree-based scheme does not need any statistics. Besides, this scheme benefits from low structure maintenance cost. In that year, Khadija Rasul, Nujhat Nuerie and Al-Sakib Khan Pathan of BRAC University, Bangladesh, presented an enhanced heterogeneous tree-based key management scheme (Rasul et al., 2010). This scheme combines different key management techniques in each architecture level and also it has a dynamic key renewal process. Here, whenever a node is compromised, key renewal is done by one-way hash functions and simple XOR operations. Also in 2010, A. S.Poornima, B. B. Amberker, H. S. Likith Raj, S. Naveen Kumar, K. N. Pradeep and S. V. Ravithej proposed simple authentication schemes based on tree-based key management scheme and secret sharing (Poornima et al., 2010). The proposed schemes identify malicious nodes acting as mobile agents and used to counter the various attacks launched by malicious nodes. These schemes identify malicious mobile data collectors and replay messages. Transferred data is encrypted using a refreshed secret key, which is known only to the cluster head and base station.

Combinatorial Design-Based Pre-Distribution Key Management Schemes

In 2005, Ling Tie, Jianhua Li of JiaoTong University, China, proposed a new hierarchical key management scheme for wireless sensor networks based on a combinatorial optimization (Zhang et al., 2016). This scheme provides a method for dealing with multiple participants leaving simultaneously by an exclusion basis system. An important contribution of this scheme is that it yields optimal results for the number of re-keying messages. In 2007, Seyit A. Çamtepe and Bülent Yener, Member, IEEE-presented novel deterministic and hybrid approaches based on combinatorial design (Çamtepe & Yener, 2007). Their approach is combinatorial based on combinatorial block designs. They showed how to map from two classes of combinatorial designs to deterministic key distribution mechanisms, re-marked the scalability issues in the deterministic constructions and proposed hybrid mechanisms. The combinatorial approach produces better connectivity with smaller key chain sizes. It has the following advantages, i.e., it increases the probability of a pair of sensor nodes to share a key and decreases the average key path length while providing scalability with hybrid approaches. In 2010, Wenqi Yu of Henan Institute of Engineering, China, presented a promising pair-wise key establishment scheme (Yu, 2010). In this proposed scheme, after pair-wise key establishment all attackers can't get any key information of un-compromised sensor nodes from compromised sensors. The novelty of this scheme is that it is combinatorial based on combinatorial design and attackers can't get any key information of non-compromised sensor nodes from the compromised sensor nodes. The main advantage of this scheme is that the sensor networks are perfectly secure again and sensor nodes capture after pair-wise keys establishment. This scheme has better network resilience against a node capture attack.

Hypercube-Based Pre-Distribution Key Management Schemes

In 2006, Wang Lei, Junyi Li, J.M. Yang, Yaping Lin and Jiaguang Sun proposed a new security mechanism for key pre-distribution by utilizing the properties of a hierarchical hypercube model (Lei et al., 2006). This hierarchical hypercube key pre-distribution scheme is based on some path key establishing algorithms. This scheme has lower communication costs, better performance and provides higher possibilities for sensors to establish a pair-wise key. In 2009, Zhao Huawei and Liu Ruixia presented a key management scheme using a hypercube model (Huawei & Ruixia, 2009). The scheme solves two problems: first, combining the structure of the hypercube and two 1-way functions, and giving an establishment scheme of pair-wise keys. Second, designing an algorithm of finding neighbor nodes in the path of delivering a cluster key, and when some sensor nodes in the path are disabled, the cluster key also can be delivered efficiently in a cluster. The key storage of this scheme is lower, and secure connectivity is good. Fault tolerance is a character of their delivery method, and when some nodes in the delivery path are disabled, the active nodes in a hypercube can also receive a cluster key. In that year, Yen Hua Liao, Chin Laung Lei and Ai Nung Wang of National Taiwan University, Taiwan, introduced a hypercube-based pair-wise key establishment for sensor networks (Liao et al., 2009). They improved the hypercube-based scheme based on this tame-based approach. It is able to fulfill fundamental authentication requirement in sensor networks, and still has the nice features of the hypercube-based scheme. Two sensor nodes need to find a key path for establishing an indirect pair-wise key if their hamming distance is bigger than one.

ID-Based Pre-Distribution Key Management Schemes

In 2009, Zhiming Zhang, Jiangang Deng and Changgen Jiang of Jiangxi Normal University, China, proposed a security and efficient key management scheme by using node-ID and bilinear pairings for wireless sensor networks based on the network structure of clustering (Zhang et al., 2015). This scheme establishes a shared secret key by using bilinear pairings, improves network connections, storage, communication burden and ability of resistance against node capture. In 2010, Zhang Li-Ping and Wang Yi proposed an ID-based pair-wise key pre-distribution scheme for wireless sensor networks (Zhang & Wang, 2010). In this scheme, the symmetric matrix is employed by a hierarchical grid model to establish a pair-wise key. Different network zones possess different secret symmetric matrixes that are used to generate the key material. The proposed scheme improves considerably the resilience to node compromising.

Energy-Aware Pre-Distribution Key Management Schemes

In 2003, Gaurav Jolly, Mustafa C. Kuscu, Pallavi Kokate and Mohamed Younis of the University of Maryland, USA, proposed a cryptographic key management protocol (Jolly et al., 2003). This key management protocol is a symmetric key mechanism, and consists of the sub-protocols. The approach does not call for any sensor to generate keys, or to perform any extensive computation associated with key management. The protocol supports the eviction of the compromised nodes. This approach supports key revocation and renewal mechanisms. In 2006, Bidi Ying, Huifang Chen, Wendao Zhao and Peiliang Qiu of Zhejiang University, China, proposed an energy-based key management (EKM) scheme (Ying et al., 2006). This scheme stored the identifier, residual energy and the pair-wise keys into each node in the key pre-distribution phase, searched for better secure links according to the identifier and residual energy and then took multiplied times hash functions to implement the security for this scheme the view of the multi-hop communication. This scheme has lower energy consumption and longer lifetime of the network, and reduces the probability of nodes capture. In that year, Huifang Chen,Bidi Ying, Bo Chen, Hiroshi Mineno and Tadanori Mizuno improved the EKM key management scheme and named the new scheme low energy key management (LEKM) (Chen et al., 2006). In this scheme, a key cluster consisting of multi-continuous keys is stored into each sensor node in the key pre-distribution phase, and then the secure network connection is searched based on the overlap of key clusters. The energy consumption is reduced and the security performance is enhanced in this scheme. In 2007, Jong-Myoung Kim, Joon-Sic Cho, Sung-Min Jung and Tai-Myoung Chung of Sungkyunkwan University, Korea, proposed an energy-efficient dynamic key management scheme that performs localized re-keying to minimize overhead (Kim et al., 2007). Since this scheme uses a symmetric key between the base station and sensor node, it can authenticate the node and performs re-keying more energy efficiently. The administrator of a specific wireless sensor network based on this scheme can select the proper metrics according to the network characteristics and the node characteristics. In that year, Kwang-Jin Paek, Jongwan Kim, Chong-Sun Hwang and Ui-Sung Song proposed an energy-efficient key management protocol (EEKM) (Paek et al., 2007). This protocol supports the revocation of the compromised nodes and the energy-efficient re-keying, the broadcast-based re-keying for low-energy key management and high resilience. For increasing complexity of an encryption key, they use the dynamic composition key scheme. Also in 2007, Tim Landstra, Maciej Zawodniok and S. Jagannathan of the University of Missouri-Rolla, USA, proposed a sub-network key management strategy in which the heterogeneous security requirements of a wireless sensor network are considered to provide differing levels of security with minimum communication overhead (Landstra et al., 2007). Additionally, it allows the dynamic creation of high security sub-networks within the wireless sensor network and provides sub-networks with a mechanism for dynamically creating a secure key using a novel and dynamic group key management protocol. In 2009, C. Gnana Kousalya and Dr. J. Raja of Anna University, India, developed a novel traffic-aware key management (EETKM) scheme for wireless sensor networks, which only establishes shared keys for active sensors and participate in direct communication (Kousalya & Raja, 2009). This key management scheme achieves stronger resilience against node capture and low-energy consumption. In that year, Xing Zhang, Jingsha He and Qian Wei of Beijing University of Technology, China, presented an energy-efficient dynamic key management scheme in which new sensor nodes can join a sensor network securely and compromised nodes can be isolated from the network in time (Zhang et al., 2011). This scheme does not depend on such infrastructure as base stations and robots; thus, it possesses a high level of flexibility. In 2010, Lin He, Yi-Ying Zhang, Lei Shu, Athanasios V. Vasilakos and Myong-Soon Park presented a new key management scheme named energy-efficient location dependent key management scheme (ELKM) (He et al., 2010). This scheme generates keys for each node based on their relative locations. Based on loose time synchronization, it reduces energy consumption significantly on the total size of transmitted message. This scheme guarantees a high security level and good network connectivity.

Location-Based Pre-Distribution Key Management Schemes

In 2005, Yanchao Zhang, Wei Liu, Wenjing Lou and Yuguang Fang of China proposed the novel notion of location-based keys for designing compromise-tolerant security mechanisms for sensor networks (Zhang et al., 2005). This scheme has perfect resilience against node compromise, low storage overhead and good network scalability. Another nice feature of this scheme is that, once finishing mutual authentication, two involved neighboring nodes have established a pair-wise key indispensable for guaranteeing link layer security. In 2006, Cungang Yang and Jie Xiao of Ryerson University Toronto, Ontario, presented a novel key management and data authentication technique that pass sensing data securely and filter false data out on its way to the base station (Yang & Xiao, 2006). The framework of this design is to divide the sensing area into a number of location cells and a group of local cells consists of a logical cell. The established pair-wise key is included in the message authentication code and is forwarded several hops down to the base station for data authentication. In 2007, Farooq Anjum of Telcordia Technologies proposed an approach for key management in sensor networks, which takes the location of sensor nodes into consideration while deciding the keys to be deployed on each node (Anjum, 2010). This approach is called location dependent key management (LDK). This scheme starts with loading a single key on each sensor node prior to deployment. The actual keys are then derived from this single key once the sensor nodes are deployed. It allows for additions of sensor nodes to the network at any point in time and nodes to be added to the network anytime during the lifetime of the sensor network. In 2009, Mohammad Reza Faghani, S. M. Amin Motahari of Isfahan University of Technology, Iran, proposed sectorized location dependent key management (SLDK) (Faghani & Motahari, 2009). This scheme does not require any deployment knowledge of sensor nodes. Also, sensor nodes can be added at any time to the network and are capable of establishing secure links with their neighbors. They tried to minimize the number of sub-keys required to save. In that year, Kaiping Xue, Wanxing Xiong, Peilin Hong and Hancheng Lu of China proposed a novel key management scheme based on location to enhance the security of wireless sensor networks (Xue et al., 2009). Here, the location of a sensor node is described by its neighbors' logical identifiers. Taekyoung Kwon, JongHyup Lee and JooSeok Song, Member, IEEE developed a simple location-based pair-wise key pre-distribution scheme also in 2009 (Lee et al., 2009). They call this scheme full and random pair-wise key pre-distribution (FRP) scheme that uses deployment knowledge and a path key offering method. This scheme is perfectly resilient to node capture. It shows much better performance with regard to path key connectivity and communications overhead, more storage efficient and more scalable. In that year, Chunguang Ma, Guining Geng, Huiqiag Wang and Guang Yang of Harbin Engineering, University, China, proposed a location-aware and secret share-based dynamic key management scheme to effectively replace the compromised central node and enhance the security level of the network (Song et al., 2007). Even if the central node was compromised, it still can be quickly evicted and have little effect on the networks. They simplified the replacement of the central nodes, and the process of it is energy conserved. In 2010, InTai Kim, Yi-Ying Zhang and Myong-Soon Park of Korea University, South Korea, proposed an efficient location dependent key management scheme (Kim et al., 2010). In this scheme, each pair of nodes finds common keys by transmitting key indexes through successive applications of a one-way hash function. Nodes generate keys depending on the location without any pre-deployment knowledge. The security effects of compromise ratio common keys through transmitting key indexes instead of all key materials while the security level does not degraded, but also message authentication is provided. In that year, MinLi, Jianping Yin and Yongan Wu of the National University of Defense Technology, China, proposed a localized key management scheme for wireless sensor networks, i.e., LEBKM. This scheme employs the localized strategy (Li et al., 2010). The key for each node is integrated from two keys separately provided by two other key managements. It limits the impacts of a betrayed node within a single cluster, which makes it support large-scale wireless sensor networks. It can greatly enhance the resilience without changing the probability of secure connection. Hye-Young Kim and Young-Sik Jeong proposed a key management scheme in sensor networks also in 2010 using an allocation of a location-based group key for secure group communication (Kim et al., 2010). This scheme provides the revocation of compromised nodes and energy-efficient re-keying. It addresses the main function using a broadcast-based re-keying for low-energy key management and high resilience.

Cluster-Based Pre-Distribution Key Management Schemes

In 2004, Sencun Zhu Sanjeev Setia and Sushil Jajodia of George Mason University, USA, described localized encryption and authentication protocol (LEAP), a key management protocol for sensor networks that is designed to support in-network processing (Zhu et al., 2006). The design of the protocol is motivated by the observation that different types of messages exchanged between sensor nodes have different security requirements, and that a single keying mechanism is not suitable for meeting these different security requirements. This scheme supports the establishment of four types of keys for each sensor node. This scheme also includes an efficient protocol for inter-node traffic authentication based on the use of one-way key chains. A salient feature of the authentication protocol is that it supports source authentication. In 2008, Reza Azarderakhsh, Arash Reyhani-Masoleh and Zine-Eddine Abid of The University of Western Ontario, Canada, developed a key management in cluster-based wireless sensor networks (Azarderakhsh et al., 2008). The goal of this scheme is to introduce a platform in which public key cryptography is used to establish a secure link between sensor nodes and gateways. Instead of pre-loading a large number of keys into the sensor nodes, each node requests a session key from the gateway to establish a secure link with its neighbors after the clustering phase. This scheme has significant savings in storage space, transmission overhead and perfect resilience against node capture. In 2009, Qingqi Pei, Lei Wang, Hao Yin, Liaojun Pang and Hong Tang introduced a hierarchical key management scheme based on the different abilities of different sensor nodes in the clustered wireless sensor network (Pei et al., 2009). In this scheme, the nodes are distributed into several clusters, and a cluster head must be elected for each cluster. Private communication between cluster heads is realized through the encryption system based on the identity of each head while private communication between cluster nodes in the same cluster head is achieved through the random key preliminary distribution system. In 2010, Yuan Zhang, Yongluo Shen and SangKeun Lee proposed a cluster-based group key management scheme for wireless sensor networks that targets to reduce the communication overhead and storage cost of sensor nodes (Zhang et al., 2010). In this scheme, a group key is generated by the collaboration of a cluster head and nodes within the cluster. Only cluster heads are responsible for reconstructing and delivering the group key. This scheme maintains a good level of security while significantly reducing the communication overhead compared with the existing schemes, especially in a large-scale wireless sensor network. In that year, Yao Nianmin, Ma Baoying and Fan Shuping proposed a clustering key management scheme (Yao et al., 2009). The key update in this scheme is based on the inclusion of a single node. This scheme can ensure the security of the network and reduce the communication traffic as well as the overhead, thereby prolonging the life cycle of the network. A. S. Poornima and B. B. Amberker proposed two schemes for key management (Poornima & Amberker, 2011) in clustered sensor networks, i.e., simple secure logical ring (SSLR) and Burmester Desmedt Logical Ring (BDLR), also in 2010. In SSLR scheme communication and computation cost incurred for key establishment is constant, whereas in the BDLR scheme, key establishment is achieved by performing many multiplications and communications. These schemes establish a key between the nodes of a cluster every time when the role of the cluster head is changed. In these schemes, without exchanging any additional information, a compromised node is revoked and a new cluster key is computed.

Other Pre-Distribution Key Management Schemes

In 2002, Adrian Perrig, Robert Szewczyk, Victor Wen, David Culler and J. D. Tygar presented a suite of optimized security building blocks (SPINS) for resource-constrained environments and wireless communication (Perrig et al., 2002). This model has two building blocks: SNEP and μ-TESLA. SNEP provides several security primitives, i.e., data confidentiality, two-party data authentication and data freshness and μ-TESLA provides an authenticated broadcast for severely resource-constrained environments. μ-TESLA is the micro-version of the timed, efficient, streaming, loss-tolerant authentication protocol. In 2004, Mohamed Eltoweissy, Mohamed Youois and Kajaldeep Ghumman proposed a new hierarchical key management scheme (Eltoweissy et al., 2004) for wireless sensor networks based on a combinatorial optimization of the group key management problem. Their solution uses symmetric encryption and re-keying to support current, forward and backward secrecy. An important contribution of their solution is that it yields optimal results for the number of administrative keys per network granule and the number of re-key messages. In that year, Ashraf Wadaa, Stephan Olariu, Larry Wilson and Mohamed Eltoweissy proposed a scalable key management scheme for sensor networks (Wadaa et al., 2005) consisting of a large-scale random deployment of commodity sensor nodes. In this key management scheme, any arbitrary sub-set of clone sets can be organized into a secure communication group. This protocol uses no communications, and thus is maximally efficient in terms of communications overhead. It scales well in the size of the network and supports dynamic setup and management of arbitrary structures of secure group communications in a large-scale wireless sensor network. In 2005, Jaemin Park, Zeen Kim and Kwangjo Kim of Information and Communications University (ICU), Korea, proposed a novel random key pre-distribution scheme (Park et al., 2005) that exploits new deployment knowledge, state of sensors, to avoid unnecessary key assignments and reduce the number of required keys that each sensor node should carry while supporting higher connectivity and better resilience against node captures. They expect to save large memory space for each sensor node and also improve resilience against node captures. In 2006, Mohamed F. Younis, Kajaldeep Ghumman and Mohamed Eltoweissy, Senior Member, IEEE proposed a novel distributed key management scheme based on exclusion basis systems (Younis et al., 2006). This scheme is termed SHELL because it is scalable, hierarchical, efficient, location-aware and lightweight. This scheme supports re-keying and, thus, enhances network security and survivability against node capture. It distributes key management functionality among multiple nodes and minimizes the memory and energy consumption through trading off the number of keys and re-keying messages. It employs a novel key assignment scheme that reduces the potential of collusion among compromised sensor nodes. This scheme exploits the physical proximity of nodes so that a node would share most keys with reachable nodes. In 2007, Yi Qian, Kejie Lu, Bo Rong and Hua Zhu formulated the key management problem as a multi-objective optimization problem, in which the cost of the sensor network and the security and survivability metrics of the sensor network are taken into account (Qian et al., 2007). To solve the multi-objective optimization model, they develop a genetic algorithm (GA) based approach that can efficiently obtain near-optimal solutions. In that year, Jamil Ibriq and Imad Mahgoub of Florida Atlantic University presented Hierarchical Key Establishment Scheme (HIKES) for wireless sensor networks (Ibriq & Mahgoub, 2007). In this scheme, the base station, acting as the central trust authority, empowers randomly selected sensors to act as local trust authorities authenticating on its behalf the cluster members and issuing all secret keys. It uses a partial key escrow scheme that enables any sensor node selected as a cluster head to generate all the cryptographic keys needed to authenticate other sensors within its cluster. This scheme localizes authentication and key distribution, provides a one-step broadcast authentication mechanism and defends the network against most known attacks. Amin Y. Teymorian, Liran Ma, Xiuzhen Cheng of George Washington University, USA, developed a cellular automata (CA) based key management scheme for wireless sensor networks termed CAB in 2007 (Teymorian et al., 2007). This scheme allows sensors to establish pair-wise keys during any stage of the network operation using pre-loaded cellular automata. A sensor computes pair-wise keys with its neighbors after deployment by applying some initial parameters to their shared cellular automata. It has several nice properties, i.e., it is computationally efficient, it achieves quasi-perfect resilience against node compromise and it is the first scheme that inherently provides re-keying capabilities. In 2008, Qing Yang, Qiaoliang Li and Sujun Li proposed an efficient key management scheme based on public key cryptography to establish distinct symmetric keys between communicating neighbor nodes (Yang et al., 2008). This scheme releases the assumption of prior knowledge of the sensor deployment location. It preloads a small number of keys in more capable high-end sensors and utilizes Rabin's scheme. It can significantly reduce sensor node memory and computation overheads. In that year, Jiann-Liang Chen, YinFu Lai, Hsi-Feng Lu and Quan-Cheng Kuo presented a public key-based pre-distribution scheme with time position nodes for simultaneous exchange of secure keys (Chen et al., 2008). The proposed defend attack and key management mechanism for sensor network applications can successfully handle sink mobility and can continually deliver data to neighboring nodes and sinks. A node can detect jamming broadcast messages with the number of data packets arriving at the nodes exceeds an acceptable level and then switch to sleep mode instantly. The traditional cipher function with stream cipher is adopted to save code space, computational capability, power and memory. Quazi Ehsanul Kabir Mamun and Sita Ramakrishnan of Monash University, Australia, presented two versions of a secured key management protocol in 2008 (Mamun & Ramakrishnan, 2008). This scheme uses partial key pre-distribution and symmetric cryptography techniques, whereas one version of this protocol uses shared partial keys in a sensor chain and the other version uses private partial keys. The protocol outperforms other random key pre-distribution protocols in the sense that it requires lower space, lower communication overhead and offers very high session key candidates. Yoon-Su Jeong, Ki-Soo Kim, Yong-Tae Kim, Gil-Cheol Park and Sang-Ho Lee of Korea proposed a protocol for wireless sensor network in 2008 (Jeong et al., 2008). This scheme is more helpful in secure sessions established between sensor nodes and gateways. In the proposed protocol, efficiency was maximized by maintaining a hop-by-hop routing function between sensor nodes using a lightweighted group key-based mechanism. In particular, an internal node plays a role of key management so that it can safely collect data with decreasing power load of a sensor node, and that malicious action can be minimized in a sensor network. In 2009, A. S. Poornima, B. B. Amberker and Harihar Baburao Jadhav proposed an energy-efficient deterministic key establishment scheme that ensures there exists a secret key between the node and its cluster head (Poornima et al., 2009). The proposed scheme is a deterministic scheme that establishes a key in an efficient manner every time a cluster head is changed. Storage at each node is optimized in this scheme. This scheme performs the task of establishing a common key for node-to-cluster head communication in an efficient manner with respect to communication, computation and storage. Every time a cluster head is changed, a key can be established by performing two transmit and two receive operations and it ensures that a key can be computed between every node and its cluster head. In that year, Huyen Thi Thanh Nguyen, Mohsen Guizani, Minho Jo, Member and Eui-Nam Huh proposed a probabilistic key pre-distribution scheme that guarantees a higher probability of sharing keys between nodes that are within the signal range than that of other schemes (Nguyen et al., 2008).

Studying the signal ranges of the sensor nodes might significantly improve the performance of the key sharing mechanism. With such knowledge of signal range, each node needs to carry fewer keys, and achieve greater connectivity with less communication overhead and better resilience from diverse attacks. Manel Boujelben, Omar Cheikhrouhou, Mohamed Abid and Habib Youssef proposed a key management protocol also in 2009 for heterogeneous sensor networks based on an asymmetric cryptosystem named pairing identity-based cryptography (Boujelben et al., 2009). This protocol includes pair-wise key establishment and also cluster keys and group key transport protocol. It assures key update and forward secrecy. This protocol has low communication and storage overhead. Zhang Jian-hua and Zhang Nan of the Southwest University for Nationalities, China, proposed a chaos scheme of key pre-distribution and management in 2009 (Jian-Hua & Nan, 2011). In this scheme, the chaos overspread character was used to enlarge the key space and increase the anti-decipher capacity. The chaos initial value sensitivity was used to spend smaller costs while greatly enhanced the security of system. This scheme was put forward based on the non-linearity character of chaos, including inscrutability, inseparability and initial value sensitivity, etc. In this scheme, the ergodicity of chaos was used to void the key of being decrypted, and the chaos initial value sensitivity was used to ensure the key can be altered safely in communications. This scheme has advantages of small amount of computation, less energy consumption, low cost and easy hardware implementation. Syed Muhammad Khaliq-ur-Rahman Raazi, Sungyoung Lee, Young-Koo Lee and Heejo Lee proposed an efficient key management scheme, BARI, also in 2009 (Raazi et al., 2010), which makes use of biometrics and is specifically designed for a wireless body area networks (WBAN) domain. It provides a required level of security in WBAN by exploiting the application characteristics of wireless body area networks. In 2010, Taogai Zhang and Hongshan Qu of Henan Institute of Engineering, China, presented a lightweight key management scheme for wireless sensor networks (Zhang & Qu, 2010). In this scheme, the hash function is used to alleviate the effect of compromised sensor nodes on the uncompromised sensor nodes and at the same time, this method does not affect the connectivity between neighboring sensor nodes. With the one-way hash function, this scheme can make attackers get less key information from the compromised sensor nodes. This scheme is substantially more resilient against sensor nodes capture. In that year, Su Meibo, Yang Xiaoyuan, Wei Lixian and Yang Heng of the Engineering College of Armed Police Force, ShanXi Xi'an, designed a key management scheme, which is based on the geometric properties of circle (Su et al., 2010). This scheme can guarantee that without changing the information stored in the nodes, it is possible to update the key. This scheme is simple, convenient and efficient; it has greater advantages in storage overhead, computation overhead, communication overhead and the dynamic topology. Beibei Kong, Hongyang Chen, Xiaohu Tang and Kaoru Sezaki first used node's deployment knowledge to propose a hexagon scheme in 2010, and then combine it with the bivariate-polynomial to realize a new key agreement scheme (Kong et al., 2010). This scheme achieves better local connectivity, stronger attack-resistant ability and supports larger scale networks. Guohua Ou, Jie Huang and Juan Li proposed a keychain-based key management scheme for heterogeneous sensor networks also in 2010 (Ou et al., 2011). This scheme handles various events, such as pair-wise key establishment, cluster key distribution and renovation. It released the assumption of prior knowledge of sensor deployment location. In this scheme, the sensor only needs to pre-load an initial key. It can significantly reduce the storage requirements, computation costs and support network extension or node mobility. Tao Liu and MingZheng Zhou of An Hui Polytechnic University, China, proposed a self-organizing key management scheme based on trust model and bilinear pairing, called behavior trust-based keying (BTBK) in 2010 (Liu & Zhou, 2010). The administrative services provided by this scheme ensure the survivability of the network. According to behavior trust degree of the communicating node, this scheme provides security mechanisms including pair-wise key establishment, update and revocation dynamically, which does not need base sites or special nodes. Bing Zhang and Li Chen of Suqian College, China, proposed an improved key management mechanism for a large-scale ZigBee network in 2010 (Zhang & Chen, 2010). Based on the ZigBee public profiles, ZigBee is expected to be deployed in significantly large numbers of service application clusters for a metering system as well as smart energy systems. This key management mechanism reduces battery cost, simplifies the key management procedures and has a better performance in resistance to the attack.

IN SITU KEY MANAGEMENT SCHEMES

Sensors compute shared keys with their neighbors after deployment instead of pre-loading key information. Subsequently, the schemes all scale well with the size of the network and each of them can obtain a highly connected key-sharing graph with low storage overhead. However, a drawback of these schemes is that the shared key computation consumes a lot of energy compared to key pre-distribution schemes that do not employ random key spaces. In 2006, Fang Liu and Xiuzhen Cheng, Member, IEEE proposed LKE, a self-configuring in situ key establishment scheme targeting large-scale sensor networks. This scheme employs location information for a deterministic key space generation and keying information distribution. For uniformly distributed networks, this scheme exhibits strong resilience against node capture attacks and achieves a high key-sharing probability. The design of this scheme targets large-scale sensor networks with severely constrained resources. In this scheme, sensors determine their roles and configure themselves automatically based on a pure localized algorithm. This scheme has a good performance in terms of key-sharing probability, keying information storage overhead and resilience against node capture attacks. In 2007, Fang Liu, Xiuzhen (Susan) Cheng, Liran Ma and Kai Xing, Member, IEEE proposed an in situ self-configuring framework for bootstrapping keys in large-scale sensor networks (Liu et al., 2008). It does not require keying information. In this scheme, sensors differentiate their roles as either service nodes or worker nodes after deployment. Service sensors construct key spaces and distribute keying information in order for worker sensors to bootstrap pair-wise keys. This scheme achieves good performance in scalability, key sharing probability, storage overhead and resilience against node capture attacks. In that year, Liran Ma, Xiuzhen Cheng, Fang Liu, Fengguang An and Jose Rivera proposed an in situ pair-wise key bootstrapping scheme for large-scale wireless sensor networks. The design of this scheme targets large-scale wireless sensor networks with constrained resources, i.e., battery, memory, CPU, etc. Worker sensors bear no key space information before deployment. They acquire keying pairs from service sensors in the neighborhood after deployment. This scheme is more favorable when high-power service nodes are available in a heterogeneous sensor network. This scheme can achieve a high key-sharing probability between neighboring sensors and a strong resilience against node-capture attacks at the cost of low storage overhead.

CHALLENGES FACED BY KEY MANAGEMENT IN A WSN

There are various challenges or constraints in a WSN that is faced in designing and implementation of an effective security solution for a WSN such as key management. These are as follows:

a. Lack of defined infrastructure
b. Very large and dense deployment
c. Vulnerability of node to physical capture
d. Vulnerability due to over-reliance on BS
e. Lack of prior deployment knowledge
f. Limited memory and computation capacity
g. Impaired wireless channel and limited bandwidth

These challenges induce several constraints in implementing security solutions for such networks.

Evaluation Metrics for KMS in a WSN

To evaluate the performance and effectiveness of a particular KMS in WSN security, several metrics are defined in KMS literature. These metrics are broadly classified as the security, efficiency and flexibility metrics. Security metrics are required to evaluate the security of the scheme during node capture attacks or collusion keys, etc. Efficiency metrics relates with the efficient execution of KMS on the sensor nodes based on the energy, memory and bandwidth. Flexibility deals with mobility support, extensibility, ability to support large networks and key connectivity among sensor nodes. These are explained below.

Security Metrics

a. Node revocation: KMS should dynamically remove the misbehaving node from the network. This prevents the compromise of other non-compromised nodes during a node capture.
b. Secrecy of forward and backward communication: Forward secrecy prevents the node to decrypt the new message with a previous key, whereas backward secrecy refers to decrypting old messages with a new key.
c. It should support both backward and forward secrecy to resist attacks.
d. Collusion resistance: Due to random pre-distribution of keys, keys stored in compromised nodes may collude with keys stored in non-compromised nodes. Thus, the whole network may be compromised.
e. Resilience against node capture: It is the fraction of the total secure links compromised by capturing n nodes by an attacker. Key management should minimize the key exposure problem.
f. Resilience against node replication: Adversary may introduce clone nodes in a WSN. It may prevent the other legitimate nodes to communicate. Thus, key management should resist against node replication attacks.

Efficiency Metric

a. Memory footprint/storage overhead (SO): It is one of the most important efficiency metrics. It is the keying information to be assigned to each sensor node in the network (<4 kB of data memory and <48 kB of instruction memory). It shows the complexity of the underlying application running in the sensor node. It is significant to identify the exact amount of memory used for storing security credentials of a KMS.
b. Bandwidth: It refers to the quantity of exchanged messages during the key generation, node eviction and re-keying process in a KMS to determine the overall performance of the network.
c. Energy: The amount of energy consumed during the key establishment of pair-wise security credentials between sensor nodes is also an important metric.

Flexibility Metric

a. Mobility: Most of KMS assume that a node is stationary. However, mobility of BS or sensor nodes is required for some applications. Thus, key management should support the mobility of nodes.

b. Scalability: The sensor nodes are placed in a huge quantity in the sensor fields. Thus, KMS should be able to support large-sized networks. The protocols should be developed to handle a network of huge number of nodes.

c. Extensibility: A network should support addition of new nodes after its initial deployment. It becomes very important when they have hostile deployment of external entity.

d. Key connectivity: It is the probability by which neighboring nodes are connected in a WSN. It is the characteristic that relates with capacity of two sensor nodes to have common security credentials. It is of three types: global connectivity, local connectivity and node connectivity. The ratio of the largest size of isolated components in network to the size of whole network contributes to global connectivity of sensors. The connectivity among neighboring nodes after shared key discovery phase is over is the local connectivity. The neighboring nodes should ideally communicate without any communication overhead or negotiation. The probability that two nodes share at least one key identifier irrespective of their location in sensor field is the node connectivity. It becomes important when the network survivability of the network is of great concern in any real-time application.

PROPOSED ADVANCED EG SCHEME FOR WSN SECURITY

This proposed scheme is based on the modification of the basic scheme EG to achieve a better network security. In this scheme, the change appeared in the initialization of the key pre-distribution phase. The scheme consists of three phases: key pre-distribution phase, the key discovery phase and the path key establishment phase.

KEY PRE-DISTRIBUTION PHASE

This phase is performed by a key distribution server and offline. Before deployment of sensor nodes, the server generates a large pool of key S and identifiers. Subsequently, he/she applies a one-way hash function for all keys to this pool. Hence, the generation of a derived pool S' of the original pool keeping the same identifiers of the original keys. By this method, we allow the security of keys even before network deployment. Then, the server loads each sensor node by a key ring m randomly selected from the pool derived key S', which contains the derived keys and their IDs.

k' = H (k) where k' is the derived key, H is the hash function and k is the original key.

SHARED KEY DISCOVERY PHASE

After the deployment of sensor nodes in a target field; to build a network, nodes must communicate together securely by a shared key. In this phase, each node broadcasts their key identifiers in its communication port to establish a shared key with its neighbors. If both nodes have the same key identities in each key ring, then these two nodes can communicate with this shared common key.

PATH KEY ESTABLISHMENT PHASE

The failure of the shared key discovery phase leads to this phase. If there are two nodes in the same communication port that do not have a common key and both nodes want to communicate, an intermediate node is used between the sensor nodes, which is used to assign a pairwise key to accept connection establishment with both nodes. The intermediate node appeared during the key discovery phase (Figure 5.1).

ANALYSIS AND SIMULATION RESULT

The evaluation of the proposed scheme is performed by the performance analysis. Various analyses include local connectivity of the network and resilience against node capture attack for the safety analysis presents the evaluation parameters in this section.

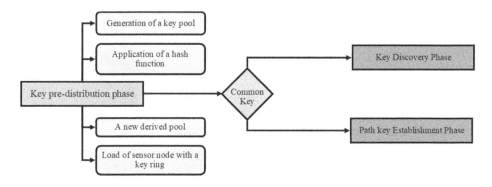

FIGURE 5.1 The principle of the proposed scheme.

Connectivity

A pre-distribution scheme is evaluated by network connectivity. The local connectivity higher than a threshold value will allow a better global connectivity.

Local connectivity Pl is the probability when two neighboring nodes established a pair-wise key in the key-shared discovery phase, which means both nodes admit a common key in each key ring. The probability is calculated by Equation (5.1):

$$P_l = 1 - P_r(\textit{Two nodes do not share any common key identity})$$

$$P_l = 1 - \frac{\binom{|S|}{m}\binom{|S| - m}{m}}{\binom{|S|}{m}^2} = \frac{((|S| - m)!)^2}{|S|!(|S| - 2m)!} \qquad (5.1)$$

where $|S|$ is the size of the key pool and m is the key ring of each sensor node.

Figure 5.2 illustrates the local probability to establish a pair-wise key between two neighboring nodes according to the size key ring and depending on different sizes of the key pool. Figure 5.2 explains several results; the increase in the size of the key ring maintains an increase of the local probability, which means the existence of the same common key identifier in two neighboring nodes. In this stage, it is necessary to take into account the sensor node memory during the choice of the size of the key ring. The

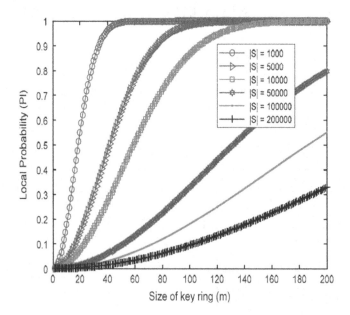

FIGURE 5.2   Local probability to establish a pair-wise key between two nodes according to the size of the key ring and key pool.

second variation, based on the size of the key pool, states that the larger the pool is to achieve the required level of connectivity, the larger the key ring must be proportional to the same size.

Safety Analysis: Resilience against Attack Capture Nodes

The safety analysis is a very important factor in assessing the performance of a proposed scheme. Because of the constraints of the sensor nodes' deployment in a hostile environment, they are subject to several attacks. During the capture of a node, all the key information is compromised. A measure of resilience against node capture is the fraction of all the links that the adversary can capture on the total number of links from the network given some nodes captured x.

A study of probability also shows that not all secure links between two nodes can be compromised, while X nodes can be occupied, which is represented by Equation (5.2):

$$R = 1 - \left(1 - \frac{m}{|S|}\right)^x \qquad (5.2)$$

Figure 5.3 shows the fraction of compromised links for nodes not compromised according to the captured nodes and the local probability 0.3 and 0.5. The increase of the compromised nodes allows the increase of the compromised secure links.

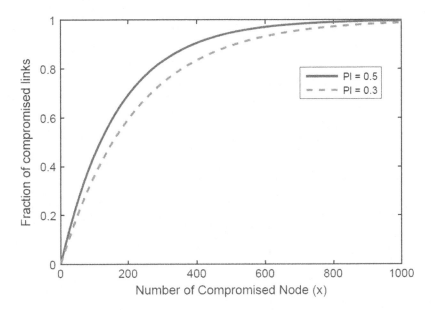

FIGURE 5.3 The fraction of compromised links for nodes not compromised according to captured nodes and Pl = 0.3, Pl = 0.5.

CONCLUSION

As each scheme was reviewed, the ability to analyze and comprehend the various key management schemes was proven to be a quite non-trivial task. Since many of the key management schemes are heavily based on mathematical computations, being a proficient researcher in this field requires a strong mathematical skill set covering such areas as calculus and discrete mathematics. Taking a step back, it was discovered that understanding the different deployments of wireless sensor networks could be considered a precursor to developing new or modifying existing key management schemes. We have seen that most of the probabilistic schemes are scalable in nature while most deterministic schemes are not scalable. However, deterministic schemes have the advantage of being simpler in terms of computation and they are better in terms of resiliency and connectivity because of its certainty. Schemes using basic schemes of Blom or Blundo et al. have a good trade-off between security and storage. Schemes using combinatorial structures are good in terms of resiliency. In situ schemes require no pre-loaded keying information but let sensors compute pair-wise keys after deployment. In situ schemes scale well to large sensor networks. We reviewed many key management schemes starting with the classic Eschenauer-Gligor (EG) scheme and moved to the more recent schemes published in 2010. It is clear that numerous trade-offs exist between different key management schemes, and the vast number of proposals make it difficult to compare them. This chapter proposed a new key pre-distribution scheme and more security is realized. The scheme is based on the modification of the initialization phase. This scheme is more efficient for resilience compared to previous schemes, as shown in the simulation.

REFERENCES

Akyildiz, I. F., Su, W., Sankarasubramaniam, Y., & Cayirci, E. (2002). A survey on sensor networks. *IEEE Communications Magazine*, *40*(8), 102–114.

Anjum, F. (2010). Location dependent key management in sensor networks without using deployment knowledge. *Wireless Networks*, *16*(6), 1587–1600.

Anokye, S., Semong, T., Li, Q., & Hu, Q. (2009). Groupwise Pairwise Scheme for Wireless Sensor Networks. *2009 International Conference on New Trends in Information and Service Science*, 695–699.

Azarderakhsh, R., Reyhani-Masoleh, A., & Abid, Z.-E. (2008). A key management scheme for cluster based wireless sensor networks. *2008 IEEE/IFIP International Conference on Embedded and Ubiquitous Computing*, *2*, 222–227.

Bandara, H. M. N. D., Jayasumana, A. P., & Ray, I. (2008). Key pre-distribution based secure backbone formation in wireless sensor networks. *2008 33rd IEEE Conference on Local Computer Networks (LCN)*, 786–793.

Bechkit, W., Challal, Y., & Bouabdallah, A. (2013). A new class of Hash-Chain based key pre-distribution schemes for WSN. *Computer Communications*, *36*(3), 243–255.

Bhushan, B., & Sahoo, G. (2018). Recent advances in attacks, technical challenges, vulnerabilities and their countermeasures in wireless sensor networks. *Wireless Personal Communications*, *98*(2), 2037–2077.

Blundo, C., De Santis, A., Herzberg, A., Kutten, S., Vaccaro, U., & Yung, M. (1992). Perfectly-secure key distribution for dynamic conferences. *Annual International Cryptology Conference*, 471–486.

Boujelben, M., Cheikhrouhou, O., Abid, M., & Youssef, H. (2009). Establishing pairwise keys in heterogeneous two-tiered wireless sensor networks. *2009 Third International Conference on Sensor Technologies and Applications*, 442–448.

Camtepe, S. A., & Yener, B. (2005). *Key distribution mechanisms for wireless sensor networks: A survey*. Troy, New York: Rensselaer Polytechnic Institute, *Technical Report* (pp. 5–7).

Çamtepe, S. A., & Yener, B. (2007). Combinatorial design of key distribution mechanisms for wireless sensor networks. *IEEE/ACM Transactions on Networking*, *15*(2), 346–358.

Canh, N. T., Van Phuong, T., Lee, Y.-K., Lee, S., & Lee, H. (2007). A location-aware key predistribution scheme for distributed wireless sensor networks. *2007 15th IEEE International Conference on Networks*, 188–193.

Chan, H., & Perrig, A. (2005). PIKE: Peer intermediaries for key establishment in sensor networks. *Proceedings IEEE 24th Annual Joint Conference of the IEEE Computer and Communications Societies*, *1*, 524–535.

Chan, H., Perrig, A., & Song, D. (2003). Random key predistribution schemes for sensor networks. *2003 Symposium on Security and Privacy, 2003*, 197–213.

Chen, H., Ying, B., Chen, B., Mineno, H., & Mizuno, T. (2006). A Low Energy Key Management Scheme in Wireless Sensor Networks. *2006 First International Conference on Communications and Networking in China*, 1–5.

Chen, J.-L., Lai, Y.-F., Lu, H.-F., & Kuo, Q.-C. (2008). Public-key based security scheme for Wireless Sensor Network. *2008 IEEE Radio and Wireless Symposium*, 255–258.

Das, A. K., & Sengupta, I. (2007). A key establishment scheme for large-scale mobile wireless sensor networks. *International Conference on Distributed Computing and Internet Technology*, 79–88.

Deng, J., & Han, Y. S. (2013). Cooperative secret delivery in wireless sensor networks. *International Journal of Ad Hoc and Ubiquitous Computing*, *14*(4), 226–237.

Du, W., Deng, J., Han, Y. S., Chen, S., & Varshney, P. K. (2004). A key management scheme for wireless sensor networks using deployment knowledge. *IEEE INFOCOM 2004*, *1*.

Du, W., Deng, J., Han, Y. S., Varshney, P. K., Katz, J., & Khalili, A. (2005). A pairwise key predistribution scheme for wireless sensor networks. *ACM Transactions on Information and System Security (TISSEC)*, *8*(2), 228–258.

Du, X., Xiao, Y., Ci, S., Guizani, M., & Chen, H.-H. (2007). A routing-driven key management scheme for heterogeneous sensor networks. *2007 IEEE International Conference on Communications*, 3407–3412.

Eltoweissy, M., Younis, M., & Ghumman, K. (2004). Lightweight key management for wireless sensor networks. *IEEE International Conference on Performance, Computing, and Communications, 2004*, 813–818.

Eschenauer, L., & Gligor, V. D. (2002). A key-management scheme for distributed sensor networks. *Proceedings of the 9th ACM Conference on Computer and Communications Security*, 41–47.

Faghani, M. R., & Motahari, S. M. A. (2009). Sectorized location dependent key management. *2009 IEEE International Conference on Wireless and Mobile Computing, Networking and Communications*, 388–393.

Ghafoor, A., Sher, M., Imran, M., & Baig, I. (2016). Disjoint Key Establishment Protocol for Wireless Sensor and Actor Networks. *Journal of Sensors, 2016.*

Gupta, A., Kuri, J., & Nuggehalli, P. (2006). A new scheme for establishing pairwise keys for wireless sensor networks. *International Conference on Distributed Computing and Networking,* 522–533.

Hayajneh, T., Doomun, R., Al-Mashaqbeh, G., & Mohd, B. J. (2014). An energy-efficient and security aware route selection protocol for wireless sensor networks. *Security and Communication Networks, 7*(11), 2015–2038.

He, L., Zhang, Y.-Y., Shu, L., Vasilakos, A. V., & Park, M.-S. (2010). Energy-efficient location-dependent key management scheme for wireless sensor networks. *2010 IEEE Global Telecommunications Conference GLOBECOM 2010,* 1–5.

Huawei, Z., & Ruixia, L. (2009). A scheme to improve security of SSL. *2009 Pacific-Asia Conference on Circuits, Communications and Systems,* 401–404.

Huh, E.-N., & Sultana, N. (2007). Application Driven Cluster Based Group Key Management with Identifier in Mobile Wireless Sensor Networks. *KSII Transactions on Internet and Information Systems, 1*(1).

Hui, L., Kefei, C., Yanfei, Z., & Mi, W. (2006). A locally group key management with revocation and self-healing capability for sensor networks. *2006 International Conference on Systems and Networks Communications (ICSNC'06), 29.*

Ibriq, J., & Mahgoub, I. (2007). A hierarchical key establishment scheme forwireless sensor networks. *21st International Conference on Advanced Information Networking and Applications (AINA'07),* 210–219.

Jeong, Y.-S., Kim, K.-S., Kim, Y.-T., Park, G.-C., & Lee, S.-H. (2008). A key management protocol for securing stability of an intermediate node in wireless sensor networks. *2008 IEEE 8th International Conference on Computer and Information Technology Workshops,* 471–476.

Jian-Hua, Z., & Nan, Z. (2011). Cloud computing-based data storage and disaster recovery. *2011 International Conference on Future Computer Science and Education,* 629–632.

Jolly, G., Kuşçu, M. C., Kokate, P., & Younis, M. (2003). A low-energy key management protocol for wireless sensor networks. *Proceedings of the Eighth IEEE Symposium on Computers and Communications. ISCC 2003,* 335–340.

Kahn, J. M., Katz, R. H., & Pister, K. S. J. (1999). Next century challenges: Mobile networking for "Smart Dust." *Proceedings of the 5th Annual ACM/IEEE International Conference on Mobile Computing and Networking,* 271–278.

Kalindi, R., Kannan, R., Iyengar, S. S., & Durresi, A. (2006). Sub-grid based key vector assignment: A key pre-distribution scheme for distributed sensor networks. *International Journal of Pervasive Computing and Communications, 2*(1), 35.

Kim, I.-T., Zhang, Y.-Y., & Park, M.-S. (2010). An efficient location-dependent key management scheme for wireless sensor networks. *2010 Sixth International Conference on Intelligent Sensors, Sensor Networks and Information Processing,* 245–250.

Kim, J.-M., Cho, J.-S., Jung, S.-M., & Chung, T.-M. (2007). An energy-efficient dynamic key management in wireless sensor networks. *The 9th International Conference on Advanced Communication Technology, 3,* 2148–2153.

Kong, B., Chen, H., Tang, X., & Sezaki, K. (2010). Key pre-distribution schemes for large-scale wireless sensor networks using hexagon partition. *2010 IEEE Wireless Communication and Networking Conference,* 1–5.

Kousalya, C. G., & Raja, J. (2009). An energy efficient traffic-based key management scheme for wireless sensor networks. *2009 International Conference on Networking and Digital Society, 2,* 156–161.

Landstra, T., Zawodniok, M., & Jagannathan, S. (2007). Energy-efficient hybrid key management protocol for wireless sensor networks. *32nd IEEE Conference on Local Computer Networks (LCN 2007)*, 1009–1016.

Law, C.-F., Hung, K.-S., & Kwok, Y.-K. (2007). A novel key redistribution scheme for wireless sensor networks. *2007 IEEE International Conference on Communications*, 3437–3442.

Lee, J., Kwon, T., & Song, J. (2009). Group connectivity model for industrial wireless sensor networks. *IEEE Transactions on Industrial Electronics*, 57(5), 1835–1844.

Lee, J. C., Leung, V. C. M., Wong, K. H., Cao, J., & Chan, H. C. B. (2007). Key management issues in wireless sensor networks: Current proposals and future developments. *IEEE Wireless Communications*, 14(5), 76–84.

Lei, W., Li, J., Yang, J. M., Lin, Y., & Sun, J. (2006). Hierarchical hypercube-based pairwise key establishment schemes for sensor networks. *Asia-Pacific Web Conference*, 186–195.

Li, Guanfeng, Ling, H., & Znati, T. (2005). Path key establishment using multiple secured paths in wireless sensor networks. *Proceedings of the 2005 ACM Conference on Emerging Network Experiment and Technology*, 43–49.

Li, Guanfeng, Ling, H., Znati, T., & Wu, W. (2006). A robust on-demand path-key establishment framework via random key predistribution for wireless sensor networks. *EURASIP Journal on Wireless Communications and Networking*, 2006(1), 91304.

Li, Guorui, He, J., & Fu, Y. (2007). A group-based dynamic key management scheme in wireless sensor networks. *21st International Conference on Advanced Information Networking and Applications Workshops (AINAW'07)*, 2, 127–132.

Li, Guorui, Wang, Y., & He, J. (2010). Efficient group key management scheme in wireless sensor networks. *2010 Third International Symposium on Intelligent Information Technology and Security Informatics*, 411–415.

Li, L., Li, J., Wu, Y., & Yi, P. (2008). A group key management scheme with revocation and loss-tolerance capability for wireless sensor networks. *2008 Sixth Annual IEEE International Conference on Pervasive Computing and Communications (PerCom)*, 324–329.

Li, M., Long, J., Yin, J., Wu, Y., & Cheng, J. (2010). An efficient key management based on dynamic generation of polynomials for heterogeneous sensor networks. *2010 2nd International Conference on Computer Engineering and Technology*, 5, V5–460.

Li, M., Yin, J., & Wu, Y. (2010). A localized key management for Wireless Sensor Networks. *2010 3rd International Conference on Computer Science and Information Technology*, 7, 569–573.

Li, S., Yang, S., Zhu, S., & Yan, F. (2010). A new pairwise key establishment scheme for sensor networks. *2010 International Conference on Computer Application and System Modeling (ICCASM 2010)*, 12, V12–281.

Liao, Y.-H., Lei, C.-L., Wang, A.-N., & Tsai, W.-C. (2009). Tame pool-based pairwise key predistribution for large-scale sensor networks. *GLOBECOM 2009-2009 IEEE Global Telecommunications Conference*, 1–6.

Lim, S. Y., Lim, M.-H., Lee, S. G., & Lee, H. J. (2008). Secure Hybrid Group Key Management for Hierarchical Self-Organizing Sensor Network. *2008 The Fourth International Conference on Information Assurance and Security*, 43–49.

Lin, C., Qiu, T., Obaidat, M. S., Yu, C. W., Yao, L., & Wu, G. (2016). MREA: A minimum resource expenditure node capture attack in wireless sensor networks. *Security and Communication Networks*, 9(18), 5502–5517.

Lin, C., Wu, G., Xia, F., & Yao, L. (2013). Enhancing efficiency of node compromise attacks in vehicular ad-hoc networks using connected dominating set. *Mobile Networks and Applications*, 18(6), 908–922.

Lin, C., Wu, G., Yu, C. W., & Yao, L. (2015). Maximizing destructiveness of node capture attack in wireless sensor networks. *The Journal of Supercomputing*, 71(8), 3181–3212.

Lin, C.-Y. (2010). A quadtree-based location management scheme for wireless sensor networks. *2010 IEEE Network Operations and Management Symposium-NOMS 2010*, 850–853.

Lin, H.-Y., Pan, D.-J., Zhao, X.-X., & Qiu, Z.-R. (2008). A rapid and efficient pre-deployment key scheme for secure data transmissions in sensor networks using lagrange interpolation polynomial. *2008 International Conference on Information Security and Assurance (Isa 2008)*, 261–265.

Ling, H., & Znati, T. (2007). End-to-end pairwise key establishment using node disjoint secure paths in wireless sensor networks. *International Journal of Security and Networks*, 2(1–2), 109–121.

Liu, D., & Ning, P. (2003). Location-based pairwise key establishments for static sensor networks. *Proceedings of the 1st ACM Workshop on Security of Ad Hoc and Sensor Networks*, 72–82.

Liu, D., Ning, P., & Li, R. (2005). Establishing pairwise keys in distributed sensor networks. *ACM Transactions on Information and System Security (TISSEC)*, 8(1), 41–77.

Liu, F., Cheng, X., Ma, L., & Xing, K. (2008). SBK: A self-configuring framework for bootstrapping keys in sensor networks. *IEEE Transactions on Mobile Computing*, 7(7), 858–868.

Liu, T., & Zhou, M.-Z. (2010). A key management scheme in wireless sensor networks based on Behavior Trust. *2010 IEEE International Conference on Progress in Informatics and Computing*, 1, 556–559.

Loree, P., Nygard, K., & Du, X. (2009). An efficient post-deployment key establishment scheme for heterogeneous sensor networks. *GLOBECOM 2009-2009 IEEE Global Telecommunications Conference*, 1–6.

Mamun, Q. E. K., & Ramakrishnan, S. (2008). SecCOSEn–a key management scheme for securing chain oriented sensor networks. *6th Annual Communication Networks and Services Research Conference (Cnsr 2008)*, 584–592.

Nabavi, S. R., & Mousavi, S. M. (2018). A review of distributed dynamic key management schemes in wireless sensor networks. *JCP*, 13(1), 77–89.

Newell, A., Yao, H., Ryker, A., Ho, T., & Nita-Rotaru, C. (2014). Node-capture resilient key establishment in sensor networks: Design space and new protocols. *ACM Computing Surveys (CSUR)*, 47(2), 1–34.

Nguyen, H. T. T., Guizani, M., Jo, M., & Huh, E.-N. (2008). An efficient signal-range-based probabilistic key predistribution scheme in a wireless sensor network. *IEEE Transactions on Vehicular Technology*, 58(5), 2482–2497.

Ou, G., Huang, J., & Li, J. (2011). *A key-chain based key management scheme for heterogeneous sensor network*. 10.1109/ICITIS.2010.5689600

Paek, K.-J., Kim, J., Song, U.-S., & Hwang, C.-S. (2007). Priority-based medium access control protocol for providing QoS in wireless sensor networks. *IEICE Transactions on Information and Systems*, 90(9), 1448–1451.

Pandey, A., Pant, P. K., & Tripathi, R. C. (2016). A system and method for authentication in wireless local area networks (WLANs). *Proceedings of the National Academy of Sciences, India Section A: Physical Sciences* 86(2), 149–156.

Panja, B., Madria, S. K., & Bhargava, B. (2006). Energy and communication efficient group key management protocol for hierarchical sensor networks. *IEEE International Conference on Sensor Networks, Ubiquitous, and Trustworthy Computing (SUTC'06)*, 1, 8 pp.

Park, J., Kim, Z., & Kim, K. (2005). State-based key management scheme for wireless sensor networks. *IEEE International Conference on Mobile Adhoc and Sensor Systems Conference, 2005*, 7 pp.

Pei, Q., Wang, L., Yin, H., Pang, L., & Tang, H. (2009). Layer key management scheme on wireless sensor networks. *2009 Fifth International Conference on Information Assurance and Security*, 2, 427–431.

Perrig, A., Szewczyk, R., Tygar, J. D., Wen, V., & Culler, D. E. (2002). SPINS: Security protocols for sensor networks. *Wireless Networks*, 8(5), 521–534.

Poornima, A. S., & Amberker, B. B. (2008). Tree-based key management scheme for heterogeneous sensor networks. *2008 16th IEEE International Conference on Networks*, 1–6.

Poornima, A. S., & Amberker, B. B. (2011). Secure data collection using mobile data collector in clustered wireless sensor networks. *IET Wireless Sensor Systems*, 1(2), 85–95.

Poornima, A. S., Amberker, B. B., & Jadhav, H. B. (2009). An energy efficient deterministic key establishment scheme for clustered Wireless Sensor Networks. *2009 International Conference on High Performance Computing (HiPC)*, 189–194.

Poornima, A. S., Amberker, B. B., Raj, H. S. L., Kumar, S. N., Pradeep, K. N., & Ravithej, S. V. (2010). Secure data collection in Sensor Networks using tree based key management scheme and secret sharing. *2010 International Conference on Computer Information Systems and Industrial Management Applications (CISIM)*, 491–496.

Pottie, G. J., & Kaiser, W. J. (2000). Wireless integrated network sensors. *Communications of the ACM*, 43(5), 51–58.

Qian, Y., Lu, K., Rong, B., & Zhu, H. (2007). Optimal key management for secure and survivable heterogeneous wireless sensor networks. *IEEE GLOBECOM 2007-IEEE Global Telecommunications Conference*, 996–1000.

Quy, N. X., Kumar, V., Park, Y., Choi, E., & Min, D. (2008). A high connectivity predistribution key management scheme in grid-based wireless sensor networks. *2008 International Conference on Convergence and Hybrid Information Technology*, 35–42.

Raazi, S. M. K.-R., Lee, H., Lee, S., & Lee, Y.-K. (2010). BARI+: A biometric based distributed key management approach for wireless body area networks. *Sensors*, 10(4), 3911–3933.

Rai, A. K., & Tewari, R. R. (2012). A secure framework for integrated manet-internet communication. *Proceedings of the National Academy of Sciences, India Section A: Physical Sciences*, 82(3), 251–255.

Rasul, K., Nuerie, N., & Pathan, A.-S. K. (2010). An enhanced tree-based key management scheme for secure communication in wireless sensor network. *2010 IEEE 12th International Conference on High Performance Computing and Communications (HPCC)*, 671–676.

Sadi, M. G., Kim, D. S., & Park, J. S. (2005). GBR: Grid based random key predistribution for wireless sensor network. *11th International Conference on Parallel and Distributed Systems (ICPADS'05)*, 2, 310–315.

Sheu, J.-P., & Cheng, J.-C. (2007). Pair-wise path key establishment in wireless sensor networks. *Computer Communications*, 30(11–12), 2365–2374.

Simplício Jr, M. A., Barreto, P. S. L. M., Margi, C. B., & Carvalho, T. C. M. B. (2010). A survey on key management mechanisms for distributed wireless sensor networks. *Computer Networks*, 54(15), 2591–2612.

Song, Z., Zhong, J., & Ma, J. (2007). Design of Climbing Rope and Cable Pneumatic Robot Based on Bionics. *Ordnance Industry Automation*, 6, 32.

Stavrou, E., & Pitsillides, A. (2010). A survey on secure multipath routing protocols in WSNs. *Computer Networks*, 54(13), 2215–2238.

Su, M., Yang, X., Wei, L., & Yang, H. (2010). Key management scheme in WSN based on property of circle. *2010 International Conference on Computational Intelligence and Software Engineering*, 1–4.

Sun, D., & He, B. (2006). Review of key management mechanisms in wireless sensor networks. *Acta Automatica Sinica*, 32(6), 900.

Sun, H.-M., Lin, Y.-H., Yang, C.-T., & Wu, M.-E. (2009). A pair-wise key establishment for wireless sensor networks. *2009 Fifth International Conference on Intelligent Information Hiding and Multimedia Signal Processing*, 1152–1155.

Sun, Y., Zhang, J., Ji, H., & Yang, T. (2008). KMSGC: A Key Management Scheme for Clustered Wireless Sensor Networks Based on Group-oriented Cryptography. *2008 IEEE International Conference on Networking, Sensing and Control*, 1259–1262.

Talawar, S. H., & Hansdah, R. C. (2015). A protocol for end-to-end key establishment during route discovery in MANETs. *2015 IEEE 29th International Conference on Advanced Information Networking and Applications*, 176–184.

Teymorian, A. Y., Ma, L., & Cheng, X. (2007). CAB: A cellular automata-based key management scheme for wireless sensor networks. *MILCOM 2007-IEEE Military Communications Conference*, 1–7.

Tong-Sen, H., Deng, C., & Xian-Zhong, T. (2008). An enhanced polynomial-based key establishment scheme for wireless sensor networks. *2008 International Workshop on Education Technology and Training & 2008 International Workshop on Geoscience and Remote Sensing*, 2, 809–812.

Wadaa, A., Olariu, S., Wilson, L., Eltoweissy, M., & Jones, K. (2005). Training a wireless sensor network. *Mobile Networks and Applications*, *10*(1–2), 151–168.

Xiao, Y., Rayi, V. K., Sun, B., Du, X., Hu, F., & Galloway, M. (2007). A survey of key management schemes in wireless sensor networks. *Computer Communications*, *30*(11–12), 2314–2341.

Xue, K., Xiong, W., Hong, P., & Lu, H. (2009). NBK: A novel neighborhood based key distribution scheme for wireless sensor networks. *2009 Fifth International Conference on Networking and Services*, 175–179.

Yang, C., & Xiao, J. (2006). Location-based pairwise key establishment and data authentication for wireless sensor networks. *2006 IEEE Information Assurance Workshop*, 247–252.

Yang, Q., Li, Q., & Li, S. (2008). An efficient key management scheme for heterogeneous sensor networks. *2008 4th International Conference on Wireless Communications, Networking and Mobile Computing*, 1–4.

Yao, N., Ma, B., & Fan, S. (2009). A New Key Management Scheme in Clustering Wireless Sensor Networks. *2009 Fourth International Conference on Internet Computing for Science and Engineering*, 227–230.

Ying, B., Chen, H., Zhao, W., & Qiu, P. (2006). A Diagonal-based TTDD in Wireless Sensor Networks. *2006 6th World Congress on Intelligent Control and Automation*, *1*, 257–260.

Younis, M. F., Ghumman, K., & Eltoweissy, M. (2006). Location-aware combinatorial key management scheme for clustered sensor networks. *IEEE Transactions on Parallel and Distributed Systems*, *17*(8), 865–882.

Yu, C.-M., Li, C.-C., Lu, C.-S., & Kuo, S.-Y. (2011). An application-driven attack probability-based deterministic pairwise key pre-distribution scheme for non-uniformly deployed sensor networks. *International Journal of Sensor Networks*, *9*(2), 89–106.

Yu, W. (2010). A promising pairwise key establishment scheme for wireless sensor networks in hostile environments. *2010 International Conference on Multimedia Information Networking and Security*, 809–812.

Yu, Z., & Guan, Y. (2005). A robust group-based key management scheme for wireless sensor networks. *IEEE Wireless Communications and Networking Conference*, *2005*, *4*, 1915–1920.

Yuan, T., Ma, J., & Zhang, S. (2008). Random key management using group deployment in large-scale sensor networks. *2008 Third International Conference on Communications and Networking in China*, 1167–1171.

Yuan, T., Zhang, S., & Zhong, Y. (2007). A Matrix-Based Random Key Pre-distribution Scheme for Wireless Sensor Networks. *7th IEEE International Conference on Computer and Information Technology (CIT 2007)*, 991–996.

Yuan Yang, X., Wang, L., & Zhang, Q. (2010). A New Group Key Management Protocol in WSNs Based on Secret Sharing. *2010 Asia-Pacific Power and Energy Engineering Conference*, 1–4.

Zeng, Y., Xia, Y., & Su, J. (2009). A new group key management scheme based on DMST for Wireless Sensor Networks. *2009 IEEE 6th International Conference on Mobile Adhoc and Sensor Systems*, 989–994.

Zhang, B., & Chen, L. (2010). An improved key management of zigbee protocol. *2010 Third International Symposium on Intelligent Information Technology and Security Informatics*, 416–418.

Zhang, J., & Ding, Y. (2010). Pairwise Key Management Scheme Using Sub Key Pool for Wireless Sensor Networks. *2010 Second International Conference on Information Technology and Computer Science*, 21–24.

Zhang, J., & Varadharajan, V. (2010). Wireless sensor network key management survey and taxonomy. *Journal of Network and Computer Applications*, *33*(2), 63–75.

Zhang, K., & Gao, H. (2013). Efficient distributed algorithm for correctly finding disjoint paths in wireless sensor networks. *International Journal of Sensor Networks*, *13*(3), 173–184.

Zhang, K., Han, Q., Yin, G., & Pan, H. (2016). OFDP: A distributed algorithm for finding disjoint paths with minimum total length in wireless sensor networks. *Journal of Combinatorial Optimization*, *31*(4), 1623–1641.

Zhang, L.-P., & Wang, Y. (2010). An ID-based pairwise key predistribution scheme for wireless sensor networks. *2010 6th International Conference on Wireless Communications Networking and Mobile Computing (WiCOM)*, 1–4.

Zhang, T., & Qu, H. (2010). A lightweight key management scheme for wireless sensor networks. *2010 Second International Workshop on Education Technology and Computer Science*, *1*, 272–275.

Zhang, X., He, J., & Wei, Q. (2011). EDDK: Energy-efficient distributed deterministic key management for wireless sensor networks. *EURASIP Journal on Wireless Communications and Networking*, *2011*, 1–11.

Zhang, Y.-Y., Yang, W.-C., Kim, K.-B., & Park, M.-S. (2008). An AVL tree-based dynamic key management in hierarchical wireless sensor network. *2008 International Conference on Intelligent Information Hiding and Multimedia Signal Processing*, 298–303.

Zhang, Yanchao, Liu, W., Lou, W., & Fang, Y. (2005). Securing sensor networks with location-based keys. *IEEE Wireless Communications and Networking Conference*, *2005*, *4*, 1909–1914.

Zhang, Yuan, Shen, Y., & Lee, S. (2010). A cluster-based group key management scheme for wireless sensor networks. *2010 12th International Asia-Pacific Web Conference*, 386–388.

Zhang, Z., Wu, F., Jiang, C., & Deng, J. (2015). An efficient detection scheme of node replication attacks for wireless sensor networks. *International Journal of Security and Networks*, *10*(4), 228–238.

Zheng, M., Zhou, H., & Cui, G. (2008). A LU Matrix-based Key Pre-distribution Scheme for WSNs. *2008 4th International Conference on Wireless Communications, Networking and Mobile Computing*, 1–4.

Zhu, S., Setia, S., & Jajodia, S. (2006). LEAP+ Efficient security mechanisms for large-scale distributed sensor networks. *ACM Transactions on Sensor Networks (TOSN)*, *2*(4), 500–528.

Secure Routing Algorithms (SRAs) in Sensor Networks

6

INTRODUCTION

The routing protocol is a process to select a suitable path for the data to travel from source to destination. The process encounters several difficulties while selecting the route, which depends upon type of network, channel characteristics and the performance metrics.

The data sensed by the sensor nodes in a wireless sensor network (WSN) is typically forwarded to the base station that connects the sensor network with the other networks (may be internet) where the data is collected, analyzed and some action is taken accordingly.

In very small sensor networks where the base station and motes (sensor nodes) are so close that they can communicate directly with each other, this is single-hop communication, but in most WSN applications the coverage area is so large that it requires thousands of nodes to be placed and this scenario requires multi-hop communication because most of the sensor nodes are so far from the sink node (gateway) so that they cannot communicate directly with the base station. The single-hop communication is also called direct communication and multi-hop communication is called indirect communication.

In multi-hop communication, the sensor nodes not only produce and deliver their material but also serve as a path for other sensor nodes towards the base station. The process of finding a suitable path from source node to destination node is called routing and this is the primary responsibility of the network layer.

DOI: 10.1201/9781003257608-6

CHALLENGES OF DESIGN TASKS OF ROUTING PROTOCOL FOR A WSN

The design task of routing protocols for a WSN is quite challenging because of multiple characteristics, which differentiate them from wireless infrastructure-less networks. Due to reduced computing, radio and battery resources of sensors, routing protocols in wireless sensor network are expected to fulfill the following requirements:

a. Data delivery model: Data delivery model overcomes the problem of a fault tolerance domain by providing the alternative path to save its data packets from nodes or link failures (Al-Karaki & Kamal, 2004). It severely affects the routing protocol in a wireless sensor network, especially with regard to use of the limited energy of the node, security purpose (Farmer, 2001), energy consumption and route immobility.

b. Scalability: A system is said to be scalable if its effectiveness increases when the hardware is put on and proportional to the capacity added (Muthukarpagam et al., 2010). Routing schemes make efforts with the vast collection of motes in WSNs which should be scalable enough to talk back to the events take place in the environment.

c. Resilience: Sometimes, due to an environment problem or battery consumption, sensors erratically stop working (Sharma et al., 2015). This problem is overcome by finding the alternate path when current in use nodes stop operating.

d. Production cost: The cost of a single node is enough to justify the overall cost of the sensor network. So, the cost of each sensor node should be kept low.

e. Operating environment: A sensor network can be set up inside large machinery, at the base of the ocean, in a biologically or chemically contaminated field, in the battlefield behind an enemy line, in a big building or warehouse, etc.

f. Power consumption: The requirement such as a long lifetime of sensor networks and restricted storage capacity of sensor nodes has directed a search to a new scope to alleviate power consumption. Sidra Aslam discussed several schemes such as power aware protocol, cross-layer optimization and harvesting technologies that help in reducing power consumption constraints in WSNs (Aslam et al., 2009). In multi-hop sensor networks, the multi-functioning of some nodes such as data sender and data router can cause a topology change due to power failure, which requires a new path for data transfer and restructuring the network.

g. Data aggression/fusion: The main goal of data aggregation algorithms is to gather and aggregate data from different sources by using different functions such as suppression, min, max and average to achieve energy-efficient and traffic optimization in routing protocols so that the network lifetime is enhanced (Feng et al., 2011).

CLASSIFICATION OF ROUTING PROTOCOLS IN A WSN

The sensor nodes are constrained to limited resources itself, so the main target is to design an effective and energy aware protocol in order to enhance the network lifetime for specific application environment. Since sensor nodes are not given a unified ID for identification and much redundant data collected at destination nodes. So, energy efficiency, scalability, latency, fault-tolerance, accuracy and QoS are some aspects that must be kept in mind while designing the routing protocols in wireless sensor networks.

Classically, most routing protocols are classified as data-centric, hierarchical and location-based protocols depending on the network structure and applications. In data-centric routing, the sink sends queries to certain regions and waits for data from the sensors located in the selected regions. Since data is being requested through queries, attribute-based naming is necessary to specify the properties of data. Here, data is usually transmitted from every sensor node within the deployment region with significant redundancy. Hierarchical or cluster-based methods are well-known techniques with special advantages of scalability and efficient communication. Nodes play different roles in the network. In location-aware routing, nodes know where they are in a geographical region. Location information is used to improve the performance of routing and to provide new types of services.

In simple words, the routing protocols define how nodes will communicate with each other and how the information will be disseminated through the network. There are many ways to classify the routing protocols of WSN. The basic classification of routing protocols is illustrated in Figure 6.1.

Attribute-Based or Data-Centric Routing Protocols

In most of the wireless sensor networks, the sensed data or information is far more valuable than the actual node itself. Therefore, for data-centric routing techniques the prime focus is on the transmission of information specified by certain attributes rather than collecting data from certain nodes.

In data-centric routing, the sink node queries to specific regions to collect data of some specific characteristics so naming a scheme based on attributes is necessary to describe the characteristics of data. The following protocols are considered and discussed in this category.

Flooding and Gossiping

Flooding and gossiping are the most traditional network routing (Heinzelman et al., 1999). They do not need to know the network topology or any routing algorithms. In a flooding mechanism, each sensor receives a data packet and then broadcasts it to all

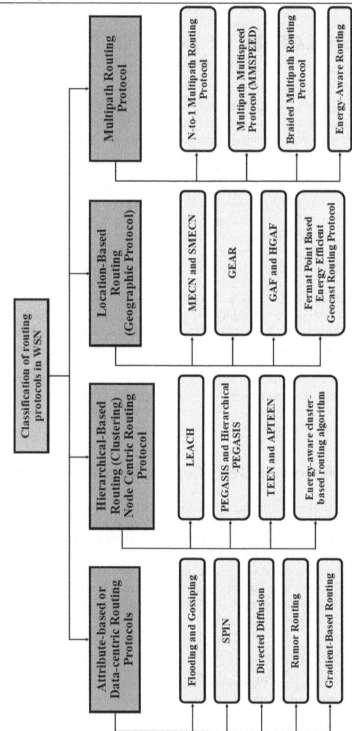

FIGURE 6.1   Classification of routing protocol in a WSN.

neighboring nodes. When the packet arrives at the destination or the maximum number of hops is reached, the broadcasting process is stopped. On the other hand, gossiping is a slightly enhanced version of flooding where the receiving node sends the packet to randomly selected neighbors, which pick another random neighbor to forward the packet to and so on. Although flooding is very easy, it has several drawbacks like implosion, overlap and resource blindness problem.

Gossiping avoids the problem of implosion by sending information to a random neighbor instead of a classic broadcasting mechanism which send packets to all neighbors. However, gossiping creates another problem of delay in a propagation of data among sensor nodes.

SPIN

Joanna Kulik et al. in Heinzelman et al. (1999) proposed a family of adaptive protocols, called SPIN (Sensor Protocol for Information via Negotiation) that efficiently disseminate information among sensors in an energy-constrained wireless sensor network and overcome the problem of implosion and overlap that occurred in classic flooding. Nodes running a SPIN communication protocol name their data using high-level data descriptors, called metadata. SPIN nodes negotiate with each other before transmitting data. Negotiation helps to ensure that the transmission of redundant data throughout the network is eliminated and only useful information will be transferred.

The SPIN family of protocols includes many protocols that disseminate information with low latency and conserve energy at the same time. The main two are called SPIN-1 and SPIN-2. Simulation results show that SPIN-1 uses negotiation to solve the difficulty of implosion and overlap. It reduces energy consumption by a factor of 3.5 when compared to flooding. As shown in Figure 6.2, SPIN-2 is able to deliver even more data per unit energy than SPIN-1 and incorporates a threshold-based resource-awareness mechanism in addition to negotiation and disseminates 60% more data per unit energy than flooding. The simulation result also shows that nodes with a higher degree tend to dissipate more energy than nodes with a lower degree, creating potential weak points in a battery-operated network.

The disadvantage of a SPIN protocol is that it is not sure the data will certainly reach the target or not and it is also not good for high-density distribution of nodes. Another drawback is that if the nodes that are interested in the data are far away from the source node and the nodes between the source and destination are not interested in that data, such data will not be delivered to the destination at all. Therefore, SPIN is not a good choice for applications.

Directed Diffusion

Ramesh Govindan et al. in Intanagonwiwat et al. (2003) proposed a popular data aggregation paradigm for wireless sensor networks called directed diffusion. Directed diffusion is data-centric and all nodes in a directed diffusion-based network are application-aware. This enables diffusion to achieve energy savings by selecting empirically good paths and by caching and processing data in a network (e.g., data aggregation).

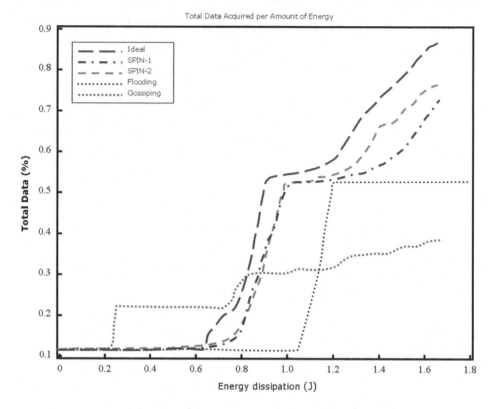

FIGURE 6.2   Data acquired for a given amount of energy. SPIN-2 distributes 10% more data per unit energy than SPIN-1 and 60% more data per unit energy than flooding.

Directed diffusion is composed of several elements: interests, data messages, gradients and reinforcements, as shown in Figure 6.3. An interest message is a query that specifies what a user wants and contains a summary of a sensing task that is supported by a sensor network for acquiring data. Typically, data in sensor networks is the collected data of a physical phenomenon. Such data can be an event that is a short description of the sensed phenomenon. In directed diffusion, data is named using attribute-value pairs.

The SPIN protocol allow sensors to advertise the availability of data and the nodes that are interested query that data, but in directed diffusion the sink queries the sensor nodes if a specific data is available by flooding.

The main advantages of directed diffusion are as follows:

Since it is data-centric, communication is neighbor-to-neighbor with no need for a node-addressing mechanism. Each node can do aggregation and caching, in addition to sensing. Caching is a big advantage in terms of energy efficiency and delay.

Direct diffusion is highly energy efficient since it is on demand and there is no need for maintaining global network topology.

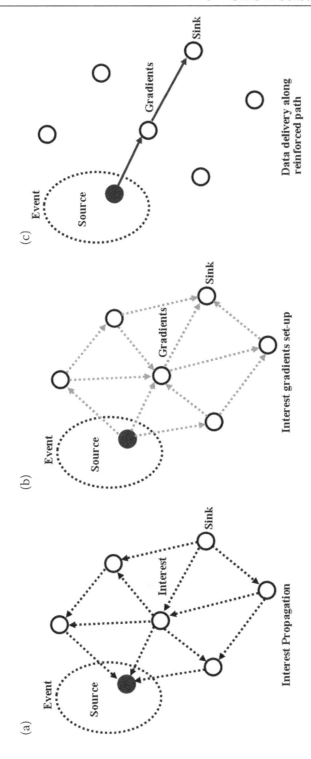

FIGURE 6.3 A simplified schematic for directed diffusion: (a) interest propagation, (b) interest gradients set-up and (c) Data delivery along reinforced path.

Directed diffusion is not a good choice for the application such as environmental monitoring because it require continuous data delivery to the sink and will not work efficiently with a query driven on a demand data model.

Rumor Routing

Rumor routing is proposed in Braginsky and Estrin (2002), which allows queries to be delivered to events in the network. It is mainly determined for a context in which geographic routing criteria is not applicable. Rumor routing is a logical compromise between flooding queries and flooding events notification.

Rumor routing is tunable and allows for a trade-off between setup overhead and delivery reliability. Generally, directed diffusion floods the queries to the entire network and data can be sent through multiple paths at lower rates, but rumor routing maintains only one path between the source and destination, as shown in Figure 6.4. In this protocol, paths are created for queries to be delivered and when a query is generated it is sent for a random walk until it finds the path, instead of flooding it throughout the network. When the event path is discovered by the query, it can be routed directly to the event.

When events are flooded through the network, a node detects an event, maintains its event table and creates an agent. The table entries contain the information about source node, events and last hop node. The main job of the agent is to propagate the information about local events to distant nodes.

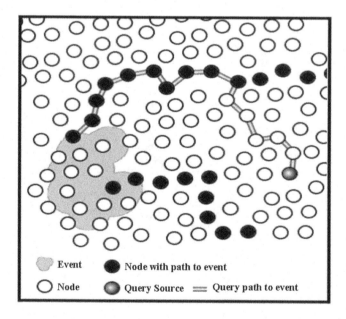

FIGURE 6.4 Query is originated from the query source and searches for a path to the event. As soon as it finds a node on the path, it is routed directly to the event.

The simulation result shows that a rumor routing protocol is reliable in terms of delivering queries to events in a large network, handles the node failure very smoothly and degrades its delivery rate linearly with the number of failure nodes. It also achieves significant energy saving over event flooding.

Gradient-Based Routing

The algorithm makes an improvement on directed diffusion in order to get the total minimum hop other than the total shortest time. In the traditional gradient minimum hop count algorithm, the hop count is the only metric, which measures the quality of route. Li Xia in Xia et al. (2004) proposed a new gradient routing protocol that not only considers the hop count but also uses the remaining energy of each node while relaying data from the source node to the sink. This scheme is helpful in handling the frequent changes of the topology of the network due to node failure.

A new gradient routing scheme also aims to establish the cost field and find a minimum cost path from the source node to the sink. Figure 6.5 illustrates a simple example of the procedure of generating a minimum cost gradient.

The source node has three routes to reach the sink, route 1: S→D→A, route 2: S→B and route 3: S→E→C. At the routing setup stage, the source node will receive three different setup messages. The cost metric of route 1 is: $\frac{1}{40} + \frac{1}{40} = \frac{1}{20}$. It is the smallest cost in these three routes. So the source node will choose route 1 as its optimal route. It records node D as its previous relay node. After a period, the node in route 1 may have low energy level. In this situation, route 2 may be chosen as the good route.

In the route setup stage, when one node receives the setup message, it waits for a short time T_{wait} for message with better metric, which may arrive during this period. When T_{wait} expires, the node rebroadcasts the message with the best metrics in all messages it has received. By this way, the number of setup messages in the whole network can decrease greatly. This scheme aggregates similar packets into one packet and transmits the information, which is energy efficient and helps to prolong the network's lifetime.

The simulation result shows the relationship between the number of relayed setup messages and the back-off waiting time T_{wait}, as shown in Figure 6.6. When T_{wait} is large,

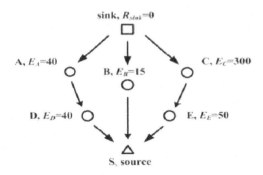

FIGURE 6.5 The procedure of generating minimum cost gradient.

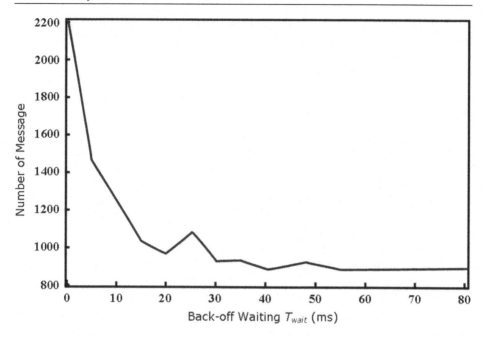

FIGURE 6.6   The relationship between the number of setup messages and T$_{wait}$.

the total messages for setting up the network's route will be small in number. So the back-off waiting scheme is quite effective for saving the energy consumption when establishing the network's routes. However, it delays the establishment of routes for a while. The size of such a delay is basically proportional to T$_{wait}$, as illustrated in Figure 6.7.

Hierarchical-Based Routing (Clustering) or Node-Centric Routing Protocol

Hierarchical routing is a guaranteed approach for point-to-point routing with a very small routing state (Iwanicki & Van Steen, 2009). Scalability is one of the essential design features of the sensor networks. A single gateway architecture can cause the gateway to overload, which might cause a break in communication and tracking of events is unhealthy. Another major disadvantage is that long-haul communication is not possible because it is not scalable for a large set of sensors. To overcome these drawbacks, network clustering has been pursued in some routing approaches.

Hierarchical or cluster-based methods are well-known techniques with special advantages of scalability and efficient communication. Nodes play different roles in the network. Hierarchical routing maintains the energy consumption of sensor nodes and performs data aggregation, which helps in decreasing the number of transmitted messages to the base station. The whole WSN is divided into a number of clusters in terms of specific rules. Some hierarchical protocols are discussed here.

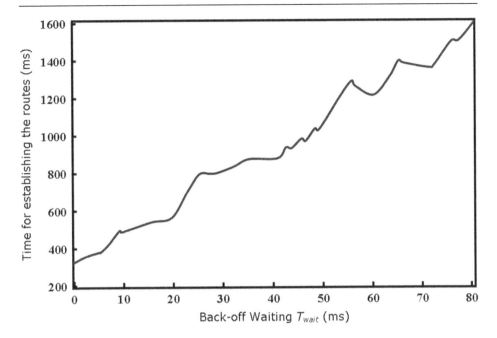

FIGURE 6.7   The relationship between route establishment time and T_{wait}.

LEACH

LEACH (Joshi & Priya, 2011) stands for low-energy adaptive clustering hierarchy, and is one of the first hierarchical protocols. When the node in the network fails or its battery stops working, then the LEACH protocol is used in the network. LEACH is a self-organizing, adaptive clustering protocol in which sensor nodes will organize themselves into local clusters and cluster members elect a cluster head (CH) to avoid excessive energy consumption and incorporate data aggregation, which reduces the amount of messages sent to the base station, to increase the lifetime of the network. Therefore, this algorithm has an effect on energy saving.

The cluster head is responsible for collecting data from its cluster members. To reduce inter-cluster and intra-cluster collisions, LEACH uses a TDMA/code-division multiple access (CDMA). The decision whether a node elevates to a cluster head is made dynamically at a time interval. However, data collection is performed periodically. Therefore, the LEACH protocol is mainly used for constant tracking by the sensor networks. When the node becomes a cluster head for the current round, then each elected cluster head broadcasts information to rest of the nodes in the network.

To balance the energy dissipation of nodes, cluster heads change randomly over time (Akkaya & Younis, 2005). The node makes this decision by choosing a random number between 0 and 1. The node becomes a cluster head for the current round if the number is less than the following threshold:

$$T(n) = \frac{p}{1 - p\left(r \bmod \left(\frac{1}{p}\right)\right)} \quad \text{if } n \in G$$

where n is the given node, P is the a priori probability of a node being elected as a cluster head, r is the current round number and G is the set of nodes that has not been elected as a cluster head in the last $1/P$ rounds.

Table 6.1 shows the comparison between SPIN, LEACH and directed diffusion according to different parameters. A centralized version of this protocol is Leach-C. This scheme is divided into two phases: the setup phase and the steady-phase. In the setup phase, sensors communicate with the base station and tell it about their current position and about their energy level. In the steady-state phase, the actual data transfer to the base station takes place. The duration of steady-phase is longer than the setup phase to minimize overhead.

Two-Level Hierarchy LEACH (TL-LEACH) is a modified form of the LEACH algorithm that consists of two levels of cluster heads (primary and secondary) instead of a single one. The advantage of a two-level structure of TL-LEACH is that it reduces the amount of nodes that transmit information to the base station, effectively reducing the total energy usage.

PEGASIS and Hierarchical-PEGASIS

PEGASIS (Power-Efficient Gathering in Sensor Information Systems), a near optimal chain-based protocol, is an improvement over LEACH. Instead of forming multiple clusters, PEAGSIS constructs a node chain when nodes are placed randomly in a play field and then each node communicates only with a close neighbor and takes turns transmitting to the base station, thus reducing the amount of energy spent per round (Lindsey & Raghavendra, 2002). The chain construction is performed in a greedy way. Figure 6.8 shows node 0 connected to node 3, node 3 connected to node 1 and node 1 connected to node 2. When a node fails, the chain is reconstructed in the same manner by avoiding the dead node (Figure 6.9).

TABLE 6.1 Comparison between SPIN, LEACH and directed diffusion

	SPIN	LEACH	DIRECTED DIFFUSION
Optimal Routing	No	No	Yes
Network Lifetime	Good	Very Good	Good
Resource Awareness	Yes	Yes	Yes
Use of Meta-Data	Yes	No	Yes

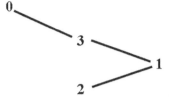

FIGURE 6.8 Chain construction using the greedy algorithm.

Hierarchical-PEGASIS conducts a further improvement; it allows concurrent transmission with the nodes that are not adjacent. Compared with LEACH, the two algorithms eliminate the overhead of forming a cluster, but both of them do not take the energy condition of next hop into consideration when choosing a routing path, so they are not suitable for a heavy-loaded network. When the amount of nodes is very large in WSNs, the delay of data transmission is very obvious, so they do not scale well and also are not suitable for sensor networks where such global knowledge is not easy to obtain.

TEEN and APTEEN

TEEN stands for threshold sensitive energy efficient sensor network protocol. It is the first protocol developed for reactive networks and used in temperature sensing applications (Manjeshwar & Agrawal, 2001). Based on LEACH, TEEN is based on hierarchical grouping that divides sensor nodes twice for a grouping cluster in order to detect the scene of sudden changes in the sensed attributes such as temperature. After the clusters are formed, TEEN separates the cluster head into the second-level cluster head and uses hard threshold and soft threshold to detect the sudden changes. The model is depicted in Figure 6.10.

Thus, the hard threshold tries to reduce the number of transmissions by allowing the nodes to transmit only when the sensed attribute is in the range of interest. The soft threshold further reduces the number of transmissions by eliminating all the transmissions which might have otherwise occurred when there is little or no change in the sensed attribute after the hard threshold.

The main drawback of this scheme is that it is not well suited for applications where the user needs to get data on a regular basis. Another possible problem with this scheme is that a practical implementation would have to ensure that there are no collisions in the cluster. TDMA scheduling of the nodes can be used to avoid this problem but this causes a delay in the reporting of the time-critical data. CDMA is another possible solution to this problem. This protocol is best suited for time-critical applications such as intrusion detection, explosion detection, etc.

The adaptive threshold sensitive energy efficient sensor network (APTEEN) protocol is an extension of TEEN and aims at both capturing periodic data collections and reacting to time-critical events. The architecture is the same as in TEEN. In APTEEN, once the CHs are decided, in each cluster period, the cluster head broadcasts the parameter such as attributes, threshold, and schedule and count time to all nodes (Manjeshwar & Agrawal, 2002).

Simulation results compare APTEEN with TEEN and LEACH (leach and leach-c) with respect to energy consumption, as shown in Figure 6.11. The performance of APTEEN lies between TEEN and LEACH in terms of energy consumption and

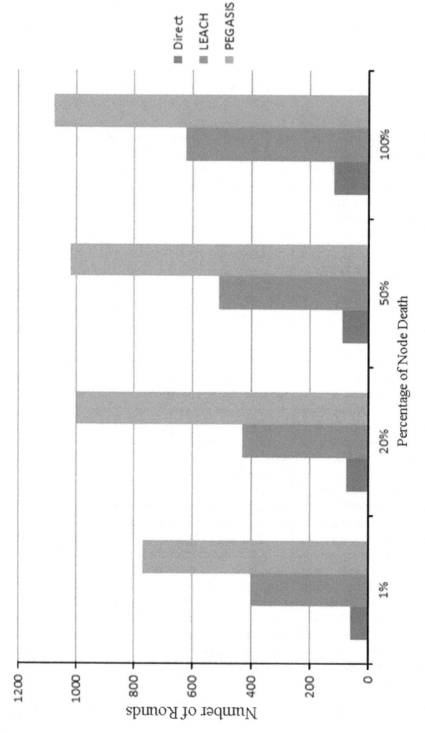

FIGURE 6.9   Performance results for 50 m × 50 m network with initial energy f0.25 J/node.

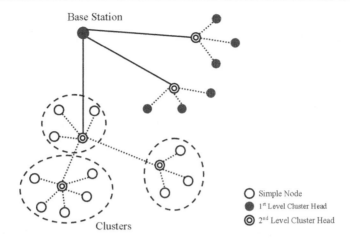

FIGURE 6.10   Hierarchical clustering in TEEN and APTEEN.

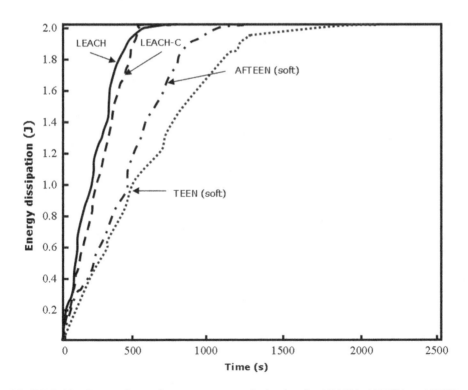

FIGURE 6.11   Comparison of average energy dissipation for LEACH, APTEEN and TEEN.

longevity of the network. While sensing the environment, TEEN only transmits time-critical data. APTEEN makes an improvement over TEEN by supporting periodic reports for time-critical events. The main disadvantages of the two algorithms are the overhead and complexity of forming clusters.

Energy-Aware Cluster-Based Routing Algorithm

Jyh-Huei Chang et al. in Chang and Jan (2005) proposed energy-aware, cluster-based routing algorithm (ECRA) for wireless sensor networks to maximize the network's lifetime. The ECRA selects some nodes as a cluster head to construct Voronoi diagrams and a cluster head is rotated to balance the load in each cluster.

LEACH may have several problems: first, if the coverage of the cluster heads is too small, then some cluster heads may not have any members in their clusters. Second, LEACH has a long transmission range between the cluster heads and the sink node. Third, LEACH requires global cluster head rotations. This cluster head selection greatly increases processing and communication overhead, thereby consuming more energy. Therefore, this protocol is used to overcome LEACH's problems and reduce the overhead of cluster head rotation for cluster-based wireless sensor networks. Clustering, data transmission and intra-cluster head rotation are the phases of energy-aware cluster-based routing protocol.

It is shown in Figure 6.12 that the cluster members of the cluster transmit their sensing data to cluster heads, which forward the aggregated data to the sink node. ECRA helps in balancing the load for all sensors and avoids too many cluster heads focusing on a small area by choosing a sensor node from the previous cluster as a cluster head, called an intra-cluster head rotation.

ECRA-2T is a two-tier architecture for ECRA that is used to enhance the performance of the original ECRA. The ECRA can be advanced by adding an extra tier called a high tier. The high tier has only one cluster and all cluster heads in the low tier are also the members in the high tier. The nodes in the high tier forward their aggregated data to the node with the maximal remaining energy, called the main cluster head.

The main cluster head transmits the aggregated data to the sink. When a round is over, rotate the cluster head of the low tier in the sensing field based on the parameter Oij:

$$Q_{ij} = \frac{E_{ij}^{new}}{E_{d_{ij}}}, \; i = 1,\ldots,n, \; j = 1,\ldots,|C_i|$$

The members of the high tier in the next round consist of these cluster heads. In the current round T, CH2 is the main cluster head. In the next round, T + d, CH3 has a maximal remaining energy that is selected as the main cluster head, and so on.

The simulation result shows that both ECRA-2T and ECRA outperform all other routing schemes: direct communication, static clustering and LEACH. The system lifetime of ECRA2T is approximately 2.5 times that of LEACH. ECRA-2T also requires much less energy consumption than that of direct communication, as shown in Figure 6.13.

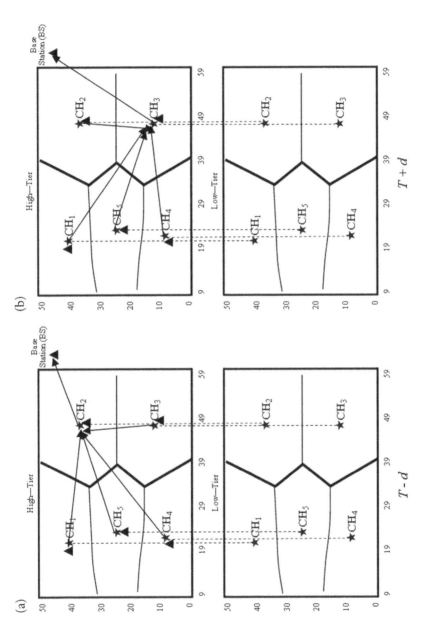

FIGURE 6.12 The operation of high-tier architecture in enhanced ECRA, where T is the current round and T + d is the next round, and so on.

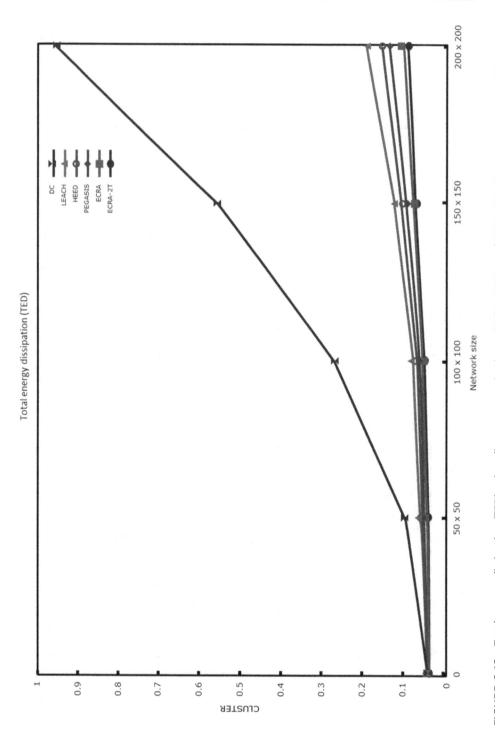

FIGURE 6.13 Total energy dissipation (TED) using direct communication, LEACH, ECRA and ECRA-2T. The messages are 2,000 bits.

Location-Based Routing (Geographic Protocol)

Most of the routing protocols require location information for sensor nodes in wireless sensor networks to calculate the distance between two particular nodes on the basis of signal strength so that energy consumption can be estimated. It is also utilized in routing data in an energy-efficient way when addressing a scheme for a sensor network is not known. It is worth noting that there have been many location-based protocols in ad hoc networks and it makes great effects when we transplant those research achievements for wireless sensor networks in some ways.

MECN and SMECN

A minimum energy communication network (MECN) (Li & Halpern, 2001) sets up and maintains a minimum energy network for wireless networks by utilizing low-power GPS. Although the protocol assumes a mobile network, it is best applicable to sensor networks, which are not mobile. A minimum power topology for stationary nodes including a master node is found. MECN assumes a master site as the information sink, which is always the case for sensor networks.

MECN identifies a relay region for every node. The relay region consists of nodes in a surrounding area where transmitting through those nodes is more energy efficient than direct transmission. The relay region for node pair (i, r) is depicted in Figure 6.14.

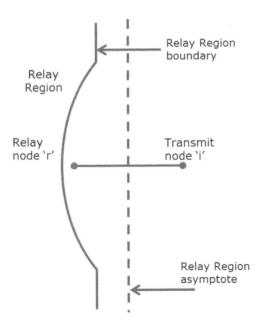

FIGURE 6.14   Relay region of transmit relay node pair (i, r) in MECN.

The enclosure of a node is then created by taking the union of all relay regions that node i can reach. The main idea of MECN is to find a sub-network, which will have less numbers of nodes and require less power for transmission between any two particular nodes. In this way, global minimum power paths are found without considering all the nodes in the network. This is performed using a localized search for each node considering its relay region.

MECN is self-reconfiguring and thus can manically adapt to node failure or the deployment of new sensors. Between two successive wakeups of the nodes, each node can execute the first phase of the algorithm and the minimum cost links are updated by considering leaving or newly joining nodes.

The small minimum energy communication network (SMECN) (Li & Halpern, 2001) is an extension to MECN. In MECN, it is assumed that every node can transmit to every other node, which is not possible every time. In SMECN, possible obstacles between any pairs of nodes are considered. However, the network is still assumed to be fully connected as in the case of MECN. The subnetwork constructed by SMECN for minimum energy relaying is provably smaller (in terms of number of edges) than the one constructed in MECN if broadcasts are able to reach to all nodes in a circular region around the broadcaster. As a result, the number of hops for transmissions will decrease. Simulation results show that SMECN uses less energy than MECN and the maintenance cost of the links is less. However, finding a sub-network with smaller numbers of edges introduces more overhead in the algorithm.

GEAR (Geographic and EnergyAware Routing)

The aim is to reduce the interest in directed diffusion and add geographic information into an interest packet by only considering a certain region rather than sending interest to the whole network by means of flooding. GEAR uses energy aware and geographically informed neighbor selection heuristics to route a packet towards the target region (Yu et al., 2001). Therefore, GEAR helps in balancing energy consumption in this way and increases the network lifetime. When a closer neighbor to the destination exists, GEAR forwards the packet to the destination by picking a next-hop among all neighbors that are closer to the destination. When all neighbors are far away, there is a hole and then GEAR forwards the packet by picking a next-hop node that minimizes a cost value of this neighbor. A recursive geographic forwarding algorithm is used to disseminate the packet within the region.

GEAR is compared to a similar non-energy aware routing protocol GPSR, which is one of the earlier works in geographic routing that uses planar graphs to solve the problem of holes. The simulation results show that for uneven traffic distributions, GEAR delivers 70% to 80% more packets than GPSR. For uniform traffic pairs, GEAR delivers 25–35% more packets than GPSR, as shown in Figure 6.15.

GAF and HGAF

A GAF (Geographic Adaptive Fidelity) (Inagaki & Ishihara, 2009) is an adaptive fidelity algorithm in which large numbers of sensor nodes are placed in an observed area

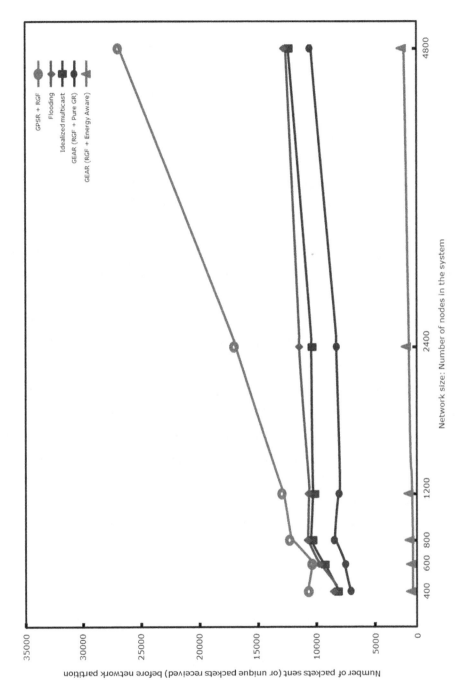

FIGURE 6.15   Comparison for uniform traffic.

and only a few nodes in the observed area are selected to transmit messages, while the other nodes sleep. In this way, GAF reduces the number of nodes needed to form a network and saves the nodes' batteries.

Hierarchical geographical adaptive fidelity (HGAF) saves much more battery by enlarging the cell of a GAF by adding a layered structure for selecting an active node in each cell. A GAF saves battery power by enlarging the size of the cell. The connectivity between active nodes in two adjacent cells must be guaranteed because active nodes work as cluster heads to deliver packets between cells. Because of this limitation, a GAF needs an active node in every area whose maximum size is R2/5.

A HGAF limits the position of active node in a cell and synchronizes the position in each cell among all cells. Through this modification, the connectivity between active nodes in two adjacent cells can be guaranteed for a larger cell than in a GAF.

A simulation result shows that a HGAF outperforms a GAF in terms of survived nodes and the packet delivery ratio when the node density is high. The lifetime of dense and randomly distributed networks with a HGAF is about 200% as long as ones with a GAF.

Fermat Point-Based Energy-Efficient Geocast Routing Protocol

A geocast routing protocol is used to deliver packets to a group of nodes that are within a specified geographical area, i.e., the geocast region. Fermat point-based protocols are adapted for reducing the energy consumption of a WASN by reducing the total transmission distance in a multi hop-multi sink scenario. A congested environment around a WASN expands the chance of multipath propagation and it in turn acquaints multipath fading. In Ghosh et al. (2012), the effects of both of these factors are considered on the performance of I-Min routing protocol designed for WASNs. I-MIN is the energy-efficient scheme as it increases the probability that a node with higher residual energy is selected even if its distance from the destination is somewhat more as compared to that for another node with a lesser value for residual energy.

After modifying the radio model with considerations for changed propagation environmental effects and multi-path fading, the consumption of energy in a geocast routing protocol is shown to vary considerably. The higher the number of geocast regions, the larger is the total distance that a data packet has to travel and thereby greater is the effect of the propagation environment combined with the effect of multi-path fading on the performance of an energy-aware algorithm.

Multi-Path Routing Protocol

Due to the limited capacity of a multi-hop path (Radi et al., 2012) and the high dynamics of wireless links, single-path routing approach is unable to provide efficient high data rate transmission in wireless sensor networks. Nowadays, the multi-path routing approach is broadly utilized as one of the possible solutions to cope with this limitation. This section discusses some of the multi-path routing protocols.

N-to-1 Multi-Path Routing Protocol

The N-to-1 multi-path routing protocol (Lou, 2005) is proposed to converge the cast traffic pattern of wireless sensor networks. In this technique, multiple node disjoint paths are simultaneously discovered from all sensor nodes towards a single sink node. In this protocol, the sink node discovers a route by sending a route update message. This stage is called branch-aware flooding, which discovers several paths from a sensor node towards a single sink tree and constructs a spanning tree. Then, each sensor node that receives a route update message for the first time selects the sender of this message as its parent towards the sink node. In addition, if an intermediate node overhears a route update message from another neighboring node that introduces an alternative node-disjoint path through a different branch of the spanning tree, it adds this path to its routing table. This process continues until all sensor nodes discover their primary path towards the sink node and the spanning tree is constructed through all the nodes, as shown in Figure 6.16(a). After that, a multi-path extension flooding technique is used to discover more paths from each sensor node towards the sink node. As shown in Figure 6.16(b), each link between two individual nodes that belong to different branches of the constructed spanning tree can help to establish an additional path from these nodes towards the sink node.

This protocol utilizes the single-path forwarding strategy for transmitting each data segment, while all the intermediate nodes use an adaptive per-hop packet salvaging technique to provide fast data recovery from node or link failures along the active paths.

The N-to-1 multi-path routing protocol profits from the availability of several paths at the intermediate nodes to improve reliability of packet delivery by employing a per-hop packet salvaging strategy. Nevertheless, using such a simple flooding strategy cannot result in constructing high-quality paths with minimum interference. According to the operation of this protocol, concurrent data transmission over constructed paths may reduce the network performance.

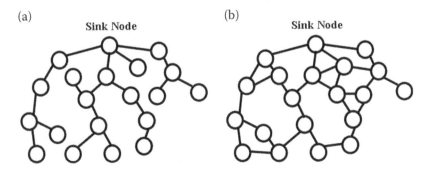

FIGURE 6.16   (a) Spanning tree constructed by initial flooding in N-to-1 multi-path routing protocol. (b) Multi-path discovery using multi-path extension flooding mechanism.

Multi-Path Multi-Speed Protocol (MMSPEED)

A MMSPEED (Felemban et al., 2006) is designed based on the cross-layer design approach between a network and MAC layer to provide QoS differentiation in terms of reliability and timeliness. A MMSPEED is the extension of the SPEED protocol (He et al., 2003), which guarantees timeliness packet delivery by introducing multiple speed levels and provides different speed layers over a single network. In this protocol, data packets are assigned to the appropriate speed layer to be placed in the suitable queue according to their speed category. After that, data packets are serviced in the first come first serve (FCFS) policy.

From a reliability perspective, MMSPEED benefits from path diversity property of multipath routing approach to guarantee reliability requirements of each data packet. This protocol provides reliability differentiation through controlling number of active paths and sending multiple copies of the original data packets over several paths. Accordingly, each intermediate node selects a set of next-hop neighboring nodes towards the destination node based on the estimated packet loss rate over each link and their geographic distance from itself.

A MMSPEED satisfies the delay requirements of various applications. To satisfy different delay requirements, each intermediate node tries to forward its received data packet to the neighboring node, which is closer to the destination node in order to provide good speed progress. However, according to the experimental results provided in Woo et al. (2003), the probability of successful data transmission over low-power wireless links highly depends on the sender receiver distance and interference power of the receiver. Therefore, using geographic routing with greedy forwarding does not necessarily improve network performance metrics. Moreover, since data transmission over long links exacerbates the required energy for data transmission, this protocol cannot support long-life applications.

Braided Multi-Path Routing Protocol

A braided multi-path routing protocol (Ganesan et al., 2001) is a seminal multi-path routing protocol proposed to provide fault-tolerant routing in wireless sensor networks. This protocol uses the same technique as in directed diffusion; it uses two types of path reinforcement messages to construct several partially disjointed paths.

The sink node sends a primary path reinforcement message to its best neighboring node to initiate the path. When an intermediate node receives a primary path reinforcement message, it forwards this message to its best next-hop neighboring node towards the source node. This process is repeated until the primary path reinforcement message reaches the source node. Whenever the sink and intermediate nodes send out the primary path reinforcement message, they also generate an alternative path reinforcement message and send this message to their next preferred neighboring node towards the source node. Through establishing a set of partially disjointed paths between the source and sink nodes, whenever the primary path fails to forward data packets towards the sink node, one of the constructed alternative paths can be utilized to avoid data transmission failure.

Simulation results show the comparison of the lower overhead of a braided multipath routing with the idealized node-disjoint multipath protocol. The proposed approach provides about 50% higher resilience against path failures, compared to the idealized node disjoint multi-path protocol. Besides, since this approach is designed based on the principles of directed diffusion, the drawbacks of directed diffusion can be presented in this protocol.

Energy-Aware Routing

An energy-aware routing protocol is an efficient method to minimize the energy cost for communication and can increase the network lifetime. Unlike directed diffusion, data transmission is done through several optimum paths at higher rates instead of transmitting through one optimal path. The transmission path selection is done by choosing a probability value of each path. The probability value balanced the initial network load and enhanced the network lifetime.

An energy-aware routing protocol is proposed in Vidhyapriya and Vanathi (2007) and provides a reliable transmission environment with low energy consumption. It is used for making decisions on which neighbor a sensor node should forward the data message. A node is selected on the basis of its residual energy level and signal strength. Ideally, the greater the energy of the node, the more likely it is to be selected on the next hop. The nodes that are not selected will move to the sleep state to conserve power. Network connectivity is shown in Figure 6.17 (Vidhyapriya & Vanathi, 2007). There are many intermediate nodes available in the network. All nodes within the radio range of the nodes receive the broadcast message at the same time. When the sink initially broadcasts the message, nodes A, E and G receive the message. Assume that the available energy at A is larger than at E and G, and also A is within the required signal strength threshold; hence, node A is selected to broadcast the message to the neighboring nodes. The process continues and node B, which is selected, sends out the broadcast message that is received by nodes F and C. It is found that both F and C have the same energy level and are within the required signal strength threshold.

So, both F and C start a back-off timer and if the back-off timer of node F ends before C, an implicit acknowledgment is sent by node F and is also received by node C;

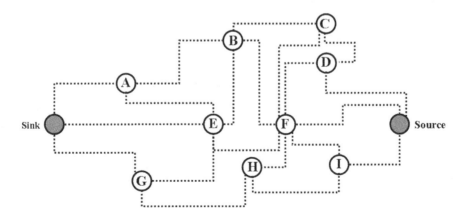

FIGURE 6.17 Network connectivity.

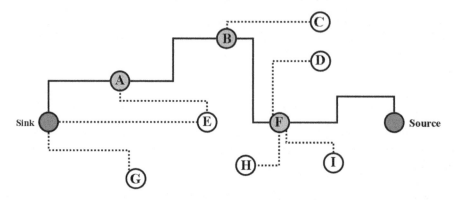

FIGURE 6.18   Path selected in energy-aware routing.

so node C stops its back-off timer, as shown in Figure 6.18. When the broadcast message reaches the target source, the source transmits the route reply packet through the nodes it received the broadcast message. This protocol provides reliable packet delivery for unicast transmission. Data is cached in the sender until an ACK is received from the receiver. If no ACK is received within a time-out period, an error report is generated and the data will be sent back to the original source of this data in order to retransmit.

The disadvantage is that energy-aware routing needs to exchange local information between neighbor nodes and all nodes have a unified address, which enlarges the price of building routing paths.

COMPARISON OF ROUTING PROTOCOLS

A detailed comparison of WSN routing protocols is given in Table 6.2 (Shabbir & Hassan, 2017).

ROUTING ATTACKS IN WIRELESS SENSOR NETWORKS

WSNs are designed in a layered form; this layered architecture makes these networks susceptible and leads to damage against many kinds of attacks. The attacks that act on the network layer are called routing attacks. These attacks occur while routing messages. We discuss the following kinds of routing attacks (Figure 6.19).

TABLE 6.2 Comparison of routing protocols

ROUTING PROTOCOLS	CLASSIFICATION	POWER USAGE	DATA AGGREGATION	SCALABILITY	QUERY BASED	OVERHEAD	DATA DELIVERY MODEL	QoS
SPIN	Flat/Source-initiated/Data-centric	Limited	Yes	Limited	Yes	Low	Event driven	No
DD	Flat/Data-centric/Destination-initiated	Limited	Yes	Limited	Yes	Low	Demand driven	No
RR	Flat	Low	Yes	Good	Yes	Low	Demand driven	No
GBR	Flat	Low	Yes	Limited	Yes	Low	Hybrid	No
CADR	Flat	Limited	Yes	Limited	Yes	Low	Continuously	No
COUGAR	Flat	Limited	Yes	Limited	Yes	High	Query driven	No
ACQUIRE	Flat/Data-centric	Low	Yes	Limited	Yes	Low	Complex query	No
LEACH	Hierarchical/Destination-initiated/Node-centric	High	Yes	Good	No	High	Cluster head	No
TEEN & APTEEN	Hierarchical	High	Yes	Good	No	High	Active threshold	No
PEGASIS	Hierarchical	Max	No	Good	No	Low	Chains based	No
VGA	Hierarchical	Low	Yes	Good	No	High	Good	No
SOP	Hierarchical	Low	No	Good	No	High	Continuously	No
GAF	Hierarchical/Location	Limited	No	Good	No	Mod	Virtual grid	No
SPAN	Hierarchical/Location	Limited	Yes	Limited	No	High	Continuously	No
GEAR	Location	Limited	No	Limited	No	Mod	Demand driven	No
SAR	Data Centric	High	Yes	Limited	Yes	High	Continuously	Yes
SPEED	Location/Data Centric	Limited	No	Limited	Yes	Low	Geographic	Yes

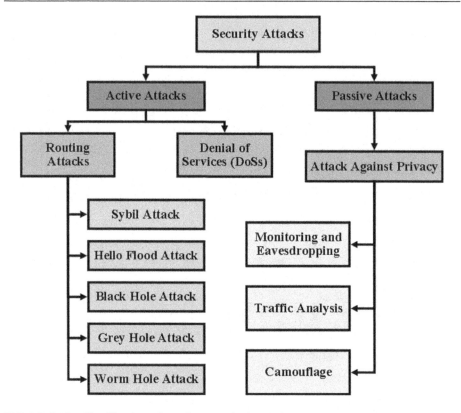

FIGURE 6.19 Classification of routing attacks in wireless sensor networks.

Sybil Attack

Sybil attack is named after the subject of the book *Sybil*, a case study of a woman diagnosed with multiple fake identities. These fake identities are known as Sybil nodes. The Sybil nodes can out-vote the honest nodes in the system. Usually, peer-to-peer systems are vulnerable to a Sybil attack. Examples of vulnerable systems include vehicular ad hoc network, distributed storage applications in peer-to-peer systems, routing in a distributed peer-to-peer system (W. Chang & Wu, 2014), etc.

Black Hole Attack

A black hole is a malicious node that attracts all the traffic in the network by advertising that it has the shortest path in the network (Al-Shurman et al., 2004). So, it creates a metaphorical black hole with the malicious node or the adversary at the center. This black hole drops all the packets it receives from the other nodes.

In a black hole attack, malicious nodes do not send true control messages. To execute a black hole attack, a malicious node awaits the neighboring nodes to send RREQ messages. When the malicious nodes receive a RREQ message from its neighboring nodes, it immediately sends a false RREP message providing a route to the destination over itself. In this way, it assigns a high sequence number to be settled in the routing table of victim node before true nodes send a genuine reply. Therefore, requesting nodes assume that the route discovery process is completed and ignore RREP messages from other nodes and start sending packets over the malicious node. This is how malicious nodes attack all the RREQ messages and take over all the routes in the network. Therefore, all the packets are sent to the malicious node from where they are never forwarded and eventually dropped. This is called a black hole, akin to the real meaning of swallowing all objects and matter (Dokurer, 2006).

Denial of Service Attack

A denial of service (DoS) attack is one that attempts to prevent the victim from being able to use all or part of his/her network connection (Soomro, 2010). A DoS attack allows an adversary to subvert, disrupt or destroy a network, and also to diminish a network's capability to provide a service.

DoS attacks extend to all the layers of the protocol stack. They are usually very difficult to prevent because they exist in many forms inside the network. For example, a malicious node can send a huge number of requests to a server that has to test the legitimacy of the nodes. Due to the huge number of requests, the server will be busy in testing illegal requests and so it will not be available for the legal users. This causes performance degradation of the entire network as the network gets congested because of illegal requests.

Wormhole Attack

A wormhole attack is an attack on the routing protocol in which the packets or individual bits of the packets are captured at one location, tunneled to another location and then replayed at another location (Hu et al., 2003a and b; Mahajan et al., 2008). In this attack, the two colluding nodes create an illusion that the locations involved are directly connected, even though they are actually distant.

Hello Flood Attack

Most protocols require nodes to broadcast HELLO PACKETS to show their presence to their neighbors and the receiving nodes may assume that it is within the RF range of the sender. This assumption may prove to be false when a laptop-class attacker transmits routing information with an abnormally high transmission power to prove every other node in the network that the malicious node is its neighbor. Such an attack in the network is called a hello flood attack (Singh et al., 2010).

Grey Hole Attack

A grey hole attack is a variation of a black hole attack in which the nodes selectively drop packets (Mohammadi & Jadidoleslamy, 2011). There are two ways in which a node can drop packets:

- It can drop all UDP packets while transmitting all TCP packets.
- It can drop 50% of the packets or it can drop them with probabilistic distribution.

In a grey hole attack, a normal node can be prevented from behaving normally and therefore this attack is difficult to detect. A grey hole attack affects one or two nodes in the network, whereas a black hole attack affects the whole network.

For each layer, there are some attacks and defensive mechanisms. Thus, WSNs are vulnerable against different routing attacks, such as DoS attacks, traffic analysis, privacy violation, sinkholes and other attacks to routing protocols (Sharma & Ghose, 2010; Zhou et al., 2008) since sensor notes in WSNs collaborate with each other for routing, the collaboration between sensors is susceptible to routing attacks. Attackers can gain access to routing paths and redirect the traffic, or propagate or broadcast false routing information into the WSNs or launch DoS attacks against routing. Table 6.3 presents the definitions of routing attacks on WSNs, and then it classifies and compares them to each other based on their strategies and effects.

CONCLUSION

Routing in sensor networks is a new research area, with a limited but rapidly growing set of results. In this paper, routing protocols are discussed based on three categories: flat-based routing, hierarchical-based routing and location-based routing on the basis of network structure. They have the common objective of trying to extend the lifetime of the sensor network. Rumor routing discussed in the paper is tunable and allows for trade-off between setup overhead and delivery reliability. In gradient-based routing, the back-off waiting scheme is quite effective for saving the energy consumption when establishing the network's routes. Hierarchical-based techniques have special advantages of scalability and efficient communication. Hierarchical routing maintains the energy consumption of sensor nodes and performs data aggregation, which helps in decreasing the number of transmitted messages to the base station. Most of the routing protocols require location information for sensor nodes in wireless sensor networks to calculate the distance between two particular nodes on the basis of signal strength, so that energy consumption can be estimated. A single-path routing approach is unable to provide efficient high data rate transmission in wireless sensor networks due to the

TABLE 6.3   The definitions, techniques and effects of routing attacks on WSNs

ATTACKS/ CRITERIA	ATTACK DEFINITION	ATTACK TECHNIQUES	ATTACK EFFECTS
Homing	Regular traffic monitoring and analyzing the messages transferred, communication patterns and sensor node activities > identify and locate critical resources that provide critical/vital services to the WSN > launching active attack	Regular monitoring and traffic analysis, including rate monitoring attack and time correlation attack; plug into the wireless channel within the sender's transmission range; use powerful resources or strong devices	Identify, locate and destroy critical resources; extract the sensitive network information; launch active attacks (wormhole, blackhole, sinkhole); threaten data confidentiality and privacy
Neglect and greed	Malicious node drops incoming packets, randomly or arbitrarily (neglectful node); malicious node gives undue priority to its own messages (greedy node)	Selective forwarding and blackhole attacks techniques; misuse from routing protocols	Consistently degrade or block traffic; packet drop/losses; Influence/limit the WSN traffic; low reliability
Rushing	Quick broadcast the false advertisings of route request through the WSN (Hu et al., 2003a&b); an attacker exploits a duplicate suppression in broadcasts to suppress legitimate packets by quickly forwarding its own packets	Forwarding route requests more quickly than any normal nodes (Hu et al., 2003a&b); use of duplicate suppression in routing protocols; sends forged or modified route requests to the entire WSN; keeps the network interface transmission queues of nearby nodes full; employs a wormhole; misuse from properties of all on-demand protocols; forwards requests without checking signature; use of a longer	Discards correct requests; launches other attacks such as blackhole or wormhole; partitions the network; unable to discover any usable/useful routes; provides a significant latency advantage; strengthens the attackers' position; forms/establishes a wormhole tunnel

(Continued)

TABLE 6.3 (Continued)   The definitions, techniques and effects of routing attacks on WSNs

ATTACKS/ CRITERIA	ATTACK DEFINITION	ATTACK TECHNIQUES	ATTACK EFFECTS
		transmission range; ignores MAC layer's delays	
Gratuitous detour attack	Makes a route through attacker appear longer where a shorter route exists and would otherwise be used, by adding virtual nodes to the route	Routing information modification or replication or injection (unauthenticated injection); fakes routing information; discards/ignores routing information; misdirection (traffic direction to wrong path)	Non-cooperation between nodes; resource exhaustion; routing loops; routing inconsistencies; traffic attraction/repel; network partition; misdirection; extends or shortens source routes; low reliability
Node malfunction	Inaccurate data generation	Malicious data injection	Integrity destruction; degrades the WSN efficiency; takes over the WSN; resource exhaustion
HELLO flood	Bombs/floods whole network with routing protocol HELLO packets (Padmavathi & Shanmugapriya, 2009) (with more energy), that announce false neighbor status using powerful radio transmitter (Karlof & Wagner, 2003)	Lures sensors; broadcasts high-power HELLO message to legitimate nodes; forges/false advertising high-quality route to sink (Karlof & Wagner, 2003)	Disrupts topology construction; network and routing confusion/ destruction; exhausts nodes' energy; decreases efficiency and cooperation; increases the WSN latency
Flooding attack or packet replication attack	Floodx application layer: exhausting the resources of sensors (Khokhar et al., 2008); floods routing layer: a node generates and propagates numerous route requests	Simple broadcast flooding; simple target flooding; false identity broadcast flooding; false identity target flooding; enforces additional processing to nodes; compromises routing information	Resource exhaustion; reduces WSN's availability; blows up the traffic statistics of the WSN or a certain node and leads to considerable damage costs

(Continued)

TABLE 6.3 (Continued)   The definitions, techniques and effects of routing attacks on WSNs

ATTACKS/ CRITERIA	ATTACK DEFINITION	ATTACK TECHNIQUES	ATTACK EFFECTS
Sinkhole	A special selective forwarding attack; more complex than blackhole attack; attracts (Padmavathi & Shanmugapriya, 2009) or draws all possible network traffic to a compromised node by placing a malicious node closer to the base station (Krontiris et al., 2008) and enabling selective forwarding; centralizes traffic into the malicious node; possible design of another attack during this attack; sinkhole detection is very hard	Lures or compromises nodes (Karlof & Wagner, 2003); tampers with application data along the packet flow path (selective forwarding); receives traffic and altering or fabricating information (Krontiris et al., 2008); identities spoofing for a short time; uses the communication pattern; creates a large sphere of influence; based on used routing protocol: MintRoute or MultiHopLQI protocol	Lures and attracts almost all the traffic; triggers other attacks, such as eavesdropping, trivial selective forwarding, blackhole and wormhole; usurps the base station's position; message modification; information fabrication and packet dropping; suppresses messages in a certain area; routing information modification/fake; resource exhaustion
Blackhole	A form of selective forwarding attack; a kind of DoS attack that the attacker swallows all the received messages; drops all incoming packets	Drops all incoming packets from neighboring/children nodes; reduces the latency and deceiving/luring the neighboring nodes; advertises/ broadcasts or propagates spoofed/ false information such as routing information, to neighboring nodes (Khokhar et al., 2008)	Decreases the throughput of a subset of nodes (especially the neighboring nodes); loses blackhole's neighbors; network partition; packet loss; influences the network traffic; limits or prevents send/receive traffic
Spoofed, altered or replayed routing information	Makes a path cycle between the source and the destination nodes (so the data message will go	Node identity replication/ fabrication; generates false and misleading	Network partition; misdirection; resource exhaustion; decreases network

(Continued)

ATTACKS/ CRITERIA	ATTACK DEFINITION	ATTACK TECHNIQUES	ATTACK EFFECTS
	around in circle, possibly forever); its target is the routing information exchanged between nodes (Karlof & Wagner, 2003); a type of DoS attack that injects fake or false routing information into the WSN	messages; spoofing, altering or replaying routing information; misdirection; unauthenticated injections; overflowing routing tables; routing table poisoning; route cache poisoning	lifetime; false error message generation; low reliability; discards routing information; wrong routing tables
Acknowledge spoofing	An adversary can spoof link layer acknowledgments (ACKs) of overheard packets (Karlof & Wagner, 2003)	ACKs replication; forges/spoofs link layer ACKs of neighbor nodes	False view/ information of the WSN; launches selective forwarding attack; packet loss/ corruption
Impersonation	Malicious node impersonates a cluster leader and lures nodes to a wrong position; impersonates a node within the path of the data flow of attacker's interest by modifying routing data or implying itself as a trustworthy communication partner to neighboring nodes in parallel	The WSN reconfiguration; access to encryption keys and authentication information; man-in-the-middle attack and fake MAC addresses; node replication (Parno et al., 2005); physical access to the WSN; false or malicious node attack techniques; Sybil attacks techniques; misdirection/ misrouting; modifies routing information; lures/convinces nodes	Routing information modification; false sensor readings; makes network congestion or collapse; discloses secret keys; network partition; false and misleading messages generated; resource exhaustion; degrades the WSN performance; invasion; carries out further attacks to disrupt operation of the WSN; confuses and takes over the entire WSN
Eavesdropping	Detects the contents of communication by overhearing/stealthy attempt to data	Interception; abuses wireless nature of WSNs' transmission medium; uses powerful resources and strong devices,	Launches other attacks (wormhole, blackhole); extracts sensitive WSN information; deletes the privacy

TABLE 6.3 (Continued)   The definitions, techniques and effects of routing attacks on WSNs

ATTACKS/ CRITERIA	ATTACK DEFINITION	ATTACK TECHNIQUES	ATTACK EFFECTS
		such as powerful receivers and well-designed antennas	protection and reducing data confidentiality
Traffic Analysis	An attack against privacy (privacy violation); regular monitoring, detecting and analyzing the messages transferred, contents of communication patterns and sensor nodes activities > extracting and revealing the sensitive information > harming to the WSN	Rate monitoring attack techniques; time correlation attack techniques; compromises the base station or the nodes which they are near to the base station; misuse from the wireless nature of WSNs' transmission medium; uses powerful resources	Monitors and accesses the WSN information; WSN partial disruption/destruction; launches other attacks (wormhole and blackhole); privacy protection elimination; data confidentiality deletion
Selective forwarding	In application layer (message selective forwarding): the attacker selectively sends the information of a particular sensor; in network layer (sensor selective forwarding): the attacker sends/discards the information from selected sensors; there are two modes of this attack: simple mode attack and complex mode attack	In application layer: understands the semantics of the payload of the application layer packets; but in routing layer: reduces the latency and deceives the neighboring nodes; misuse of nodes' faithful (which forward all received messages); packet dropping or modification or suppression; the attacker is on the route of packet transfer in a multi-hop network; otherwise, needs to position itself in the routing path using other attacks (Sybil, sinkhole and routing	Drops/alters certain messages; influences the WSN traffic; impossibility verifying malicious nodes

(Continued)

TABLE 6.3 (Continued)   The definitions, techniques and effects of routing attacks on WSNs

ATTACKS/ CRITERIA	ATTACK DEFINITION	ATTACK TECHNIQUES	ATTACK EFFECTS
		table poisoning attack)	
Misdirection	Misroutes the received packets or traffic flows in one direction to a distant node; forwards messages to/along wrong paths	Generates wrong messages; routing information modification, fabrication, replication or discard; Internet smurf attack techniques	Packet misdirection; floods its network link; wrong routing tables (false routing information); non-cooperation; resource exhaustion; network partition; low reliability; reduces the WSN's availability
DoS attacks	A general attack includes several types of other attacks in different layers of WSN, simultaneously; reduces the WSN's availability	Physical layer attack techniques; link layer attack techniques; routing layer attack techniques; transport layer attack techniques; application layer attack techniques	Effects of physical layer, link layer, routing layer, transport layer and application layer attacks

limited capacity of a multi-hop path and the high dynamics of wireless links. This problem can be overcome by using multi-path routing. Many routing protocols have been proposed that are not suitable for all applications in WSNs. Many issues and challenges still exist that need to be solved in the sensor networks.

REFERENCES

Akkaya, K., & Younis, M. (2005). A survey on routing protocols for wireless sensor networks. *Ad Hoc Networks*, *3*(3), 325–349.

Al-Karaki, J. N., & Kamal, A. E. (2004). Routing techniques in wireless sensor networks: A survey. *IEEE Wireless Communications*, *11*(6), 6–28.

Al-Shurman, M., Yoo, S.-M., & Park, S. (2004). Black hole attack in mobile ad hoc networks. *Proceedings of the 42nd Annual Southeast Regional Conference*, 96–97.

Aslam, S., Farooq, F., & Sarwar, S. (2009). Power consumption in wireless sensor networks. *Proceedings of the 7th International Conference on Frontiers of Information Technology*, 1–9.

Braginsky, D., & Estrin, D. (2002). Rumor routing algorthim for sensor networks. *Proceedings of the 1st ACM International Workshop on Wireless Sensor Networks and Applications*, 22–31.

Chang, J.-H., & Jan, R.-H. (2005). An energy aware, cluster-based routing algorithm for wireless sensor networks. *International Conference on Embedded and Ubiquitous Computing*, 255–266.

Chang, W., & Wu, J. (2014). A survey of sybil attacks in networks. In *Sensor networks for sustainable development* (pp. 497–534). CRC Press.

Dokurer, S. (2006). *Simulation of Black hole attack in wireless Ad-hoc networks*. Atılım University Ankara.

Farmer, J. (2001, August). *Managing secure data delivery: A data roundhouse model*.

Felemban, E., Lee, C.-G., & Ekici, E. (2006). MMSPEED: Multipath Multi-SPEED protocol for QoS guarantee of reliability and. Timeliness in wireless sensor networks. *IEEE Transactions on Mobile Computing*, 5(6), 738–754.

Feng, Y., Tang, S., & Dai, G. (2011). Fault tolerant data aggregation scheduling with local information in wireless sensor networks. *Tsinghua Science and Technology*, 16(5), 451–463.

Ganesan, D., Govindan, R., Shenker, S., & Estrin, D. (2001). Highly-resilient, energy-efficient multipath routing in wireless sensor networks. *ACM SIGMOBILE Mobile Computing and Communications Review*, 5(4), 11–25.

Ghosh, K., Bhattacharya, P. P., & Das, P. K. (2012). Effect of multipath fading and propagation environment on the performance of a Fermat point based energy efficient geocast routing protocol. *International Journal of Wireless & Mobile Networks*, 4(1), 215.

He, T., Stankovic, J. A., Lu, C., & Abdelzaher, T. (2003). SPEED: A stateless protocol for real-time communication in sensor networks. *23rd International Conference on Distributed Computing Systems, 2003. Proceedings*, 46–55.

Heinzelman, W. R., Kulik, J., & Balakrishnan, H. (1999). Adaptive protocols for information dissemination in wireless sensor networks. *Proceedings of the 5th Annual ACM/IEEE International Conference on Mobile Computing and Networking*, 174–185.

Hu, Y.-C., Perrig, A., & Johnson, D. B. (2003a). Packet leashes: A defense against wormhole attacks in wireless networks. *IEEE INFOCOM 2003. Twenty-Second Annual Joint Conference of the IEEE Computer and Communications Societies (IEEE Cat. No. 03CH37428)*, 3, 1976–1986.

Hu, Y.-C., Perrig, A., & Johnson, D. B. (2003b). Rushing attacks and defense in wireless ad hoc network routing protocols. *Proceedings of the 2nd ACM Workshop on Wireless Security*, 30–40.

Inagaki, T., & Ishihara, S. (2009). HGAF: A power saving scheme for wireless sensor networks. *Information and Media Technologies*, 4(4), 1086–1097.

Intanagonwiwat, C., Govindan, R., Estrin, D., Heidemann, J., & Silva, F. (2003). Directed diffusion for wireless sensor networking. *IEEE/ACM Transactions on Networking*, 11(1), 2–16.

Iwanicki, K., & Van Steen, M. (2009). On hierarchical routing in wireless sensor networks. *2009 International Conference on Information Processing in Sensor Networks*, 133–144.

Joshi, A., & Priya, L. (2011). A survey of hierarchical routing protocols in wireless sensor network. *MES Journal of Technology and Management*, 2(1), 67–71.

Karlof, C., & Wagner, D. (2003). Secure routing in wireless sensor networks: Attacks and countermeasures. *Ad Hoc Networks*, 1(2–3), 293–315.

Khokhar, R. H., Ngadi, M. A., & Mandala, S. (2008). A review of current routing attacks in mobile ad hoc networks. *International Journal of Computer Science and Security*, 2(3), 18–29.

Krontiris, I., Giannetsos, T., & Dimitriou, T. (2008). Launching a sinkhole attack in wireless sensor networks; the intruder side. *2008 IEEE International Conference on Wireless and Mobile Computing, Networking and Communications*, 526–531.

Li, L., & Halpern, J. Y. (2001). Minimum-energy mobile wireless networks revisited. *ICC 2001. IEEE International Conference on Communications. Conference Record (Cat. No. 01CH37240)*, *1*, 278–283.

Lindsey, S., & Raghavendra, C. S. (2002). PEGASIS: Power-efficient gathering in sensor information systems. *Proceedings, IEEE Aerospace Conference*, *3*, 3.

Lou, W. (2005). An efficient N-to-1 multipath routing protocol in wireless sensor networks. *IEEE International Conference on Mobile Adhoc and Sensor Systems Conference, 2005.*, 8-pp.

Mahajan, V., Natu, M., & Sethi, A. (2008). Analysis of wormhole intrusion attacks in MANETS. *MILCOM 2008–2008 IEEE Military Communications Conference*, 1–7.

Manjeshwar, A., & Agrawal, D. P. (2001). TEEN: A routing protocol for enhanced efficiency in wireless sensor networks. *Ipdps*, *1*, 189.

Manjeshwar, A., & Agrawal, D. P. (2002). APTEEN: A hybrid protocol for efficient routing and comprehensive information retrieval in wireless sensor networks. *Ipdps*, 0195b.

Mohammadi, S., & Jadidoleslamy, H. (2011). A comparison of link layer attacks on wireless sensor networks. *ArXiv Preprint ArXiv:1103.5589*.

Muthukarpagam, S., Niveditta, V., & Neduncheliyan, S. (2010). Design issues, topology issues, quality of service support for wireless sensor networks: Survey and research challenges. *International Journal of Computer Applications*, *1*(6), 1–4.

Padmavathi, D. G., & Shanmugapriya, M. (2009). A survey of attacks, security mechanisms and challenges in wireless sensor networks. *ArXiv Preprint ArXiv:0909.0576*.

Parno, B., Perrig, A., & Gligor, V. (2005). Distributed detection of node replication attacks in sensor networks. *2005 IEEE Symposium on Security and Privacy (S&P'05)*, 49–63.

Radi, M., Dezfouli, B., Bakar, K. A., & Lee, M. (2012). Multipath routing in wireless sensor networks: Survey and research challenges. *Sensors*, *12*(1), 650–685.

Shabbir, N., & Hassan, S. R. (2017). Routing protocols for wireless sensor networks (WSNs). *Wireless Sensor Networks-Insights and Innovations*.

Sharma, K., & Ghose, M. K. (2010). Wireless sensor networks: An overview on its security threats. *IJCA, Special Issue on "Mobile Ad-Hoc Networks" MANETs*, 42–45.

Sharma, T., Singh, H., & Sharma, A. (2015). A comparative review on routing protocols in wireless sensor networks. *International Journal of Computer Applications*, *123*(14).

Singh, V. P., Jain, S., & Singhai, J. (2010). Hello flood attack and its countermeasures in wireless sensor networks. *International Journal of Computer Science Issues (IJCSI)*, *7*(3), 23.

Soomro, S. A. (2010). Denial of service attacks in wireless ad hoc networks. *Journal of Information & Communication Technology (JICT)*, *4*(2), 10.

Vidhyapriya, R., & Vanathi, P. T. (2007). Energy aware routing for wireless sensor networks. *2007 International Conference on Signal Processing, Communications and Networking*, 545–550.

Woo, A., Tong, T., & Culler, D. (2003). Taming the underlying challenges of reliable multihop routing in sensor networks. *Proceedings of the 1st International Conference on Embedded Networked Sensor Systems*, 14–27.

Xia, L., Chen, X., & Guan, X. (2004). A new gradient-based routing protocol in wireless sensor networks. *International Conference on Embedded Software and Systems*, 318–325.

Yu, Y., Govindan, R., & Estrin, D. (2001). *Geographical and energy aware routing: A recursive data dissemination protocol for wireless sensor networks*.

Zhou, Y., Fang, Y., & Zhang, Y. (2008). Securing wireless sensor networks: A survey. *IEEE Communications Surveys & Tutorials*, *10*(3), 6–28.

Secure Localization Technique (SLT)

7

INTRODUCTION

Wireless sensor networks (WSNs) are shaping many activities in our society, as they have become the epitome of pervasive technology. WSNs have an endless array of potential applications in both military and civilian applications, including robotic land-mine detection, battlefield surveillance, target tracking, environmental monitoring, wildfire detection and traffic regulation, to name just a few. One common feature shared by all of these critical applications is the vitality of sensor location. The core function of a WSN is to detect and report events which can be meaningfully assimi-lated and responded to only if the accurate location of the event is known. Also, in any WSN, the location information of nodes plays a vital role in understanding the ap-plication context. There are three visible advantages of knowing the location in-formation of sensor nodes. First, location information is needed to identify the location of an event of interest. For instance, the location of an intruder, the location of a fire or the location of enemy tanks in a battlefield is of critical importance for deploying rescue and relief troops. Second, location awareness facilitates numerous application services, such as location directory services that provide doctors with the information of nearby medical equipment and personnel in a smart hospital, target-tracking ap-plications for locating survivors in debris or enemy tanks in a battlefield. Third, lo-cation information can assist in various system functionalities, such as geographical routing (Karp & Kung, 2000; Ko & Vaidya, 2000; Mauve et al., 2001; Navas & Imielinski, 1997; Yu et al., 2001), network coverage checking (Yan et al., 2003) and location-based information querying (Gupta et al., 2006). Hence, with these ad-vantages and much more, it is but natural for location-aware sensor devices to become the de facto standard in WSNs in all application domains that provide location-based service.

A straightforward solution is to equip each sensor with a GPS receiver that can ac-curately provide the sensors with their exact location. This, however, is not a feasible

DOI: 10.1201/9781003257608-7

solution from an economic perspective since sensors are often deployed in very large numbers and manual configuration is too cumbersome and hence not feasible. Therefore, localization in sensor networks is very challenging. Over the years, many protocols have been devised to enable the location discovery process in WSNs to be autonomous and able to function independently of GPS and other manual techniques (Bulusu et al., 2000; Doherty, 2001; Nagpal et al., 2003; Nasipuri & Li, 2002; Savvides et al., 2001). In all of these literatures, the focal point of location discovery has been a set of specialty nodes known as *beacon nodes*, which have been referred to by some researchers as anchor, locator or seed nodes. However, in this chapter, we shall use the term *beacon node* without loss of generality. These beacon nodes know their location, either through a GPS receiver or through manual configuration, which they provide to other sensor nodes. Using this location of beacon nodes, sensor nodes compute their location using various techniques discussed in a further section. It is, therefore, critical that malicious beacon nodes be prevented from providing false location information since sensor nodes completely rely on the information provided to them for computing their location.

There are three important metrics associated with localization: *energy efficiency, accuracy* and *security*. Though the first two metrics have been researched extensively, the security metric has drawn the attention of researchers only recently, and as such has not been addressed adequately. As security is a key metric, we are motivated to survey the existing techniques focusing on secure localization. This chapter, in which we review secure localization techniques that have been featured in literature thus far, is intended to be a single point of reference for researchers interested in secure localization.

Operational Challenges in WSNs

WSNs, unlike their counterparts, are often deployed to operate in unattended and hostile environments rarely encountered by typical computing devices: rain, snow, humidity and high temperature. When used for military applications like landmine detection, battlefield surveillance or target tracking, the conditions further deteriorate. In such unique operational environments, WSNs have to operate autonomously and consequently are faced with unique challenges. An adversary can now capture and compromise one or more sensors physically. Once captured, a node is at the mercy of the adversary. The adversary can now tamper with the sensor node by injecting malicious code, forcing the node to malfunction, extracting the cryptographic information held by the node to bypass security hurdles like authentication and verification and so on and so forth. Now, the adversary can launch attacks from within the system as an insider, and most existing systems would fail in the face of such inside attacks.

For instance, consider a beacon-based localization model. Now, since sensor nodes are not capable of determining their own location, they have no way of determining which beacon nodes are being truthful in providing accurate location information. There could be malicious beacon nodes that give false location information to sensor nodes compelling them to compute incorrect location. This situation, in which one entity has more information than the other, is referred to as information asymmetry. The information asymmetry in beacon-based localization models has been addressed in Srinivasan et al. (2006). Srinivasan et al. (2006) also presents an effective way of resolving insider attacks. The attacker can also launch Sybil, wormhole, or replay attacks to disrupt the localization process.

SECURE LOCALIZATION PROCESS

Localization (Meguerdichian et al., 2001; Niculescu & Nath, 2003b) defines the calculation of the location or position of sensor nodes in wireless sensor networks (WSNs). The dynamic need of the applications has made the deployment of WSNs extended from static to mobile. Such networks are dynamic and therefore the localization of nodes is also changeable and thus makes the process a critical factor in WSNs. The knowledge of the physical location of a network entity helps in different applications and services (Boukerche et al., 2008; Chintalapudi et al., 2003; Patwari et al., 2003). The main consideration of location discovery is a set of special nodes known as anchor nodes, which are resource privileged with more storage and computational capacity. Using the location of anchor nodes, other unknown nodes compute their location in different ways. Therefore, it is critical that malicious anchor nodes need to be prevented from providing false location information as the unknown nodes completely depend on the anchor nodes for computing their own location (Kumar & Rai, 2017). WSNs attract the adversaries in a very general way. Attacks are executed by the internal nodes as well as external nodes. Therefore, it is compulsory that the localization techniques should be secure enough (Xiao-Mei et al., 2008). The secured localization process must prevent both malicious insider nodes from misrepresenting their location and outside entities from performing intrusion with the location determination process. The security requirements for localization techniques must include privacy of the location information, authorization for legitimate nodes and the integrity to identify any kind of deviation from true location. Further, information availability to compute proper location is also required for a secured localization process. The accuracy of nodes' locations can be considered on the basis of two aspects. On one hand, nodes (anchor or unknown) need to calculate their correct position depending upon some references, which is called localization estimation (Figure 7.1(a)). On the other hand, the base station (BS) also needs to ensure that the location estimations it has received are correct. Thus, we need to verify the locations received from the nodes. This is called location verification (Figure 7.1(b)).

Additionally, localization is a mechanism for discovering spatial relationships between objects. The various approaches taken in literature to solve this localization problem differ in the assumptions they make about their respective network and sensor capabilities. A detailed, but not exhaustive, list of assumptions made include

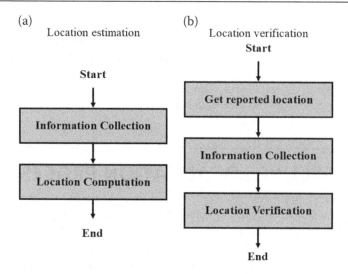

FIGURE 7.1 Localization system: (a) location estimation and (b) location verification.

assumptions about device hardware, signal propagation models, timing and energy requirements and composition of network viz homogeneous vs. heterogeneous, operational environment viz indoor vs. outdoor, beacon density, time synchronization, communication costs, error requirements and node mobility (He et al., 2003). In node mobility, four different scenarios arise. First, both sensor and beacon nodes are static. Second, sensor nodes are static while beacon nodes move. Third, sensor nodes move while beacon nodes are static. Fourth, both sensor and beacon nodes move.

In localization models that use GPS as the source, the localization process is straightforward. However, in a localization model that uses beacon nodes to help sensor nodes with location discovery, the beacon nodes are either manually configured with their location or equipped with a GPS receiver that they can use to determine their location. Beacon nodes then provide their location information to sensor nodes and help them in computing their location. The idea of beacon-based localization is presented in Figure 7.2.

The localization process itself can be classified into two stages. In the first stage, a node merely estimates its distance to other nodes in its vicinity using one or more features of the received signal. In the second stage, a node uses all the distance estimates to compute its actual location. The method employed in stage two to compute the actual location depends on the signal feature used in stage one, and can be classified into three main groups, as presented in Figure 7.3 and described as follows:

1. **Triangulation:** A large number of localization algorithms fall into this class. In simple terms, the triangulation method involves gathering angle of arrival (AoA) measurements at the sensor node from at least three sources. Then, using the AoA references, simple geometric relationships and properties are applied to compute the location of the sensor node.

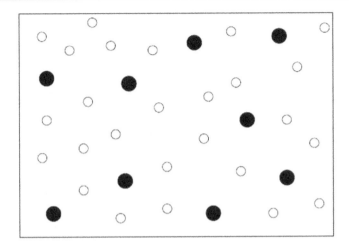

FIGURE 7.2 A network with sensor and beacon nodes. Sensor nodes are represented by hollow circles and beacon nodes are represented by shaded circles.

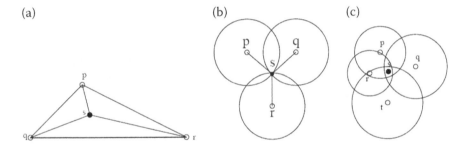

FIGURE 7.3 (a) Triangulation; (b) trilateration; (c) multilateration.

2. **Trilateration:** Trilateration is a method of determining the relative positions of objects using the geometry of triangles similar to triangulation. Unlike triangulation, which uses AoA measurements to calculate a subject's location, trilateration involves gathering a number of reference tuples of the form (x, y, d). In this tuple, d represents an estimated distance between the source providing the location reference from (x, y) and the sensor node. To accurately and uniquely determine the relative location of a point on a 2-D plane using trilateration, a minimum of three reference points is needed.

3. **Multilateration:** Multilateration is the process of localization by solving for the mathematical intersection of multiple hyperbolas based on the time difference of arrival (TDoA). In multilateration, the TDoA of a signal emitted from the object to three or more receivers is computed accurately with tightly synchronized clocks. When N receivers are used, it results in

N − 1 hyperbolas, the intersection of which uniquely positions the object in a 3-D space. When a large number of receivers are used, N > 4, then the localization problem can be posed as an optimization problem that can be solved using, among others, a least squares method.

Secure localization in sensor networks has become a major focus of research in recent years. Like any other process, localization also has security requirements, which are listed below. The breach of any of these security requirements is a harbinger of compromise in the localization process.

1. **Authentication:** Information for localization must be provided only by authorized sources. Therefore, before accepting location-related information, the provider has to be authenticated.
2. **Integrity:** The information provided by the source should be untampered before the sensor nodes can use it to discover their location.
3. **Availability:** All the information required by a sensor node to compute its location must be available when needed.
4. **Non-Repudiation:** Neither the source that provides the location information nor the sensor nodes that receive the location information should be able to deny the information exchange at a later time.
5. **Privacy:** Location privacy is one of the most important security requirements. The source should only help the sensor node in determining its location. Neither the source's location nor the sensor node's location should be disclosed at any point. This constraint helps to prevent malicious nodes from claiming a different legitimate location in the network.

Error in the estimated location of a sensor can be classified into two groups: intrinsic and extrinsic (Savvides et al., 2005). Intrinsic errors are most often caused by abnormalities in the sensor hardware and software, and can cause many complications when estimating node positions. On the other hand, extrinsic errors are attributed to the physical effects on the measurement channel. This includes shadowing effects, changes in signal propagation speed, obstacles, etc. Extrinsic errors are more unpredictable and harder to handle. Measurement errors can significantly amplify the error in position estimates. Also, use of lower-precision measurement technology combined with higher uncertainty of beacon locations will augment errors in position estimates.

CLASSIFICATION OF LOCALIZATION TECHNIQUES

In this section, we shall classify localization techniques and discuss their merits and demerits.

Direct Approaches

This is also known as absolute localization. The direct approach itself can be classified into two types: manual configuration and GPS-based localization. The manual configuration method is very cumbersome and expensive. It is neither practical nor scalable for large-scale WSNs and, in particular, does not adapt well for WSNs with node mobility. On the other hand, in the GPS-based localization method, each sensor is equipped with a GPS receiver. This method adapts well for WSNs with node mobility. However, there is a downside to this method. It is not economically feasible to equip each sensor with a GPS receiver since WSNs are deployed with hundreds of thousands of sensors. This also increases the size of each sensor, rendering them unfit for pervasive environments. Also, the GPS receivers only work well outdoors on earth and have line-of-sight requirement constraints. Such WSNs cannot be used for underwater applications like habitat monitoring, water pollution level monitoring, tsunami monitoring, etc.

Indirect Approaches

The indirect approach of localization is also known as relative localization since nodes position themselves relative to other nodes in their vicinity. The indirect approaches of localization were introduced to overcome some of the drawbacks of the GPS-based direct localization techniques while retaining some of its advantages, like accuracy of localization. In this approach, a small subset of nodes in the network, called the beacon nodes, are either equipped with GPS receivers to compute their location or are manually configured with their location. These beacon nodes then send beams of signals providing their location to all sensor nodes in their vicinity that don't have a GPS receiver. Using the transmitted signal containing the location information, sensor nodes compute their location. This approach effectively reduces the overhead introduced by the GPS-based method. However, since the beacon nodes are also operating in the same hostile environment as the sensor nodes, they too are vulnerable to various threats, including physical capture by adversaries. This introduces new security threats concerning the honesty of the beacon nodes in providing location information since they could have been tampered by the adversary and misbehave by providing incorrect location information. This particular problem has been addressed well in Srinivasan et al. (2006) where a reputation and trust-based system is used to monitor such misbehavior.

Within the indirect approach, the localization process can be classified into the following two categories.

Range-Based Localization

In range-based localization, the location of a node is computed relative to other nodes in its vicinity. Range-based localization depends on the assumption that the absolute distance between a sender and a receiver can be estimated by one or more features of the communication signal from the sender to the receiver. The accuracy of such an estimation, however, is subject to the transmission medium and surrounding environment. Range-based techniques usually rely on complex hardware which is not feasible for WSNs since sensor nodes are highly resource-constrained and have to be produced at throwaway prices as they are deployed in large numbers.

Based on the distance-bounding protocols (Brands & Chaum, 1994), Capkun et al. propose the verifiable multilateration (VM) technique (Capkun & Hubaux, 2005, 2006). With a central authority and several anchor nodes that are also named verifiers, VM enables a secure computation and verification of the unknown nodes' positions in the presence of attackers. In VM, verifiers $(v_1, \ldots, v_n)$ that are in the communication range of the unknown node u perform distance bounding to the node u and obtain distance bounds $db_1, \ldots, db_n$. These distance bounds, as well as the positions of the verifiers are then reported to the central authority. The authority computes an estimate position $(\hat{x}_u, \hat{y}_u)$ of the unknown node using distance bounds. Then, the authority runs two tests: (1) σ-test: for all v_i, does the distance between $(\hat{x}_u, \hat{y}_u)$ and v_i differ from the measured distance bound db_1 by less than the expected distance measurement error σ? (2) point in the triangle test: does $(\hat{x}_u, \hat{y}_u)$ fall within at least one physical triangle formed by a triplet of verifiers? If both the σ and the point in the triangle tests are positive, the authority accepts $(\hat{x}_u, \hat{y}_u)$ as correct; else, the position is rejected.

Based on VM, the authors propose a secure cooperative positioning mechanism called SPINE (Capkun & Hubaux, 2005, 2006). SPINE is executed in three phases: (1) the unknown nodes measure distance bounds to their neighbors; (2) the distance bounds are verified through VM; and (3) the positions of the unknown nodes are computed by a distributed algorithm, or by the central authority using a centralized positioning algorithm. Therefore, nodes in SPINE cannot produce erroneous distance measurements. However, SPINE has some drawbacks, e.g., in order to perform verifiable multilateration, a high number of verifiers are required.

Capkun et al. use the covert base station (CBS) and mobile base station (MBS) to verify the positions of unknown nodes (Capkun et al., 2008, 2006). In the CBS case, for infrastructure-centric localization, the public base station (PBS) sends a nonce firstly. When a node replies to the nonce, all the CBSs compute their position together based on TDoA and check if this position is consistent with the time differences. If not, an attack is detected and the estimated position is rejected. For node-centric localization, the unknown node broadcasts a radio signal and an ultrasound signal at the same time, then each CBS obtains the estimated distance based on the arrival time differences of two signals. Also, the CBS obtains calculated distance using the nodes' reported location and the CBS's location. Finally, the CBS compares estimated and calculated distances and rejects inconsistent ones. In the MBS case, it first requires unknown nodes to broadcast a radio signal. After a given period of time, it moves to a different location to broadcast a ultrasound signal. Then the MBS implements the same operations as a CBS does.

Anjum et al. (2005) present a secure localization algorithm, called SLA. It is considered that each anchor node has a capability to vary power level. Each power level is assumed to correspond to a different communication range. When an unknown node is localized, the sink node requests anchor nodes to send a localization nonce to the node at different power levels. As a result, each unknown node receives a set of unique nonces and retransmits them back to the sink. The sink then determines the position of the unknown node. Compared with VM, the SLA does not need fine-grained time synchronization. But the model of power level and transmission range is just suitable for an outdoor environment not indoor ones (Ganu et al., 2004). In addition, a SLA has a few drawbacks: (1) anchor and sink nodes are all assumed to be trusted; (2) only considering a single sensor node being compromised and ruling out collaborative attacks between sensor nodes; (3) a SLA is a centralized approach that creates a bottleneck at the base station.

Zhang et al. (2006) propose SLS for ultra-wideband (UWB) sensor networks. To localize a node, anchor nodes first measure their respective distance to the node with a modified two-way ToA approach, called K-distance. The anchor leader then collects all the distance estimates whereby to derive a MMSE location estimate. Subsequently, SLS employs a location validity test by checking whether the location is inside the polygon formed by all the anchor nodes to detect possible attacks. Compared with VM, SLS is more robust and gernal, e.g., using mobile anchor nodes to replace static ones and making each anchor node take turns to act as the leader to balance their resource usage. However, the process of SLS is more complex than that of VM and consumes higher energy.

In He et al. (2008), based on an attack-driven model specified with the Petri net, an enhanced secure localization scheme (ESLS) is proposed, which extends the idea in Zhang et al. (2006) and defends against not only distance reduction attacks but also distance enlargement attacks. The major contribution is the first time to use the Petri net to validate a security scheme for WSNs.

Arisar and Kemp (2009) present a two-way "Greet, Meet and Locate" (GML) mechanism for secure location estimation based on geographical sectorization. GML comprises three phases: greet, meet and locate. (1) Greet: a lightweight authentication scheme, the HB+ Protocol, is used to perform two-way authentication, individually by unknown and anchor nodes. (2) Meet: the Diffie Hellman key exchange algorithm is used that allows exchange of secret shared keys between two users in an adversarial environment over an insecure communication medium. (3) Locate: the location is estimated via a ToA-based technique. Moreover, a double-averaging mechanism is also presented to minimize the localization error.

Alfaro et al. (2009) provide three algorithms that enable the unknown nodes to determine their positions in the presence of neighbor sensors that may lie about their locations. The first algorithm is called the majority-three neighbor signals. When an unknown node is localized, all the neighbor anchor nodes send their locations to it. For every three anchor nodes, the unknown node uses trilateration to calculate a position. Then, a majority decision rule is used to correct the final position of the unknown node. The second algorithm is the majority two neighbor signals. The unknown node uses only two neighbor anchor nodes; therefore, the correct location is one of the two points of intersection of the two circles centered at two neighbors. The third algorithm is called the tabulated-two neighbor signals. It is assumed the unknown node may trust one of the neighbor anchor nodes. Then, the unknown node implements the second algorithm for every neighbor anchor nodes except the trusted one. Finally, the

TABLE 7.1 Compression of range-based secure localization

ALGORITHM	TECHNIQUE	OBSERVATION
VM	Distance-bounding	Nanosecond clock
SPINE	Distance-bounding	Nanosecond clock, high number of anchor nodes
(Capkun et al., 2008)	CBS and MBS	Centralized approach, rely on locations of CBS
SLA	Distance-bounding	Centralized approach
	Vary power level	Resist only one compromised sensor node
SLS	K-distance approach, MMSE, validity test	Complex higher-energy consumption
ESLS	Petri net	Higher-energy consumption
GML	HB+ Protocol Diffie Hellman ToA	Complex
(Alfaro et al., 2009)	Trilateration Majority decision	Dense network

unknown node calculates the occurrence frequency of each position and accepts the most frequently occurring one as the correct position. The three algorithms have been extended to localize unknown nodes in Garcia-Alfaro et al. (2011).

A comparison of the above-mentioned schemes is shown in Table 7.1.

Doherty (2001), Savvides et al. (2001), Savvides et al. (2002), Nasipuri and Li (2002) and Liu et al. (2005) are some more additional examples of range-based localization techniques. The features of the communication signal that are frequently used in literature for range-based localizations are as follows:

1. Angle of Arrival (AoA): Range information is obtained by estimating and mapping relative angles between neighbors. Nasipuri and Li (2002) and Niculescu and Nath (2003) make use of AoA for localization.

2. Received Signal Strength Indicator (RSSI): Use a theoretical or empirical model to translate signal strength into distance. RADAR (Bahl & Padmanabhan, 2000) is one of the first to make use of RSSI. RSSI has also been employed for range estimation in Hightower et al. (2000), Niculescu and Nath (2003a) and Patwari et al. (2003).

3. Time of Arrival (ToA): To obtain range information using ToA, the signal propagation time from souce to destination is measured. A GPS is the most basic example that uses ToA. To use ToA for range estimation, a system needs to be synchronous, which necessitates use of expensive hardware for precise clock synchronization with the satellite. ToA is used in Patwari et al. (2003) for localization.

4. Time Difference of Arrival (TDoA): To obtain the range information using TDoA, an ultrasound is used to estimate the distance between the node and

the source. Like ToA, TDoA necessitates the use of special hardware, rendering it too expensive for WSNs. Harter et al. (2002), Priyantha et al. (2000), Savvides et al. (2001) and Savvides et al. (2002) use some localization techniques that make use of TDoA.

Range-Free Localization

Range-free localization never tries to estimate the absolute point-to-point distance based on received signal strength or other features of the received communication signal like time, angle, etc. This greatly simplifies the design of hardware, making range-free methods very appealing and a cost-effective alternative for localization in WSNs. Amorphous localization (Nagpal et al., 2003), centroid localization (Bulusu et al., 2000), APIT (He et al., 2003), DV-Hop localization (Dragoş Niculescu & Nath, 2003a), SeRLoc (Lazos & Poovendran, 2004) and ROCRSSI (Liu et al., 2004) are some examples of range-free localization techniques. Range-free techniques have also been employed in Rabaey and Langendoen (2002).

Lazos and Poovendran (2004) propose a distributed range-free localization algorithm called SeRLoc, which does not require any communication among unknown nodes. The SeRLoc uses trusted locators equipped with a set of higher-power sectored antennas to replace anchor nodes. The locators have longer transmission range than unknown nodes. They send anchor beacons to unknown nodes, which contain their positions and the sectors of the antenna. When a node hears multiple locators, it computes the center of gravity of the sectors corresponding to locators as its position. The SeRLoc is robust against severe WSN attacks, such as the wormhole attack, the Sybil attack and compromised sensor nodes. However, SeRLoc is based on the assumption that no jamming of the wireless medium is feasible. And it does not protect against attacks on locator's information, which are avoided by checking network properties such as sector uniqueness and communication range. Moreover, in order to minimize the region of sector intersection to improve localization, we need to increase the number of locators and sectored antennas.

Later, a robust positioning system (ROPE) was proposed (Lazos et al., 2005) to reduce the impact on localization accuracy in SeRLoc due to various attacks, for example, misleading anchor beacons. Combining the techniques in SeRLoc and VM (Capkun & Hubaux, 2005), ROPE provides both the location determination and location verification function. In location determination, each unknown node obtains its exact location by VM when it is inside at least one triangle formed by locators, and still estimates its location by center of gravity when it is not inside any triangle. The location verification mechanism verifies the location claims of the unknown nodes. Since every unknown node can communicate with at least one locator, when an unknown node reports data to a locator, the locator can verify the unknown node's position by the execution of the distance bounding protocol. Compared with SeRLoc, ROPE is resistant to jamming of the communication medium, limits the maximum spoofing impact and prevents location spoofing due to the Sybil attack, with relatively low density deployment of locators. However, ROPE has higher hardware requirements, e.g., nanosecond time synchronization and instantaneous processing capacity, which is not suitable for low-cost WSNs.

Based on SeRLoc, in order to minimize the region of sector intersection without increasing the number of locators and sectored antennas, the same authors propose an improved method called high-resolution range independent localization (HiRLoc) (Lazos & Poovendran, 2006), which achieves greater localization accuracy through rotatable antennas and variable transmission power, while increaseing computational and communication complexity.

Zeng et al. (2007) present a Secure HOp-Count based LOCalization scheme (SHOLOC) that is resistant to different attacks, e.g., hop-count reduction attack and forging packets. In SHOLOC, a protocol combining modified TESLA (Perrig et al., 2000) and hash mechanisms is proposed to authenticate anchor nodes' location information and protect hop-count information. In order to detect wormhole attacks, anchor nodes are responsible for checking the distance-impossibility between nodes. Finally, the least median squares (LMS) (Rousseeuw & Leroy, 2005) is used to deal with bad location references.

In Ekici et al. (2006, 2008), the probabilistic location verification (PLV) algorithm is proposed. The main idea is to leverage the statistical relationships between the number of hops in a sensor network and the Euclidean distance that is covered. First, an unknown node broadcasts a message in the network using flooding, which contains its location as well as the hop count. Each verifier receiving the message can compute the relative distance between it and the unknown node. Then, each verifier computes its probability slack and maximum probability values. Finally, a central node collects the two probability values from all verifiers and a common plausibility for the location advertisement is computed. The central node uses the plausibility to accept or reject the location.

Based on the basic DV-Hop localization process, Wu et al. propose a label-based secure localization scheme to defend against the wormhole attack by removing the packets delivered through the wormhole link (Wu et al., 2010). Firstly, the anchor nodes are differentiated and labeled according to their geographic relationship. Then, unknown nodes are further differentiated and labeled by using the labeling results of neighbor anchor nodes. After eliminating the abnormal connections among the labeled neighbor nodes that are contaminated by the wormhole attack, the DV-Hop localization procedure can be conducted. The Label-Based DV-Hop Localization scheme is capable of detecting the wormhole attack and resisting its adverse impacts with a high probability.

Labraoui and Gueroui (2011) similarly propose a Wormholefree DV-hop Localization scheme (WFDV), to thwart wormhole attacks in a DV-Hop algorithm. The main idea of WFDV is a plug-in proactive countermeasure named infection prevention to the basic DV-Hop scheme. Infection prevention consists of two phases: neighbor list construction (NLC) and neighbor list repair (NLR). NLC applies RSSI and RTT (round trip delay of a link), and utilizes local information to construct neighbor lists. NLR is applied only when a wormhole attack is suspected to remove the packet delivery through the wormhole link. In this phase, frequency hopping and the RTS/CTS mechanism are used to confirm the existence of a wormhole and repair

TABLE 7.2   Comparison of range-free secure localization.

ALGORITHM	TECHNIQUE	OBSERVATION
SeRLoc	Encryption	Extra hardware
	Sectored antennas	Totally trusted beacons
ROPE	Encryption	Extra hardware
	Sectored antennas	
HiRLoc	Encryption	Extra hardware
	Sectored antennas	Complex
SHOLOC	TESLA	Resist simple attacks
	Hash mechanisms	
PLV	Plausibility Test	Centralized approach
Wu et al. (2010)	Label-Based Scheme	Resist only wormhole attack
WFDV	NLC, NLR	Resist only wormhole attack

the neighbor lists. After eliminating the illegal connections, the DV-Hop localization procedure can be successfully conducted.

A comparison of the above-mentioned schemes is shown in Table 7.2.

ATTACK MODEL

Before reviewing the existing secure localization models, we feel it is necessary to analyze the attacker model to understand the attacker's capabilities. The attacker can either be an insider or an outsider. As an insider, the attacker has access to all of the cryptographic keying material held by a node. This is potentially dangerous since the attacker can now claim to be a legitimate part of the network. Authentication or verification via password and other mechanisms give way under this attacker model. On the other hand, in the outsider attack model, the attacker is outside the network and has no information about cryptographic keys and passwords necessary for authentication. The attacker can only capture a node but cannot extract the sensitive information. This model is comparatively less detrimental, but harmful nonetheless. So, for a localization process to be secure it has to be robust in its defense against both outsider and insider attacks. Attacks are executed in the information collection process in the location estimation phase as well as location verification phase. There are several types of elementary and combinational attacks that can be executed in localization systems.

Table 7.3 summarizes the layer-wise attacks in WSNs' localization process (Han et al., 2016). Some attacks that have been discussed for nearly a decade in literature that are the most common against localization schemes and are as follows.

TABLE 7.3   Summary of layer-wise attacks on localization in WSNs

LAYERS	ATTACKS	ATTACK BEHAVIOR	RESULTS
Physical layer	Stealing	Signal eavesdropping and tampering	Packet error and packet loss
	Jamming	Sending jamming signal in the working frequency range	Packet loss
Data link layer	Collision	Repetition of messages	Packet loss
	Exhaustion	Sending of unnecessary message	Packet loss
	Unfairness	Explicitly take the control of the channel	Packet loss
Network layer	DoS Attacks	Exhaustion of energy of the unknown nodes	Packet loss
	Selective forwarding	Selectively forward packets	Packet loss
	Sybil	Possessing multiple identities	Packet error
	Sinkhole	Maliciously tamper with routing	Packet error
	Wormhole	Shortening the distance to make a fast routing path	Packet loss
Transport layer	Flooding	Establishing false connections	Packet loss
	Tampering	Tampering localization beacons	Packet error

Elementary Attacks

Elementary attacks are the prime attacks that have their own technical aspects of execution. Some of such attacks are discussed below.

Range Change Attack

In this attack, an attacker changes the range or angle of arrival (AoA) measurements among nodes. This attack affects both localization estimation and location verification systems. For example, reducing or increasing the range measurement between node A and node B will lead to malicious estimation of locations of B shown by dotted circles in Figure 7.4.

False Beacon Location Attack

In this attack, an attacker makes the victim node receive false estimated locations. For example, an attacker gains control over a beacon or anchor node and then it makes the node broadcast false location. A false reported location attack is generally executed in a location verification system where a malicious anchor node or unknown node reports false location.

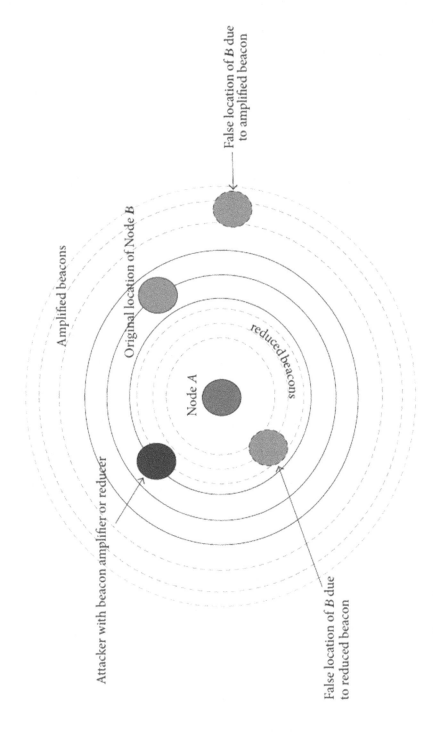

FIGURE 7.4 Effects of range change.

Combinational Attacks

Combinational attacks are those that merge different technicalities of elementary attacks and create an overall malicious affect. Some of the important combinational attacks are listed below.

Impersonation

In this attack, an attacker makes its identity a legitimate node in the network. For example, in localization systems, an attacker spoofs the anchor nodes' identity and broadcasts false locations. This leads to erroneous range measurements. In location verification systems, an attacker impersonates a victim node to make verifiers believe that the original node is at the attacker's location.

Sybil Attack

In this attack, a malicious node has the capability of presenting itself as different identities in a network to function as distinct nodes. These multiple identities are called Sybil nodes. It sends false information like position of beacon nodes and erroneous strength of signal. By masquerading and disguising as multiple identities, this type of malicious node gains control over the network.

Replay Attack

A replay attack is the easiest and most commonly used by attackers. Specifically, when an attacker's capability is limited, i.e., the attacker cannot compromise more than one node, this is the most preferred attack. In a replay attack, the attacker merely jams the transmission between a sender and a receiver and later replays the same message, posing as the sender. The other way to launch a replay attack is, as shown in Figure 7.5(a), malicious node A retransmits to node C the message it

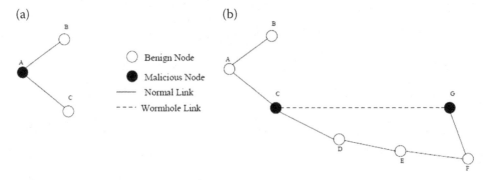

FIGURE 7.5   (a) Replay attack example. Node A replays to C the message it receives from B. (b) Wormhole attack example. Nodes C and G have a wormhole link.

receives from node B. A replay attack has a twofold consequence. First, the attacker is replaying the message of another node. Second, the attacker is transmitting stale information. In particular, the chances of the information being stale is higher in networks with higher node mobility. When replay attacks are launched on the localization process, a localizing node will receive an incorrect reference, thereby localizing incorrectly. Unlike a wormhole attack, a single node can disrupt the network with a replay attack.

Wormhole Attack

A wormhole attack is the most complicated of all the mentioned attacks. To launch a wormhole attack, the attacker has to compromise at least two nodes. In a wormhole attack, the colluding nodes in the network tunnel messages transmit in one part of the network to their colluding partners in other parts of the network. The effect of a wormhole attack on localization is depicted in Figure 7.5(b). Here, node A is sending its reference to nodes B and C. However, since there is a wormhole link between C and G, G can locally replay the location reference of A in its neighborhood, misleading node F. Consequently, F will compute its location incorrectly. Intuitively, wormhole attacks pose more serious problems in range-free localization compared to range-based localization.

Location-Reference Attack

This attack is executed against the localization phase. Each common node gets a location reference set $\langle loc_i, d_i \rangle$ for localization where loc_i is the location of beacon i and d_i is the distance between the beacon and the common node. In this attack, the attacker makes the compromised beacons broadcast false locations and distorts the distance measurements between beacons and common nodes. The attack can be classified into three types: (a) uncoordinated attack, (b) collusion attack and (c) pollution attack. Exemplary scenarios are shown in Figure 7.6(a), (b) and (c), respectively. Dark black node represents the attacker nodes, the light gray node represents the beacon nodes, and the blank white nodes represent common nodes.

In an uncoordinated attack, different false location references are provided to mislead the unknown node to different false locations; for example, P1 and P2 in Figure 7.6(a). In a collusion attack, all false location references mislead the common node to the same randomly chosen false location, say P1 in Figure 7.6(b). In a pollution attack, all false location references misguide the unknown node to a specially chosen false location P1, as in Figure 7.6(c), which still conforms to some normal location references. This attack succeeds even when normal location references are in the majority. In all the categories shown in Figure 7.6, P is the original location.

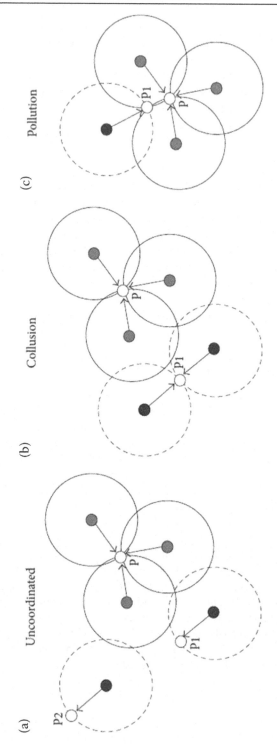

FIGURE 7.6 Location-reference attack variation: (a) uncoordinated, (b) collusion and (c) pollution.

EXISTING SOLUTIONS OF SECURE LOCALIZATION SYSTEMS

Whenever we talk about the secure localization (Srinivasan & Wu, 2007) several related problems emerge like location privacy and location reporting. To mitigate the attacks on location identification or location calculation, many researchers have proposed different schemes and approaches. They are classified into two types:

1. Node-centric
2. Infrastructure-centric

Node-Centric Secure Localization

The Prevention Method

Researchers proposed several solutions belonging to the prevention method (Capkun & Hubaux, 2005; Lazos & Poovendran, 2004; Lazos et al., 2005). In SeRLoc (Lazos & Poovendran, 2004), Lazos et al. used trusted nodes called locators to replace beacons. The locators are equipped with sectored antennas and have longer transmission range. When a node hears multiple locators, it computes the center of gravity of sectors corresponding to the locators as its location. They later proposed an improved method, HiRLoc (Lazos & Poovendran, 2006), which achieves higher accuracy by rotating locators' antennas and varying locators' transmission power in localization.

In Capkun and Hubaux (2005) and Capkun and Hubaux (2006), Capkun et al. proposed a SPINE based on the verifiable multilateration (VM) technique introduced by them. In VM, if a node is inside a triangle formed by any three nodes with known locations, through RF-based DB (radio-frequency-based distance bounding) (Brands & Chaum, 1994), the location of the node can be uniquely determined. In SPINE, all the distance measurements are verified by VM triangles formed by surrounding sensor nodes, so nodes cannot produce erroneous distance measurements.

In Lazos et al. (2005), combining the techniques in SeRLoc (Lazos & Poovendran, 2004) and VM (Capkun & Hubaux, 2005, 2006), Lazos et al. proposed ROPE. In ROPE, each node obtains its exact location by VM when it is inside at least one triangle formed by locators, or still estimates its location by center of gravity when it is not inside any triangle. Zeng et al. (2007) proposed SHOLOC to prevent the compromised nodes from reducing the hop counts in hop-count-based localization algorithms. Their method is to represent the value of the hop count by the number of hash operations on a nonce.

The Detection Method

Two solutions have been proposed in this category (Liu et al., 2005; Srinivasan et al., 2008, 2006), and they both focus on detecting malicious beacons. Liu et al. (2005)

proposed to use detecting beacons to detect malicious beacons broadcasting false locations. The detecting beacons first pretend to be common nodes and send requests to other beacons. Then they compare the distances computed by using their locations and the replied locations with the measured distances. If the distances are inconsistent, the beacons being checked are malicious and will be revoked.

In DRBTS (Srinivasan et al., 2006, 2008), Srinivasan et al. generalized the solution of Liu et al. (2005) by employing beacons to maintain reputations for their neighbor beacons. Each beacon computes reputations of its neighbor beacons based on the overheard location replies as well as the reputation values heard from other beacons. Common sensor nodes will only use beacons trusted by other beacons (i.e., such beacons' reputations are above a threshold) to compute their locations.

The Filtering Method

There are many algorithms belonging to this method (Li et al., 2005; Liu et al., 2008; Kiyavash & Koushanfar, 2007; Zhong et al., 2008). They all focus on filtering the bad location references in a location-reference set. Liu et al. (2008) proposed ARMMSE and a voting-based algorithm (Vote). The ARMMSE is to obtain a subset of location references, which satisfies that the mean square error of the location computed by the subset is below a threshold. In Vote, the minimum rectangle covering all the location references is divided into cells, and each location reference votes to the divided cells according to its observation. Then a new rectangle is selected to cover the cells with the highest vote. If the new rectangle is smaller than the previous one, it will be further divided into cells to vote. Otherwise, the algorithm outputs the centroid of current cells with the highest vote as the estimated location.

Li et al. (2005) proposed to use LMS (Rousseeuw & Leroy, 2005) to filter bad location references. Different from traditional methods that minimize the mean square error (Savvides et al., 2001), the LMS method is to minimize the median of square errors:

$$loc_0 = arg \min_{loc_o} med_i [[|loc_i - loc_0| - d_i]^2 \qquad (7.1)$$

where loc_i and d_i are the location and distance in the i location reference, respectively, and $|loc_a - loc_b|$ is the Euclidean distance between two locations loc_a and loc_b, and loc_0 is the estimated location.

Wang and Xiao (2006) proposed the i-Multihop algorithm, which aims to filter distance measurements that are larger than or smaller than their real values. The optimization computation of i-Multihop is described as below:

$$loc_0 = arg \min_{loc_0}(- \sum (|loc_0 - loc_i|^2) + k \sum \varepsilon_i) \qquad (7.2)$$

subject to $|loc_0 - loc_i| \le d_i + \varepsilon_i$

where k is a large weight coefficient (e.g., 10^6) and $\varepsilon_i s$ are slack variables.

Misra et al. (2006, 2008) proposed a method to filter compromised beacons, where distance bounding (Brands & Chaum, 1994) is used and then attackers can only enlarge distance measurements. Their method is to compute the geometric center of the intersection of circles corresponding to location references.

Zhong et al. (2008) proved that when there are no more than $\left(\frac{n-3}{2}\right)$ compromised beacons $\left((i.\ e.\ ,k \le \left(\frac{n-3}{2}\right)\right)$, we can definitely compute the location of node with an error bound, where n and k are the number of total and compromised beacons, respectively. However, such a result is proved under the condition that ϵ (i.e., the maximum measurement error) is ideally small; Zeng et al. (2009) showed that an adversary can still seriously distort the estimated location with a pollution attack, when $k \le \left(\frac{n-3}{2}\right)$ holds and ϵ is practically small. Zhong et al. (2008) also proposed two localization algorithms, based on finding a location inside $k + 3$ rings.

Infrastructure-Centric Secure Localization

Infrastructure-centric localization systems usually belongs to the prevention method, since they have a reliable infrastructure (and without vulnerable beacon nodes). Čapkun et al. (2006, 2008) proposed a method to localize nodes based on covert base stations (CBSs). The public base station (PBS) first sends a nonce to a node. When the node replies to the nonce, all the CBSs will compute their location together based on the TDoA method. Then, if the actual time differences deviate from the supposed values over a threshold, an attack is detected and the estimated location is rejected.

Zhang et al. (2006) proposed SLS for UWB (ultra-wideband) sensor networks. The authors assume that there is a set of trusted anchors that can perform group movement in the deployment field. In SLS, first, each anchor performs an algorithm called K-Distance to measure the distance between the anchor and the node to be localized. Second, anchors send the measured distances to the anchor leader to compute a node's location. Third, SLS employs a location validity test by checking whether the computed location is inside the polygon formed by all the anchors. This test is similar to, but more general than, VM (Capkun & Hubaux, 2005, 2006) since a polygon is not limited to a triangle. He et al. (2008) later proposed ESLS to improve the SLS (Zhang et al., 2006) scheme in defeating distance enlargement attacks, and used Petri net to formally verify the security of ESLS.

Anjum et al. (2005) proposed a SLA to securely localize nodes based on transmission range (TR) variation. Here, the anchors are assumed to be reliable and can vary their TRs to several values. In the localization process, the BS lets anchors transmit different nonces with different TRs. Each sensor then sends its received nonces to the BS. The BS computes sensors' locations based on the unique sets of nonces corresponding to different locations.

EXISTING SECURE LOCALIZATION SYSTEMS

In this section, we review the existing secure localization techniques, throwing light on their strengths and weaknesses.

SeRLoc

Lazos and Poovendran (2004) proposed a novel scheme for localization of nodes in WSNs in untrusted environments called SeRLoc. SeRLoc is a range-free, distributed, resource-efficient localization technique in which there is no communication requirement between nodes for location discovery. SeRLoc is robust against wormhole attacks, Sybil attacks and sensor compromise. SeRLoc considers two sets of nodes: N, which is the set of sensor nodes equipped with omnidirectional antennas, and L, which is the set of locator nodes equipped with directional antennas. The sensors determine their location based on the location information transmitted by these locators. Each locator transmits different beacons at each antenna sector with each beacon containing two pieces of information: the locator coordinates and the angles of the antenna boundary lines with respect to a common global axis. Using directional antennas improves the localization accuracy.

In SeRLoc, an attacker has to impersonate several beacon nodes to compromise the localization process. Also, since sensor nodes compute their own location without any assistance from other sensors, the adversary has no incentive to impersonate sensor nodes. Wormhole attacks are thwarted in SeRLoc due to two unique properties: sector uniqueness property and communication range violation property. In SeRLoc, to improve the localization accuracy, either more locators have to be deployed or more directional antennas have to be used. The authors also make an assumption that no jamming of the wireless medium is feasible. This is a very strong assumption for a real-world setting.

Beacon Suite

Liu et al. (2005) present a suite of techniques for detecting malicious beacon nodes that provide incorrect information to sensor nodes providing location services in critical applications. Their suite includes detection of malicious beacon signals, detection of replayed beacon signals, identification of malicious beacon nodes, avoidance of false detection and finally the revoking of malicious beacon nodes. They use beacon nodes for two purposes: to provide location information to sensor nodes and to perform detection on the beacon signals it hears from other beacon nodes. A beacon node does not necessarily need to wait passively to hear beacon signals. It can request location information. The beacon node performing the detection is called the detecting node and the beacon node being detecting is called the target node. They suggest that the detecting node should use a nonbeacon ID when requesting location information from a target node in order to observe the true behavior of the target node.

Their revocation scheme works on the basis of two counters maintained for each beacon node: alert counter and report counter. The alert counter records the suspiciousness of the corresponding beacon node and the report counter records the number of alerts this node reported and was accepted by the base station. When a detecting node determines that a target node is misbehaving, it reports to the base station. Alert reports are accepted only from detecting nodes whose report counter is below a threshold and against nodes that are not yet revoked. When this criteria is met, the report counter and the alert counter of the detecting and the target node, respectively, are incremented. These two counters work on a discrete scale and the revocation mechanism is centralized. This has been improved to be more robust in Srinivasan et al. (2006) by employing a continuous scale and a reputation and trust-based mechanism.

Attack-Resistant Location Estimation

Liu et al. (2008) put forward two range-based robust methods to tolerate malicious attacks against beacon-based location discovery in sensor networks. The first method, attack-resistant minimum mean square estimation, filters out malicious beacon signals. This is accomplished by examining the inconsistency among location references of different beacon signals, indicated by the mean square error of estimation, and defeats malicious attacks by removing such malicious data. The second method, voting-based location estimation, quantizes the deployment field into a grid of cells and has each location reference "vote" on the cells in which the node may reside. This method tolerates malicious beacon signals by adopting an iteratively refined voting scheme. Both methods survive malicious attacks even if the attacks bypass authentication.

However, there is a downside to both of these techniques. In the proposed localization technique, an attacker cannot dislodge sensors by compromising a few range estimates. Nonetheless, this localization model fails if the attacker can compromise a simple majority of range estimates. Assume there are k nodes in a neighborhood. Now, if the attacker can compromise $\frac{k}{2} + 1$ beacon nodes in that neighborhood, then he/she can generate more malicious location references than benign ones. This will lead to failure of the minimum mean square estimation technique in the neighborhood, the effects of which can propagate throughout the network. Similar attacks are possible for the voting-based location estimation technique.

Robust Statistical Methods

Li et al. (2005) introduced the idea of being tolerant to attacks rather than trying to eliminate them by exploiting redundancies at various levels within wireless networks. They examine two classes of localization: triangulation and RF-based fingerprinting.

They have presented two statistical methods for securing localization in sensor networks. Both methods are based on the simple idea of filtering out outliers in the range estimates used for location estimation used by sensors.

For the triangulation-based localization, they proposed the use of an adaptive least squares and least median squares estimator. This adaptive estimator switches to the robust mode with least mean squares estimation when attacked and enjoys the computational advantage of least squares in the absence of attacks. For the fingerprinting-based method, the traditional Euclidean distance metric is not secure enough. Hence, they proposed a median-based nearest neighbour scheme that is robust to location attacks. In this paper, the authors have also discussed attacks that are unique to localization in sensor networks. The statistical methods proposed in Li et al. (2005) are based on the assumption that benign observations at a sensor always outnumber malicious observations. This is a strong assumption in a real-world setting where an attacker can launch Sybil attacks or even wormhole attacks to outnumber the benign observations.

SPINE

Capkun and Hubaux (2005) devised secure positioning in sensor networks (SPINE), a range-based positioning system based on verifiable multilateration that enables secure computation and verification of the positions of mobile devices in the presence of attackers. SPINE works by bounding the distance of each sensor to at least three reference points. Verifiable multilateration relies on the property of distance bounding, that neither the attacker nor the claimant can reduce the measured distance of the claimant to the verifier, but only enlarge it. By using timers with nanosecond precision, each sensor can bound its distance to any reference point within range.

If the sensor is within a triangle formed by three reference points, it can compute its position via verifiable multilateration, which provides a robust position estimate. This is based on a strong assumption that any attacker does not collude with compromised nodes. Verifiable multilateration effectively prevents location spoofing attacks, wormhole and jamming attacks and prevents dishonest nodes from lying about their positions. However, SPINE has some drawbacks. In order to perform verifiable multilateration, a high number of reference points is required. SPINE is a centralized approach which creates bottleneck at the central authority or the base station. Also, it is very unlikely that an attacker will not try to collude with other compromised nodes.

ROPE

Lazos, Poovendran and Capkun designed ROPE (Lazos et al., 2005), a robust positioning system in WSNs. ROPE, a hybrid algorithm, has a twofold benefit to the system. First, it allows sensors to determine their location without any centralized computation. Second, ROPE provides a location verification mechanism by virtue of which the location claims of sensors can be verified prior to data collection. In ROPE, the network consists of two types of nodes: sensors and locators. Each sensor shares a pair-wise key with every locator. Since the number of locators is less, it does not impose a large storage overhead on the sensors.

To measure the impact of attacks on ROPE, they introduce a novel metric called maximum spoofing impact. ROPE achieves a significantly lower maximum spoofing impact while requiring the deployment of a significantly smaller number of reference points, compared to Capkun and Hubaux (2005). ROPE is second to only Capkun and Hubaux (2005) to propose a solution for jamming attacks. ROPE is also resilient to wormhole attacks and node impersonation attacks. The robustness of ROPE has been confirmed via analysis and simulation.

Transmission Range Variation

Anjum et al. (2005) show a novel transmission-based secure localization technique for sensor networks. They have presented a secure localization algorithm (SLA). Their technique does not demand any special hardware and considers a network with two sets of nodes: the sensor nodes and the beacon nodes. Their scheme works as follows. Beacon nodes associate a unique nonce to different power levels at a given time, which they transmit securely at the associated power level. As a result, each sensor node receives a set of unique nonces which it will have to transmit back to the sink via the beacon nodes. Then, the location of the sensor node can be estimated securely, based on this set of nonces. This is a centralized localization technique where the sink determines the location of the sensor node.

This model has a few drawbacks. The authors have not considered the collaboration of sensor nodes, which is crucial and has to be addressed to suit the real-world scenario. They have also assumed that all beacon nodes in the network and the sink are to be trusted and assumed the encryption between beacon nodes and sink to be stronger than that between sensor nodes and sink. They have shown that their model is resilient to replay attacks, spoofing attacks, modification attacks and response delay attacks. Another major drawback arises from the fact that this a centralized model with the base station as the single point of failure. This also causes a significant bottleneck at the base station.

DRBTS

DRBTS (Srinivasan et al., 2006) is a distributed reputation and trust-based security protocol aimed at providing a method for secure localization in sensor networks. This work is an extension of Liu et al. (2005). In this model, incorrect location information provided by malicious beacon nodes can be excluded during localization. This is achieved by enabling beacon nodes to monitor each other and provide information so that sensor nodes can choose who to trust, based on a quorum voting approach. In order to trust a beacon node's information, a sensor must get votes for its trustworthiness from at least half of their common neighbors. Specifically, sensor nodes use a simple majority principle to evaluate the published reputation values of all the beacon nodes in their range.

With this model, it is clearly demonstrated that sensors can accurately guess the misbehaving/non-misbehaving status of any given beacon node, given a certain assumption about the level of corruption in the system. The authors also show that their system grows in robustness as node density increases, and show through simulations the effects of different system parameters on robustness. This distributed model not only alleviates the burden on the base station to a great extent, but also minimizes the damage caused by the malicious nodes by enabling sensor nodes to make a decision on which beacon neighbors to trust, on the fly, when computing their location.

HiRLoc

Lazos and Poovendran propose another model, a high-resolution, range-independent localization technique called HiRLoc (Lazos & Poovendran, 2006). In HiRLoc, sensors passively determine their location without any interaction among themselves. HiRLoc also eliminates the need for increased beacon node density and specialized hardware. It is robust to security threats like wormhole attacks, Sybil attacks and compromising of the network entities by virtue of two special properties: antenna orientation variation and communication range variation. In HiRLoc, Lazos and Poovendran have used cryptographic primitives to ensure the security of beacon transmissions. Here, each beacon transmission is encrypted using a global symmetric key, an idea very similar to the one used in Srinivasan et al. (2006).

Unlike SeRLoc, in HiRLoc, sensors receive multiple beacons from the same locator. This relaxation helps in improving the accuracy of location estimation.

There are two important observations. First, since no range measurements are required for localization, they are free from attacks aimed at altering the measurements, like jamming to increase the hop count. Second, since sensors do not rely on other sensor nodes for computing their location, it is robust to sensor compromise attacks.

PROPOSED SECURE LOCALIZATION TECHNIQUE (SLT)

Our proposed algorithm considers only the anchor nodes, unknown nodes and base station where anchor nodes and unknown nodes are deployed randomly. The anchors have a variable range of transmission with an average transmission range, R_{avg}, given as

$$R_{avg} = \frac{min \sum_{e \in E} \psi(|e|)}{m} \tag{7.3}$$

where m is the number of anchor nodes in the network, e is an edge between two nodes, E is the set of the edges in the network and $\psi(|e|)$ is the weighing function of a connection between an anchor node and an unknown node and interpreted as $\psi(|e|) \sim |e|^{\alpha}$, $2 \leq \alpha \leq 4$.

The algorithm starts with an initialization phase that deals with distribution of certificates by the BS. After the distribution of the certificates, the distance estimation phase starts among the anchor nodes and the unknown nodes. Once the distances are estimated, the BS is able to localize the unknown nodes, applying the minimum mean square error (MMSE) method. The algorithm is summarized in the following steps.

ALGORITHM 7.1   DISTANCE ESTIMATION BY ANCHOR NODES

Input: anchor node set A, unknown node set U

1. BS creates identities ID_{aj} for all anchor nodes and identities ID_{ui} for all unknown nodes
2. BS provides certificates: $Cert_{aj}$, $Cert_{ui}$
3. $\forall\ a_j \in A$ do
   a. a_j sends u_i random nonce $\varkappa$, $Cert_{aj}$; for $i = 1, 2, 3, \cdots, m$
   b. a_j wants a threshold time, $t_{retransmit}$, to retransmit the message
4. $\forall\ u_i$ under R_{avg} for any $a_j \in A$
   u_i sends a_j: $[\varkappa, time_{proc_u}]_{k_{aj+}}$, $Cert_{ui}$
5. Calculate $time_{prop}$
6. $d_{ui}^{aj} = c \times time_{prop}$
7. a_j sends d_{ui}^{aj} to the base station (BS)
8. end loop
9. Apply MMSE

As we have used the speed of light, c, to estimate the distance, the process shown will prevent the generation of a high-speed link required to execute a wormhole attack because there cannot be any high-speed link in which the transmission speed will be more than that of the light. The utilization of mutual authentication with certificates provided by the BS will help to avoid or prevent any kind of authentication attack such as a Sybil attack and impersonation attack executed by the outsider nodes. The encryption method will help to securely transmit the estimated distance to the BS. The $t_{retransmit}$ value will help to detect the jamming attack so that the avoidance and detection process can apply the following the methods as shown in Xu et al. (2006). But it can be a fact that the insider nodes are compromised and can generate distance reduction or enlargement attacks. To prevent these attacks, we have to follow the further process.

Let us assume that the deviation of the true position of the unknown node due to measurement error and/or malicious distance estimates is δ, which is tolerable for the system. We know that the unknown node, (x_{u_i}, y_{u_i}), must be in the intersection region of the anchor nodes' bound circles in the range. Therefore, in the following algorithm we can validate the distance estimation provided by the anchor nodes.

ALGORITHM 7.2   VALIDATION OF DISTANCE ESTIMATION AND DETECTION OF MALICIOUS ANCHORS BY BS

Input: Set of anchor nodes A with locations, (x_{a_j}, y_{a_j}), location estimate of an unknown node, (x_{u_i}, y_{u_i}), error parameter, δ

1. $\forall\, a_j \in A,\ j = 1, 2, \ldots, m$
   If $(true_{d_{u_i}^{a_j}} - \delta)^2 \le (x_{u_i}, x_{a_j})^2 + (y_{u_i}, y_{a_j})^2 \le (true_{d_{u_i}^{a_j}} + \delta)^2$
   then exit
   else go to next step
2. Calculate the algebraic center x^* of intersection region $\mathcal{R}$
3. Initialize $r^* = 0$ //radius of the intersection region $\mathcal{R}$ as
4. $\forall\, v$ inside the region $\mathcal{R}$ do
   if $\|v - r^*\| > r^*$
   then $r^* \leftarrow \|v - r^*\|$
   end if
5. $\forall\, a_j \in A,\ j = 1, 2, \ldots, m$ do

$$\overline{true_{d_{u_i}^{a_j}}} = \frac{true_{d_{u_i}^{a_j}}}{1 + \varepsilon_{max}}$$

   if $true_{d_{u_i}^{a_j}} > \|x^* - a_j\| + r^*$ then
   Anchor node a_j is malicious
   else a_j is not malicious
6. end if

Network Model and Assumptions

The network model is considered to be self-organizing, having no central control of deploying the sensor nodes in the network. For the ease of presentation, the wireless sensor network model $\mathcal{N}$ is considered to be in 2-D and represented by a graph, $G(V, E)$, which consists of V, a set of vertices, and E a set of edges. The size of the network can be given as

$$|\mathcal{N}| = |A| + |U| \tag{7.4}$$

where $|A|$ is the size of anchor node set A and $|U|$ is the size of the unknown node set U, and $A,\ U \subseteq V$.

In the proposed algorithm, we have divided the network nodes in two categories of nodes. First, the anchor nodes, $a_j \in A$, are privileged in their storage capacity and computational capacity with additional energy resources. Secondly, the unknown nodes, $u_i \in U$, are not privileged like the anchor nodes and are able to perform minimum computational tasks. Both types of nodes are randomly deployed in the network environment. The location estimation of an unknown node is calculated by using the location information of the anchor nodes in a WSN. Therefore, the integrity of location messages as well as the reliability of message origin is very important during the localization process. Confidentiality of estimated location is also required in some applications, to protect the privacy of the corresponding sensors. In this paper, an appropriate cryptographic scheme is presented to provide the security services. The assumptions for our proposed approach have been listed:

i. The unknown nodes and anchor nodes are mobile.
ii. The base station (BS) is assumed to be trusted and is considered to be key distributor and certificate authority.
iii. Anchor nodes and unknown nodes are deployed with their private keys.
iv. The base station shares the public key only to the legitimate unknown nodes and anchor nodes predefined.

Initialization Phase:

The base station (BS) provides the identity for all anchor nodes and unknown nodes as ID_{a_j} and ID_{u_i}, where a_j is an anchor node and u_i is an unknown node. The BS also provides certificates for each anchor node and unknown node as $Cert_{a_j}$ and $Cert_{u_i}$:

$$BS \rightarrow Cert_{a_j} = \left[ID_{a_j}, K_{a_{j+}}, t, e_t\right]BS_{K-}, \tag{7.5}$$

where ID_{a_j} is the identity of an anchor node a_j, $K_{a_{j+}}$ is the public key of that anchor node, t is the timestamp when the certificate was created and e_t is the expiry time of the certificate. This total certificate is digitally signed by $BS_{K}-$, which is the private key of the BS. All anchor nodes must make them update themselves by having a fresh certificate as required. For a legitimate unknown node, u_i, we can rewrite the previous format in the following way:

$$BS \rightarrow Cert_{u_i} = \left[ID_{u_i}, K_{u_{i+}}, t, e_t\right]BS_{K-}, \tag{7.6}$$

where ID_{u_i} is the identity of an unknown node u_i, $K_{u_{i+}}$ is the public key of that unknown node and e_t is the expiry time of the certificate.

Distance Estimation Phase:

The anchor node, a_j, sends a random nonce, $\varkappa$, along with the certificate, $Cert_{a_j}$, to all the one-hop neighborhood unknown nodes, u_i, in the range, R_{avg}, and starts the timer on. When the unknown nodes receive the message, verify the certificate using the public key, BS_{K+}, given by the BS. As only legitimate anchor nodes have the certificate to provide, by verifying the certificates, the authentication of the anchor nodes can be proved. Then, the unknown nodes, u_i, respond back to the anchor node, a_j, with the same nonce, $\varkappa$, time duration between receiving the last bit of message sent by the anchor node and transmitting the first bit of message to the anchor node, given as

$time_{proc_u}$, encrypted with the anchor node's public key, $K_{a_{j+}}$, along with its own certificate.

$$a_j \rightarrow u_i: \varkappa, Cert_{u_i}$$

$$u_i \rightarrow a_j: [\varkappa, time_{proc_u}]_{K_{a_{j+}}}, Cert_{u_i} \tag{7.7}$$

When a_j sends a message to u_i, it waits for a bounded time value, $t_{retransmit}$, to retransmit the message if no response starts arriving to the anchor in that bounded time. This value is precomputed at the start of the network deployment, assuming all the favorable conditions of the network environment with a noise effect of Δt and given as:

$$t_{retransmit} = time_{normal} + \Delta t \tag{7.8}$$

where $time_{normal}$ is the normal time duration of getting a response back from the unknown node.

When the anchor node receives the response back from the unknown nodes, it decrypts the message using its own private key, $K_{a_{j-}}$; verifies the certificate of the unknown nodes; stops the timer; and calculates the signal propagation time as:

$$time_{prop} = \frac{(time_j - time_{proc_u} - time_{proc_a})}{2} \tag{7.9}$$

where $time_{prop}$ is the signal propagation time, $time_j$ is the timer interval at the anchor side and $time_{proc_a}$ is the time duration between receiving the first bit of the response and last bit of the response. The interaction between unknown node and anchor node is shown in Figure 7.7.

Once the propagation time is calculated, the estimated distance between anchor node, a_j, and unknown node, u_i, is calculated as

$$d_{u_i}^{a_j} = c \times time_{prop}, \tag{7.10}$$

where c is the speed of light.

Once the anchor node calculates this estimated distance, it is then forwarded to the BS encrypted with the public key of the BS and along with the anchor node's certificate.

$$a_j \rightarrow BS: [d_{u_i}^{a_j}]_{BS_{K+}}, Cert_{a_j} \tag{7.11}$$

After receiving the message from the anchor nodes, the BS decrypts the message with a private key and gets the estimated distances. Finally, it uses the minimum mean square error (MMSE) (Savvides et al., 2001) to estimate the location of an unknown node (x_{u_i}, y_{u_i}). One thing to remember is that we need at least three noncollinear anchor nodes to apply the MMSE. Another important attribute of our proposed algorithm deals with the mobility of the nodes. We consider that the nodes (whether the anchor or

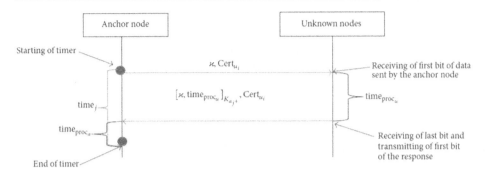

FIGURE 7.7   Propagation time estimation process.

the unknown) are mobile. The relative mobility between an unknown node, a_j, and anchor node, a_j, at a given time t is given by:

$$RM_t^{a,u} = d_{a,u_t} - d_{a,u_{t-1}}$$ (7.12)

$RM_t^{a,u}$ is positive if node u_i is moving away from a_j and negative if u_i is coming closer to a_j.

Though the mobility is incorporated in the algorithm, nodes (both the anchor nodes and the unknown nodes) are assumed to be pseudostatic; that is, they are static for a very short time interval for the localization process and this does not incorporate any significant error in the estimation.

Handling Distance Estimation Error:

Distance estimations in a wireless environment commonly have an error due to the noise or delay in the medium. Assume that the estimation error is $\epsilon \in [-\epsilon_{max}, \epsilon_{max}]$, where ϵ_{max} is a system parameter and given as $0 \leq -\epsilon_{max} \leq 1$. Therefore, the estimated distance can be given as:

$$d_{u_i}^{a_j} \epsilon \left[true_{d_{u_i}^{a_j}} \times (1 - \epsilon_{max}), \, true_{d_{u_i}^{a_j}} \times (1 + \epsilon_{max}) \right]$$ (7.13)

where $true_{d_{u_i}^{a_j}}$ is the true distance between a_j and u_i and can be calculated by applying the Euclidean method.

Further, the presence of compromised insider anchor nodes can create an error factor, θ. Following this, the estimated distance between a_j and u_i in the presence of a malicious anchor node can be given as:

$$d_{u_i}^{a_j} = true_{d_{u_i}^{a_j}} \times (1 + \epsilon_{max}) \times (1 + \theta), \, for \; \theta > 0$$ (7.14)

As we know that $\epsilon \in [-\epsilon_{max}, \epsilon_{max}]$, the value of ϵ can create both the positive estimation error and negative estimation error. Positive estimation error will create multiple intersection points of the convex region of the anchor nodes' ranges, leading to the distance enlargement attacks. On the other hand, negative estimation error creates an empty intersection region, assuming that the location of the unknown node is in the intersection of bounds of anchors leading to the distance reduction attack. This concept is shown in Figure 7.8. The black solid circles are anchor nodes and the gray circle in center is the original estimated location. If the anchor nodes are compromised and provide reduced distance estimations, the intersection will be empty and if the malicious anchor nodes provide enlarged distance estimations, the position of the unknown node deviates from the original position, which is shown as a gray circle on the outer circumference.

Distance reduction is not severe in a WSN localization. If we find the empty intersection region, $\mathcal{R}$, the distance estimates can be increased with a factor of $1/(1 - \epsilon_{max})$ to get a nonempty intersection region, $\mathcal{R}'$, where the unknown node must exist.

To prevent a distance enlargement situation, the BS needs to follow the process summarized in Algorithm 2. The tolerable error parameter, δ, can be derived from the following equation as:

$$\delta = w_1 \epsilon + w_2 \theta \tag{7.15}$$

where ϵ is the system measurement error due to noise and θ is the error included by malicious anchor nodes. We assume that the unknown nodes are error-free and do not provide any false distance estimation. w_1, w_1 are used as weighing values for the errors depending upon the network conditions. This δ will provide an upper bound and lower bound of the estimated distance in presence of error given as:

$$\left(true_{d_{u_i}^{a_j}} - \delta\right)^2 \leq \left(x_{u_i} - x_{a_j}\right)^2 + \left(y_{u_i} - y_{a_j}\right)^2 \leq \left(true_{d_{u_i}^{a_j}} + \delta\right)^2 \tag{7.16}$$

$$true_{d_{u_i}^{a_j}} = \sqrt{\left(x_{u_i} - x_{a_j}\right)^2 + \left(y_{u_i} - y_{a_j}\right)^2}$$

The algebraic center x^* in Algorithm 2 can be calculated using the barrier method on the unconstrained optimization problem given as:

$$\min(x, \delta) - \lambda \cdot \delta - \sum_{j=1}^{m} log\left[\left(\overline{true_{d_{u_i}^{a_j}}} \cdot (1 - \delta)\right)^2 - x - a_j^2\right] \tag{7.17}$$

where λ is the Lagrangian multiplier and $\overline{true_{d_{u_i}^{a_j}}}$ is given by $\overline{true_{d_{u_i}^{a_j}}} = true_{d_{u_i}^{a_j}}/(1 - \epsilon_{max})$, that is, the increased distance estimation in the case of negative estimation error.

The radius of the intersection region, $\mathcal{R}$, is initialized with 0 with an assumption that the unknown node is positioned at the intersection point itself and no convex region has been generated by the intersection. Moreover, the radius of the intersection region can be updated by verifying the distance between any point v inside the region and the algebraic center x^*. Finally, we can detect the malicious insider anchor nodes depending upon the increased estimated distance.

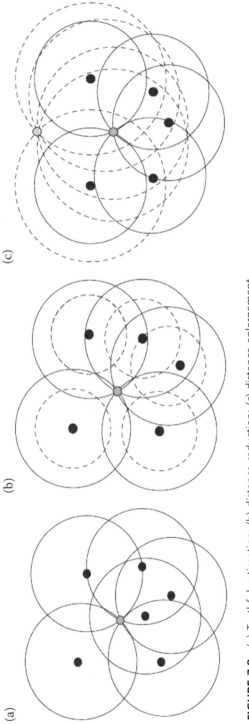

FIGURE 7.8 (a) Truthful estimation; (b) distance reduction; (c) distance enlargement.

TABLE 7.4   Prevention of attacks by the proposed model

ATTACKS	ATTACK BEHAVIOR	PREVENTION BY OUR PROPOSED MODEL
Stealing	Signal eavesdropping and tampering	Our proposed model uses encryption to prevent such attacks
Jamming	Sending jamming signal in the working frequency range	Detection is addressed in the proposed algorithm
Collision	Repetition of messages	Not applicable in the proposed model, as the maximum calculation is done by the BS and anchor node with minimum message controls
Exhaustion	Sending of unnecessary message	No scope to provide unnecessary message as transmission range is limited to and the distance estimation process is secured
Unfairness	Explicitly taking the control of the channel	Not possible due to the minimum size of the packets
DoS Attacks	Exhaustion of energy of the unknown nodes	Can be monitored directly by the BS
Selective forwarding	Selectively forward packets	Using the approach of one-hop neighborhood forwarding is not necessary
Sybil	Possessing multiple identities	Mutual authentication is used
Sinkhole	Maliciously tamper with routing	Mutual authentication is used with the certificates
Wormhole	Shortening the distance to make a fast routing path	The distance estimation is done based upon the light speed, which is the maximum speed of transmission can be and therefore no faster route can be created between an anchor and an unknown node
Flooding	Establishing false connections	Broadcasting is limited by the anchor nodes within a limited range of R_{avg}
Tampering	Tampering localization beacons	Both encryption and mutual authentication are used
Insider attack	Compromised anchor nodes may provide false information	Both the distance reduction and distance enlargement attack have been addressed
Range change attack	Changing the range or angle of arrival (AoA)	Our proposed model does not incorporate the mechanism of AoA as it works on time interval to calculate the distance and

(Continued)

TABLE 7.4 (Continued)   Prevention of attacks by the proposed model

ATTACKS	ATTACK BEHAVIOR	PREVENTION BY OUR PROPOSED MODEL
		therefore can easily avoid such an attack
False beacon location attack	Compromising a beacon and then can make the beacon broadcast false location	Authentication, limited range and validation of distance estimation in the proposed approach will help to avoid such an attack
False reported location attack	Malicious node reports false	Verification is done at the BS, so there is less chance to report falsified verification

So the attacks, as identified in the localization process shown in Table 7.3, are addressed in the proposed model. The summary of countermeasures by our proposed model is shown in Table 7.4.

Results and Discussion

This section evaluated the proposed algorithm based on the parameters, as shown in Table 7.5.

We have compared the simulated results with the three recent algorithms: (1) collaborative secure localization algorithm based on trust model (CSLT) proposed by Han et al. (2016), (2) multilateral privacy algorithm (MPA) for secured localization proposed by Shu et al. (2015) and (3) authenticated weight-based secured (AWS) DV-hop proposed by Liu et al. (2015). The performances of the algorithms are measured on the following three parameters: localization efficiency, localization accuracy and malicious detection ratio.

The attacks described in Table 7.4 are also simulated to show the efficiency of the proposed algorithm. The localization ratio is defined as the percentage of successful location estimation of unknown nodes. The result in Figure 7.9(a) shows that, with the increasing malicious nodes' percentage, every algorithm in our comparison faces a significant decrease in successful localization of unknown nodes. However, the

TABLE 7.5   Simulation parameters

Simulation area	500 m × 500 m
Number of unknown nodes	500
Communication range	120 m
Node deployment	Random
Mobility model	Random Way Point model

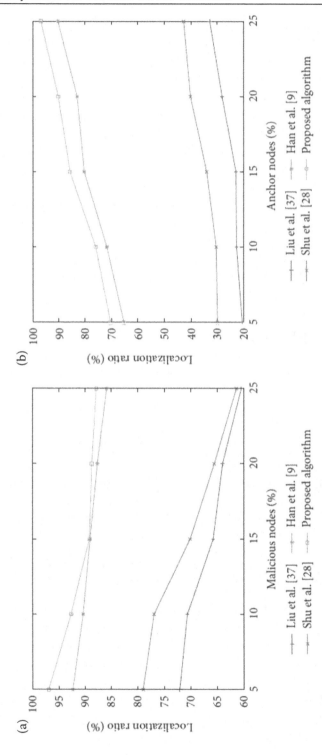

FIGURE 7.9   Comparison of localization ratio: (a) impact of malicious nodes and (b) impact of anchor nodes.

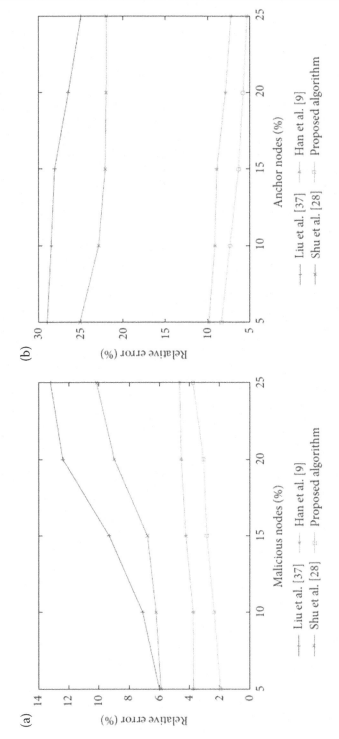

FIGURE 7.10 Comparison of localization accuracy: (a) impact of malicious nodes and (b) impact of anchor nodes.

proposed algorithm still performs better as compared to others. Figure 7.9(b) shows that the proposed algorithm outperforms the other algorithms in the successful localization of unknown nodes with the increasing percentage of anchor nodes. Localization accuracy is a valuable metric for evaluating the efficiency of localization algorithms.

In the proposed work, the localization accuracy is defined by the relative error between the actual location and the calculated node position. In our simulation, we have varied the ratio of malicious nodes from 5% to 30% with increments of 5%. Simulation result, shown in Figure 7.10(a), shows that the relative error percentage of location estimation increases with the increasing number of malicious nodes. However, the proposed algorithm proves its efficiency in location estimation accuracy. Similarly, location accuracy is also tested by varying the anchor nodes' percentage. The result shown in Figure 7.10(b) signifies the fact that the proposed algorithm significantly reduces the relative error percentage with the increasing number of anchor nodes. It is also seen in the result that the other algorithms also decrease the relative error with the increasing number of anchor nodes, but the percentage of relative error is less in our proposed algorithm.

Simulation time is defined as the time taken for the algorithms to detect a particular malicious attack. The result in Figure 7.11 shows that the proposed algorithm is efficient in detecting 90% of the malicious attacks with less time as compared to the other algorithms in comparison.

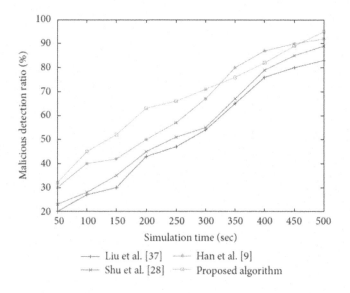

FIGURE 7.11 Comparison of malicious detection ratio.

SUMMARY

Sensor location is vital for many critical applications like battlefield surveillance, target tracking, environmental monitoring, wildfire detection and traffic regulation. Localization has three important metrics: energy efficiency, accuracy and security. Though the first two metrics have drawn the attention of researchers for nearly a decade, the security metric has been addressed only recently. In this chapter, we have discussed the unique operational challenges faced by WSNs, presented a comprehensive overview of the localization process and discussed the three localization techniques: triangulation, trilateration and multilateration. We have also delineated the security requirements of localization, and discussed the merits and demerits of both range-based and range-free localization models that have been proposed as an effective alternative for GPS-based localization. The attacker model and attacks specific to localization have also been discussed in detail. Finally, we conclude this chapter with a survey of all secure localization techniques proposed thus far. This chapter is intended to serve as a single point of reference to researchers interested in secure localization in WSNs.

REFERENCES

Alfaro, J. G., Barbeau, M., & Kranakis, E. (2009). Secure localization of nodes in wireless sensor networks with limited number of truth tellers. *2009 Seventh Annual Communication Networks and Services Research Conference*, 86–93.

Anjum, F., Pandey, S., & Agrawal, P. (2005). Secure localization in sensor networks using transmission range variation. *IEEE International Conference on Mobile Adhoc and Sensor Systems Conference, 2005*, 9 pp.

Arisar, S. H., & Kemp, A. H. (2009). Secure location estimation in large scale wireless sensor networks. *2009 Third International Conference on Next Generation Mobile Applications, Services and Technologies*, 472–476.

Bahl, P., & Padmanabhan, V. N. (2000). RADAR: An in-building RF-based user location and tracking system. *Proceedings IEEE INFOCOM 2000. Conference on Computer Communications. Nineteenth Annual Joint Conference of the IEEE Computer and Communications Societies (Cat. No. 00CH37064)*, 2, 775–784.

Boukerche, A., Oliveira, H. A. B. F., Nakamura, E. F., & Loureiro, A. A. F. (2008). Vehicular ad hoc networks: A new challenge for localization-based systems. *Computer Communications, 31*(12), 2838–2849.

Brands, S., & Chaum, D. (1994). *Distance-bounding protocols, EUROCRYPT'93: Workshop on the theory and application of cryptographic techniques on Advances in cryptology (Secaucus, NJ, USA)*. Springer-Verlag New York, Inc.

Bulusu, N., Heidemann, J., & Estrin, D. (2000). GPS-less low-cost outdoor localization for very small devices. *IEEE Personal Communications, 7*(5), 28–34.

Čapkun, S., Čagalj, M., & Srivastava, M. (2006). Secure localization with hidden and mobile base stations. In *Proceedings of IEEE INFOCOM*.

Capkun, S., & Hubaux, J.-P. (2005). Secure positioning of wireless devices with application to sensor networks. *Proceedings IEEE 24th Annual Joint Conference of the IEEE Computer and Communications Societies*, *3*, 1917–1928.

Capkun, S., & Hubaux, J.-P. (2006). Secure positioning in wireless networks. *IEEE Journal on Selected Areas in Communications*, *24*(2), 221–232.

Capkun, S., Rasmussen, K., Cagalj, M., & Srivastava, M. (2008). Secure location verification with hidden and mobile base stations. *IEEE Transactions on Mobile Computing*, *7*(4), 470–483.

Chintalapudi, K. K., Dhariwal, A., Govindan, R., & Sukhatme, G. (2003). On the feasibility of ad-hoc localization systems. *Techinal Report*.

Doherty, L. (2001). Convex optimization methods for sensor node position estimation. In *Proc. IEEE INFOCOM, April 2001*.

Ekici, E., McNair, J., & Al-Abri, D. (2006). A probabilistic approach to location verification in wireless sensor networks. *2006 IEEE International Conference on Communications*, *8*, 3485–3490.

Ekici, E., Vural, S., McNair, J., & Al-Abri, D. (2008). Secure probabilistic location verification in randomly deployed wireless sensor networks. *Ad Hoc Networks*, *6*(2), 195–209.

Ganu, S., Krishnakumar, A. S., & Krishnan, P. (2004). Infrastructure-based location estimation in WLAN networks. *IEEE Wireless Communications and Networking Conference (WCNC 2004)*, *1*, 465–470.

Garcia-Alfaro, J., Barbeau, M., & Kranakis, E. (2011). Secure geolocalization of wireless sensor nodes in the presence of misbehaving anchor nodes. *Annals of Telecommunications-Annales Des Télécommunications*, *66*(9–10), 535–552.

Gupta, H., Zhou, Z., Das, S. R., & Gu, Q. (2006). Connected sensor cover: Self-organization of sensor networks for efficient query execution. *IEEE/ACM Transactions on Networking*, *14*(1), 55–67.

Han, G., Liu, L., Jiang, J., Shu, L., & Rodrigues, J. J. P. C. (2016). A collaborative secure localization algorithm based on trust model in underwater wireless sensor networks. *Sensors*, *16*(2), 229.

Harter, A., Hopper, A., Steggles, P., Ward, A., & Webster, P. (2002). The anatomy of a context-aware application. *Wireless Networks*, *8*(2–3), 187–197.

He, D., Cui, L., Huang, H., & Ma, M. (2008). Design and verification of enhanced secure localization scheme in wireless sensor networks. *IEEE Transactions on Parallel and Distributed Systems*, *20*(7), 1050–1058.

He, T., Huang, C., Blum, B. M., Stankovic, J. A., & Abdelzaher, T. (2003). Range-free localization schemes for large scale sensor networks. *Proceedings of the 9th Annual International Conference on Mobile Computing and Networking*, 81–95.

Hightower, J., Want, R., & Borriello, G. (2000). *SpotON: An indoor 3D location sensing technology based on RF signal strength*.

Karp, B., & Kung, H.-T. (2000). GPSR: Greedy perimeter stateless routing for wireless networks. *Proceedings of the 6th Annual International Conference on Mobile Computing and Networking*, 243–254.

Kiyavash, N., & Koushanfar, F. (2007). Anti-collusion position estimation in wireless sensor networks. *2007 IEEE International Conference on Mobile Adhoc and Sensor Systems*, 1–9.

Ko, Y., & Vaidya, N. H. (2000). Location-Aided Routing (LAR) in mobile ad hoc networks. *Wireless Networks*, *6*(4), 307–321.

Kumar, G., & Rai, M. K. (2017). An energy efficient and optimized load balanced localization method using CDS with one-hop neighbourhood and genetic algorithm in WSNs. *Journal of Network and Computer Applications*, *78*, 73–82.

Labraoui, N., & Gueroui, M. (2011). Secure range-free localization scheme in wireless sensor networks. *2011 10th International Symposium on Programming and Systems*, 1–8.

Lazos, L., & Poovendran, R. (2004). SeRLoc: Secure range-independent localization for wireless sensor networks. *Proceedings of the 3rd ACM Workshop on Wireless Security*, 21–30.

Lazos, L., & Poovendran, R. (2006). HiRLoc: High-resolution robust localization for wireless sensor networks. *IEEE Journal on Selected Areas in Communications*, 24(2), 233–246.

Lazos, L., Poovendran, R., & Capkun, S. (2005). ROPE: Robust position estimation in wireless sensor networks. *IPSN 2005. Fourth International Symposium on Information Processing in Sensor Networks*, 2005, 324–331.

Li, Z., Trappe, W., Zhang, Y., & Nath, B. (2005). Robust statistical methods for securing wireless localization in sensor networks. *IPSN 2005. Fourth International Symposium on Information Processing in Sensor Networks*, 2005, 91–98.

Liu, C., Wu, K., & He, T. (2004). Sensor localization with ring overlapping based on comparison of received signal strength indicator. *2004 IEEE International Conference on Mobile Ad-Hoc and Sensor Systems (IEEE Cat. No. 04EX975)*, 516–518.

Liu, D., Ning, P., & Du, W. (2005). Detecting malicious beacon nodes for secure location discovery in wireless sensor networks. *25th IEEE International Conference on Distributed Computing Systems (ICDCS'05)*, 609–619.

Liu, D., Ning, P., Liu, A., Wang, C., & Du, W. K. (2008). Attack-resistant location estimation in wireless sensor networks. *ACM Transactions on Information and System Security (TISSEC)*, 11(4), 1–39.

Liu, X., Yang, R., & Cui, Q. (2015). An efficient secure DV-Hop localization for wireless sensor network. *International Journal of Security and Its Applications*, 9, 275–284.

Mauve, M., Widmer, J., & Hartenstein, H. (2001). A survey on position-based routing in mobile ad hoc networks. *IEEE Network*, 15(6), 30–39.

Meguerdichian, S., Slijepcevic, S., Karayan, V., & Potkonjak, M. (2001). Localized algorithms in wireless ad-hoc networks: Location discovery and sensor exposure. *Proceedings of the 2nd ACM International Symposium on Mobile Ad Hoc Networking & Computing*, 106–116.

Misra, S., Bhardwaj, S., & Xue, G. (2006). ROSETTA: Robust and secure mobile target tracking in a wireless ad hoc environment. *MILCOM 2006-2006 IEEE Military Communications Conference*, 1–7.

Misra, S., Xue, G., & Bhardwaj, S. (2008). Secure and robust localization in a wireless ad hoc environment. *IEEE Transactions on Vehicular Technology*, 58(3), 1480–1489.

Nagpal, R., Shrobe, H., & Bachrach, J. (2003). Organizing a global coordinate system from local information on an ad hoc sensor network. *Information Processing in Sensor Networks*, 333–348.

Nasipuri, A., & Li, K. (2002). A directionality based location discovery scheme for wireless sensor networks. *Proceedings of the 1st ACM International Workshop on Wireless Sensor Networks and Applications*, 105–111.

Navas, J. C., & Imielinski, T. (1997). GeoCast—geographic addressing and routing. *Proceedings of the 3rd Annual ACM/IEEE International Conference on Mobile Computing and Networking*, 66–76.

Niculescu, Dragos, & Nath, B. (2003). Ad hoc positioning system (APS) using AOA. *IEEE INFOCOM 2003. Twenty-Second Annual Joint Conference of the IEEE Computer and Communications Societies (IEEE Cat. No. 03CH37428)*, 3, 1734–1743.

Niculescu, Dragoș, & Nath, B. (2003a). DV based positioning in ad hoc networks. *Telecommunication Systems*, 22(1–4), 267–280.

Niculescu, Dragoș, & Nath, B. (2003b). Localized positioning in ad hoc networks. *Ad Hoc Networks*, 1(2–3), 247–259.

Patwari, N., Hero, A. O., Perkins, M., Correal, N. S., & O'Dea, R. J. (2003). Relative location estimation in wireless sensor networks. *IEEE Transactions on Signal Processing, 51*(8), 2137–2148.

Perrig, A., Canetti, R., Tygar, J. D., & Song, D. (2000). Efficient authentication and signing of multicast streams over lossy channels. *Proceeding 2000 IEEE Symposium on Security and Privacy. S&P 2000*, 56–73.

Priyantha, N. B., Chakraborty, A., & Balakrishnan, H. (2000). The cricket location-support system. *Proceedings of the 6th Annual International Conference on Mobile Computing and Networking*, 32–43.

Rabaey, C. S. J., & Langendoen, K. (2002). Robust positioning algorithms for distributed ad-hoc wireless sensor networks. *USENIX Technical Annual Conference*, 317–327.

Rousseeuw, P. J., & Leroy, A. M. (2005). *Robust regression and outlier detection* (Vol. 589). John Wiley & Sons.

Savvides, A., Garber, W. L., Moses, R. L., & Srivastava, M. B. (2005). An analysis of error inducing parameters in multihop sensor node localization. *IEEE Transactions on Mobile Computing, 4*(6), 567–577.

Savvides, A., Han, C.-C., & Strivastava, M. B. (2001). Dynamic fine-grained localization in ad-hoc networks of sensors. *Proceedings of the 7th Annual International Conference on Mobile Computing and Networking*, 166–179.

Savvides, A., Park, H., & Srivastava, M. B. (2002). The bits and flops of the n-hop multilateration primitive for node localization problems. *Proceedings of the 1st ACM International Workshop on Wireless Sensor Networks and Applications*, 112–121.

Shu, T., Chen, Y., & Yang, J. (2015). Protecting multi-lateral localization privacy in pervasive environments. *IEEE/ACM Transactions on Networking, 23*(5), 1688–1701.

Srinivasan, A., Teitelbaum, J., & Wu, J. (2006). DRBTS: Distributed reputation-based beacon trust system. *2006 2nd IEEE International Symposium on Dependable, Autonomic and Secure Computing*, 277–283.

Srinivasan, A., & Wu, J. (2007). A survey on secure localization in wireless sensor networks. *Encyclopedia of Wireless and Mobile Communications, 126*.

Srinivasan, A., Wu, J., & Teitelbaum, J. (2008). Distributed reputation-based secure localization in sensor networks. *Special Issue on Journal of Autonomic and Trusted Computing (JoATC), 3*, 1–13.

Wang, C., & Xiao, L. (2006). Locating sensors in concave areas. *Proceedings IEEE INFOCOM 2006. 25TH IEEE International Conference on Computer Communications*, 1–12.

Wu, J., Chen, H., Lou, W., Wang, Z., & Wang, Z. (2010). Label-based DV-Hop localization against wormhole attacks in wireless sensor networks. *2010 IEEE Fifth International Conference on Networking, Architecture, and Storage*, 79–88.

Xiao-Mei, C., Bo, Y., Gui-Hai, C., & Feng-Yuan, R. (2008). *Security analysis on node localization systems of wireless sensor networks*.

Xu, W., Ma, K., Trappe, W., & Zhang, Y. (2006). Jamming sensor networks: Attack and defense strategies. *IEEE Network, 20*(3), 41–47.

Yan, T., He, T., & Stankovic, J. A. (2003). Differentiated surveillance for sensor networks. *Proceedings of the 1st International Conference on Embedded Networked Sensor Systems*, 51–62.

Yu, Y., Govindan, R., & Estrin, D. (2001). *Geographical and energy aware routing: A recursive data dissemination protocol for wireless sensor networks*.

Zeng, Y., Cao, J., Zhang, S., Guo, S., & Xie, L. (2009). Pollution attack: A new attack against localization in wireless sensor networks. *2009 IEEE Wireless Communications and Networking Conference*, 1–6.

Zeng, Y., Zhang, S., Guo, S., & Li, X. (2007). Secure hop-count based localization in wireless sensor networks. *2007 International Conference on Computational Intelligence and Security (CIS 2007)*, 907–911.

Zhang, Y., Liu, W., Fang, Y., & Wu, D. (2006). Secure localization and authentication in ultra-wideband sensor networks. *IEEE Journal on Selected Areas in Communications*, 24(4), 829–835.

Zhong, S., Jadliwala, M., Upadhyaya, S., & Qiao, C. (2008). Towards a theory of robust localization against malicious beacon nodes. *IEEE INFOCOM 2008-The 27th Conference on Computer Communications*, 1391–1399.

Malicious Node Detection Mechanisms

8

INTRODUCTION

A wireless sensor network (WSN) consists of a set of compact and automated devices called sensing nodes. A sensing node is a computational device that has memory, battery, processor, transceiver and a sensing device. The Berkeley MICA Mote (Hill & Culler, 2002), SmartDust (Kahn et al., 1999, 2000; Warneke et al., 2001) and CotsDust (Hollar, 2000) are examples of such nodes. These nodes are distributed across an area and communicate among themselves, forming an ad hoc network. Sensor networks contain special nodes that process and store the information collected by the network; they are called sink nodes. Communication between two nodes is performed in multiple hops if they are not within each other's transmission range.

Wireless sensor networks can collect data from the environment where they are embedded. These networks can detect events such as forest fires, intruders, etc. An agent exists on each sensor node in a WSN, and the agent creates an event message and delivers it to the sink over multi-hop paths. Some of the applications envisioned for sensor networks are environmental monitoring, infrastructure management, public safety, medical, home and office security, transportation and battlefield surveillance. Given their criticality, these applications are likely to be attacked.

There are a number of ways one can attack a WSN. Because WSNs are unattended, an adversary could capture and compromise some of the sensor nodes. In so doing, the adversary can extract all information such as the secret keys stored in the nodes, and the adversary can insert malicious agents into the nodes. Then, these nodes can be used to create false messages, i.e., generate false messages on their own and/or falsify legitimate messages they have received from other nodes. They can waste a considerable amount of network resources. Moreover, they can also generate network congestion by creating many false event messages to prevent a legitimate event message from being transmitted to the sink.

Although there are many works on detecting such false messages (Cao et al., 2012; Lu et al., 2011; Ye et al., 2005), they cannot detect malicious agents that create false messages.

The malicious node detection also becomes a complicated task at this situation, since communication errors will occur. Generally, the malicious node detection methodologies so far consumed enormous energy and by these criteria, the operation of a WSN is affected (Yu et al., 2013).

Studies on trace-back in wireless sensor networks include ones (Ye et al., 2007; Zhang et al., 2007) on detecting malicious agents that create false messages. However, these methods can only be used in situations where there is only one malicious agent and the routing path from it to the sink is static. Although authenticated K-sized probabilistic packet marking (AK-PPM) (Xu et al., 2012) can be used in environments where the routing paths are changeable, it cannot identify malicious agents that falsify messages. Lightweight packet marking (LPM) (Sei & Ohsuga, 2013) can be used in situations where there are many malicious agents. However, LPM can only detect a suspicious node group, which contains a suspicious node, n, nodes that had sent messages to node n and nodes that had received messages from node n. If nodes can move, the number of nodes in a suspicious node group can be very large. Therefore, the effectiveness of LPM goes away in this case.

The packet marking method detects nodes that created false messages, that is, the source nodes that generate false messages and the nodes that falsify messages. In this method, each forwarding node appends its ID and a k-bit message authentication code (MAC) to the message. If the length of the bits of a MAC is normal, such as 128 bits (Ganesan et al., 2003), there is a lot of communication traffic for forwarding a message. In this method, a MAC set k to be small, e.g., only 1 bit. Of course, malicious agents can generate a correct MAC with high probability if k is small. Even so, we can detect malicious agents by using a statistical procedure when some false messages reach the sink.

SECURITY THREATS AGAINST WIRELESS SENSOR NETWORKS

As there is enhancement in WSN technology, also there is increase in threats. Therefore, to reduce or avoid these threats, new encryption techniques have been introduced. However, these encryption methods can protect the system from outside attackers only. Identifying these threats by the behavior of sensor nodes and their irregularity is a major concern. Security threats against wireless sensor networks are classified into two major types: passive and active attacks.

1. Passive attacks: Attackers are usually unknown and either hit the transmission path to gather information or destroy the operating elements

(Vasiliou & Economides, 2006). This attack can be sorted into node tampering or destruction, eavesdropping and node faulty and traffic analysis types.

2. Active attacks: An opponent node strikes the operations in the network. Active attacks can be grouped into denial of service, flooding attacks, Sybil attacks, jamming and hole attacks such as wormhole, black hole and sinkhole.

Resolutions to security attacks against wireless sensor networks require (Papadimitratos & Haas, 2002) the following three major elements:

1. Prevention: The goal is to prevent any attack before it occurs in the network.
2. Detection: If an attacker overtakes the prevention step, then it intends to break down to protect against the attack. The security resolution instantly identifies the attack development and recognizes the node to be compromised.
3. Mitigation: The objective of the finishing step is to alleviate the attack after encounters by withdrawing the unnatural nodes and securing the network.

Some of the well-known intrusion detection system (IDSs) are discussed herein.

Abnormality Detection

The behavior of nodes is being monitored and analyzed as typical or not. In this approach, the normal behavior of a node is studied and compared with any misbehaving node. Such unusually misbehaving nodes within the network are considered malicious nodes. The demerit of this method is that it has a high false alert rate; however, it can identify the well-known attacks.

Misuse Detection

In this system, a set of formulations is followed once an attack commences in a WSN, and is a control-based detection type. The nodes are differentiated from attackers by comparing them with already known misbehaved characteristics of malicious nodes. This detection is fruitful only for well-known attacks and fails for unknown attacks.

Specification-Based Detection

This method is a combination of standard distinguishing proofs and variations from manual acknowledgments. The methodology follows the conventional techniques for misbehavior detection in nodes. It determines a malicious node based on relevant opinions from other systems.

The next section of the chapter is going to review some of the commonly observed node failures, malicious node detection, sensor faults, etc. Faults in sensor data can occur for many reasons. The first source stems from unpredictable environmental conditions, which can often cause sensors to behave erratically. Factors such as extreme temperatures or precipitation can affect sensor performance. During a deployment, sensors can be displaced or change orientation. This can be caused, for example, by animals or humans or wind or if they are deployed in a body of water that freezes. Another type of fault occurs when the environmental conditions travel outside the range of values the sensor is able to detect. In this case, the sensor becomes saturated and is unable to report the true readings.

LITERATURE ON MALICIOUS NODE DETECTION

Singh et al. (2017) incorporated the fuzzy rules with hybrid methodology to identify the malicious nodes from normal test nodes in a large WSN environment. The mamdani fuzzy rules were incorporated by the authors for the detection and mitigation of malicious nodes in WSN. The authors achieved 99.4% detection rate for Sybil malicious attacks, 98.2% detection rate for wormhole malicious attacks and 99.2% detection rate for hellowfood malicious node attacks in WSNs. The malicious node detection results were verified and compared with conventional techniques. The main limitation of this method is that this work was not able to detect the passive malicious nodes in WSNs.

Sharma and Gambhir (2017) developed a methodology for the detection of malicious nodes using reputation-based cooperative approach. The authors implemented a cooperative technique for differentiating the trusty nodes from untrusty nodes in a WSN environment.

Nachammai and Radha (2016) proposed a trust-based approach to detect the untrusty nodes. The authors analyzed their proposed trust methodology against various kinds of attacks such as black hole attacks, gray hole attacks and DoS attacks. The authors analyzed their performance of the proposed work in terms of detection rate and classification accuracy.

Koriata (2016) used a weighted trust evaluation (WTE) technique to differentiate the trusty nodes from malicious nodes in a WSN environment. Sukanesh et al. (2016) proposed an energy-aware malicious node identification technique using dynamic probabilistic flooding (DPF). The rebroadcast probability of each node in a WSN environment is analyzed with respect to various qualities of service parameters.

Turkanović et al. (2014) proposed a key management methodology for heterogeneous wireless sensor networks to achieve high security from attackers. The authors analyzed their performance using flooding attack in the nodes of WSN environments. Various cryptographic techniques were analyzed on their proposed method to validate the results.

Malicious node detection in a wireless sensor network through detection of message transmission in a network is provided in Pires et al. (2004). A message transmission is considered suspicious if its signal strength is incompatible with its originator's geographical position. A protocol for detecting suspicious transmissions and consequent identification of malicious nodes is proposed. The two -ray model used does not model signal power loss due to obstacles, weather conditions, interference, etc. Determination of malicious nodes locations needs coordination with its neighbors. Atakli et al. (2008) proposed a novel scheme based on weighted trust evaluation to detect malicious nodes. A lightweight algorithm that incurs little overhead and hierarchical network architecture is adopted. In this approach, the base station is assumed to be trusted. In fact, if the adversary gains control over the base station, the possibility of attack is increased.

Khalil et al. (2008) has presented a countermeasure for the wormhole attack, called MOBIWORP, which alleviates the drawbacks of the previous work and efficiently mitigates the wormhole attack in mobile networks. MOBIWORP uses a secure central authority (CA) for global tracking of node positions. Local monitoring is used to detect and isolate malicious nodes locally. Additionally, when sufficient suspicion builds up at the CA, it enforces a global isolation of the malicious node from the whole network. MOBIWORP provides a technique that isolates the malicious nodes from the network, thereby removing their ability to cause future damage. The isolation is achieved in two phases, locally and globally that neutralize the capability of the malicious nodes from launching further attacks after detection, whether at the current location or at a new location. In this protocol, guard nodes are assumed to be minimum and choosing them based on their location which eliminates the causes of loss in detection coverage has not been discussed.

A specification-based intruder detection system to detect black holes and selective forwarding attacks in WSNs has been proposed by Tiwari et al. (2009). In this, nodes and their neighborhood collaborate with the cluster head to monitor malicious behavior. Watchdog nodes closely watch the behavior of nodes in the network and report their feedback to the cluster head for decision making. The probability of attacking watchdog nodes in the network disturbs the communication between the cluster head and watchdog nodes.

George and Parani (2014) proposed high-level security architecture to detect the number of false nodes using an overlay network model. The authors analyzed a probabilistic model of each sensor node in a WSN environment by analyzing its performance behavior with respect to the number of nodes. The proposed methodology was described int erms of the following terms:

* Probabilistic model
* Deterministic factor

Nakul (2013) used SVM classification methodology for the classification of nodes through various routing protocols. The authors used a linear mode in SVM classification methodology for an increasing detection rate. The nonlinear SVM classification model was not suitable for the detection of misleading packets that were passed over the nodes in the WSN environment.

Lee et al. (2013) used constructive mapped linear predictive algorithm for the computation of linear models for the entire network architecture. The functional behavior of each sensor nodes was with its surrounding nodes in a clustered area of the clustered network architecture. The location of the sensor nodes was coordinated with respect to the number of abnormal packets on each sensor node.

Thakre and Sonekar (n.d.) analyzed the behavior of the node misdetection behavior with respect to the number of malicious nodes. The authors analyzed its functional behavior using a random mode linear mapping algorithm.

Oh et al. (2012) proposed a trust-based rule computation model in order to derive the weights of the internal nodes in a WSN environment. The authors achieved a low detection rate of about 67% by varying the number of attack nodes in a WSN. This weight computation model was analyzed with respect to the number of misdetected sensor nodes. The authors applied a neighbor clustering technique on nodes that were spread over the number of regions. The nodal node of each cluster computed internal weights of node details with respect to its functional behavior. This information was sent to a centralized node that was located in a remote area. Jadidoleslamy (2011) developed an abnormal node detection technique on each sensor node in a WSN environment. The authors analyzed various abnormal detection sensor nodes with respect to the number of intruders.

Yu and Kim (2011) extended the linear prediction algorithm for the computation of trust factors in the linear mode. The authors further developed a hypothesis model that was extracted from the fuzzy model used in a WSN environment. The trust factors were computed and derived on each node, which further improved the error detection rate. The weight factor was computed from the nodal node in a certain clustered area and then its surrounding weight factor values were compared with its calculated value, which increased the detection rate. The proposed work stated in this paper classified nodes into normal and dependable nodes, which made the entire system reconfigurable.

A WSN has the least energy resources for carrying the process such as environment sensing, information processing and communication. A fuzzy-based approach for detecting a node-exhaustion attack has been proposed by Baig and Khan (2010) to achieve a trade-off between attack detection and energy utilization. This scheme has been proposed with the limitation in number of cluster heads and internode distances for the attack detecting process.

Celenk et al. (2008) presented a method of anomaly detection based on the adaptive Weiner filtering of noise followed by ARMA modeling of network flow data. Noise and traffic signal statistics are dynamically calculated using network-monitoring metrics for traffic features such as average port, high port, server ports and peered port. The port measurements are used to confirm the anomaly prediction as part of the majority voting scheme. The proposed method limits the use of multiple features and additional defense mechanisms for estimating a cyber attack, which will improve the system accuracy and reliability.

Bao et al. (2012) devised a clustering technique to cluster the entire network system in a WSN environment, which makes the entire network into linear and non-linear modes of the activities. The different quality parameters were analyzed by the authors to make the reputation in a WSN network environment. This kind of functional behavior of the network system was entirely monitored and controlled by different network controllers in the network system, which increases the performance of the system to be more active.

Sun et al. (2012) presented an anomaly detection technique for wireless sensor networks. The authors made use of several parameters like average, max, sum and min and formulated an algorithm to increase detection sensitivity by integrating a collective summary and probability ratio. In their method, both intrusion detection modules (IDMs) and system monitoring modules (SMMs) are integrated, which helps in classifying the malicious activities of nodes effectively in WSNs. WSNs are applied in real-time applications to monitor emergency crisis, such as forest fire, enemy attack in war, etc.

Gopalakrishnan and Ganeshkumar (2014) proposed two different detection methodologies, avoiding the hacking of packets in a WSN. The authors proposed a secure routing for attacker identification (SRAI) protocol to detect the attackers in the sensor network. This proposed system automatically detected the type of attack implemented in the network, thereby generating an attacker identification report periodically. Using this report, all the other nodes in the network can easily identify the attacker and the data transmission to that particular node could be terminated.

Chang et al. (2014) proposed a bait detection methodology for preventing various attacks in a WSN environment. This bait detection algorithm used a bait packet detection concept to detect the attackers using fuzzy set rules with their relative models. This ensured proper mechanisms by identifying the relative behavior of various nodes in a WSN environment. The simulated network can be verified using a NS2 simulating tool with its multi-axle network model. The functionalities of each layer in its architectural model were analyzed with its functional activities. The authors also analyzed various feature sets of each node.

Rajasegarar et al. (2008) proposed a methodology for layer detection in WSNs using a linear sensor model algorithm. The data were transmitted and received using sensor nodes with a linear mapping algorithm for the efficient data transmission and reception. Curiac et al. (2007) used autoregression methodology for the detection of abnormal behavior of each node in a WSN environment. The authors utilized data optimization algorithms for abnormal node detection and mitigation. The authors achieved 78% detection rate for the detection of malicious nodes using the regression modeling approach. Junior et al. devised a model that exhibited abnormal node detection using strength modeling methodology. The location of each sensor node in a WSN environment was analyzed for the detection of abnormal nodes in a particular area.

Deng and Xiong (2011) analyzed the working model of sensor topology using the markov regression technique. This technique classified each link in a network into either good or bad. The bad links were mitigated using a regression markov model. Atakli et al. (2008) developed a hierarchical architecture for a sensor network using trust evaluation methodology. In this methodology, the authors alloted an individual weight for each node and the malicious nodes and link failures were detected based on their individual weights in WSN environments. Ju et al. (2010) analyzed the intrusion identification methodology for the detection of intruders in WSN environments. The authors analyzed various geographic locations of each node and, based on this location analysis, the nodes were classified into either normal or abnormal.

Mao (2010) identified a multi-agent detection scheme for locating abnormal nodes in a WSN environment. The authors detected and analyzed various intruders and then these detected intruders' details were sent to all nodes in a WSN environment to alert the presence of intruders in sensor networks. The authors divided the entire network architecture into various mapping regions with a linear regression mapping technique that was based on cooperative methodology in real-time monitoring and controlling environments.

Misra et al. (2010) proposed an energy-efficient methodology for the detection of intruders in larger sensor networks. The authors analyzed the performance of these energy-efficient sensor networks using a stochastic linear mapping algorithm. The authors detected malicious packets were transferred through a number of sensor nodes in a WSN environment. The authors analyzed various learning models for all nodes in energy utilization models.

Crosby et al. (2011) developed trust-based intrusion detection models using various location mapping methodologies. The probabilistic factors were computed on each sensor node and then trust factors were then computed. Based on these computed factors, the trust of each node was classified.

In Chen et al. (2010), a method using an isolation table is proposed to isolate malicious nodes to avoid the consumption of network architecture elements. By which the network controller is rapidly analyzed which enables the whole system to establish connections with a large number of its peers by the network architecture system.

Sa and Rath (2011) developed a Bayesian-based malicious detection algorithm. Their methodology effectively detected the malicious activities and their performance improvement was analyzed based on their agent-based approaches and compared their results with other conventional methodologies.

Mamun and Kabir (2010) used various hierarchical models for the detection and classification of various intruders based on policy developing techniques. The authors applied various clustering techniques on sensor nodes and, based on the clustering, the nodes in each cluster area were classified. The layer transmission and reception behavior of sensor network architecture was analyzed by the authors.

Yan et al. (2009) used hybrid methodology for the detection of attacks in various cluster modes using different routing algorithms, such as hybrid intrusion detection system (HIDS) and heterogeneous cluster-based WSN (CWSN). Various attacks can be determined by their proposed model, such as sinkhole attack, replication attack, Sybil attack, wormhole, hello floods, etc.

In Huo and Wang (2008), a dynamic model of intrusion detection (DIDS) for a WSN was proposed. Their model for detection of malicious activity was based on a clustered network even at low energy levels. It employed a distributed defense to detect multiple intruders, even at a very larger cluster size and high energy consumption.

Chen et al. (2010) proposed malicious node detection using an energy mapping algorithm based on a lightweight technique. The authors analyzed rough map nonlinear techniques in order to detect and mitigate the malicious nodes. The authors used a SVM classification technique to detect and classify the nodes. Then, the nodes in a WSN environment were classified by locating the coordinates of all nodes in network sensor environments.

The previously discussed methods are summarized in Table 8.1.

TABLE 8.1 Analysis of existing intrusion detection systems (IDSs)

EXISTING IDS	STRENGTH	WEAKNESS	FUTURE SCOPE
Semantic IDS (Mao, 2010)	1. Agent node stores the whole ontology in its memory. 2. Energy efficient	1. Mapping of security ontology with sensor data is vague. 2. Decision-making function is not clearly specified.	Algorithms can be improved by using more complex semantics of security ontology.
Simple Learning Automata Based IDS (Misra et al., 2010)	1. Single node failure does not affect the entire system due to distributed feature. 2. Minimizes energy. 3. Improves packet sampling through self-learning feature. 4. Optimizes efficiency.	Computational complexity increases because of dynamic topology by distributed self-learning automation technique.	S-LAID solution can be tested in different application domains of sensor network.
Location Aware Trust Based IDS (Crosby et al., 2011)	1. Malicious node detection by reputation-based monitoring. 2. Accuracy is enhanced by location awareness.	Use of encryption algorithm consumes more energy.	Location verification protocol can be extended.
Isolation Table Based IDS (Chen et al., 2010)	Initial setup makes ITIDS effectively prevent attacks and enhances the transmission accuracy by increase in live nodes.	Decrease in the remaining nodes, makes the attackers penetrate a WSN more easily.	Extension of Anomaly node detection for performance upgradation.
Ranger Based IDS (Chen et al., 2010)	1. Attacker cannot assault an isolated malicious node. 2. Lightweight model in energy-efficient manner.	It mainly solves the problem of a Sybil attack.	Implementation through standard protocols for performance evaluation (e.g., Zigbee).
Hierarchical Overlay Design Based IDS (Mamun & Kabir, 2010)	1. Reliability, efficiency and effectiveness are high for a large geographical area. 2. Distributed four level hierarchy	1. IDS needs to wait for intruders to reach the core area, whereas nodes can be captured at any	Election procedure can be implemented; IDS scalability and definition of detection policy needs to be

(Continued)

TABLE 8.1 (Continued)   Analysis of existing intrusion detection systems (IDSs)

EXISTING IDS	STRENGTH	WEAKNESS	FUTURE SCOPE
	results in highly energy-saving structure. 3. ID becomes very fast and effective.	area without any notice. 2. Total cost of network setup increases with policy-based mechanism.	determined, more specifically.
Hybrid IDS (Yan et al., 2009)	1. Its detection rate and accuracy are high for using hybrid approach. Decision-making model is very simple and fast. 2. Cluster head is used to reduce energy consumption, amount of data in the entire network and to increase network lifetime.	Rules in the anomaly detection model are defined manually, so performance cannot be verified through simulation.	Feature selection in anomaly detection can be done by data mining; rule-based approach can be extended to provide anomaly detection model with better performance and flexibility.
Weighted Trust Evaluation Based IDS (Atakli et al., 2008)	1. It detects misbehaved nodes accurately with very short delay. 2. Lightweight algorithm incurs little overhead.	It gives rise to high misdetection rate.	More detailed analysis regarding the performance will be studied in ongoing research.
Dynamic Model of IDS (Huo & Wang, 2008)	1. Enhances the security, stability, robustness and network lifetime through its distributed framework. 2. Enhancement in flexibility through security update.	1. It needs more time to detect all intrusions. 2. Distributed detection consumes more energy.	It can be tested with real-life applications to ensure accuracy of the model.

From the existing techniques of malicious node detection in a WSN, the subsequent points are observed:

- The attackers in the case of both active and passive were discussed in detail with various system architectures.

- The abnormal or malicious nodes in WSN environments were analyzed using clustering algorithms.
- The flexibility behavior of the network architecture model was analyzed by varying its feature set with respect to number of nodes, which were attacked by different attackers.
- The present algorithms were able to detect fewer numbers of malicious or abnormal nodes.
- The currently existing methods cannot determine malicious nodes within a WSN environment if it is moving faster.

The conventional methodology for a malicious node detection system has several limitations as follows:

- They consumed high latency for differentiating the malicious nodes from trusty nodes.
- They obtained low PDR, which is not suitable for multimedia data transmission and reception.
- The detection and classification rate of the malicious nodes in a WSN of the conventional method is low.

The limitations of the conventional malicious node detection system are overcome by proposing a classifier-based feature that incorporates a malicious node detection system.

SUSPICIOUS NODE DETECTION BY SIGNAL STRENGTH

This section describes the approach for detecting suspicious messages and suspicious nodes based on signal strength.

The Model

This model assumes WSNs are homogeneous (all network nodes contain the same hardware and software configuration), symmetric (node A can only communicate with node B if and only if B can communicate with A) and static (network nodes do not move after deployment). In particular, the radio transceivers of all members of the network operate under the same configuration throughout the lifetime of the network (e.g., transmission power, antenna height, antenna gain).

All nodes are uniquely identified, and know their own geographical position, which can be obtained using a positioning system such as the GPS. The value of a node's geographical position as well as its identifier are included in each of the messages it sends. We assume that message exchanges in the network are protected against tampering (using some cryptographic mechanism, for example) (Stallings, 2006).

We further assume that radio propagation follows a well-defined model, such as the free space model and the two-ray ground model (Rappaport, 1996), which specify how the values of transmission power, received signal strength and distance between the transmitter and the receiver relate to each other. As an example, the two-ray ground propagation model (Equation 8.1) makes the assumption that a signal sent from one node does not arrive at another node through a unique path (a straight line), but eventually also through a reflection in the ground:

$$P_r = \frac{P_t \times G_t \times G_r \times h_t^2 \times h_r^2}{d^4 \times L} \tag{8.1}$$

In Equation 8.1, P_r is the received signal power in watts, P_t is the transmission power also in watts, G_t is the transmitter antenna gain, G_r is the receiver antenna gain, h_t is the transmitter antenna height in meters, h_r is the receiver antenna height in meters, d is the distance between the receiver and transmitter in meters and L is the system loss (a constant). A signal is only detected by a receiving node if the received signal power, P_r, is equal or greater than the received signal power threshold, P_m.

We also assume that the signal strength of a received signal can be easily acquired from a transceiver. The Chipcon SmartRF CC1000[1] transceiver, used in the latest MICA Motes series,[2] for example, has a built-in RSSI (Received Signal Strength Indicator), giving an analog output signal at its RSSI pin. When the RSSI function is enabled, the output current of this pin is inversely proportional to the input signal level. The voltage at the pin can be measured by an analog/digital converter, which is the only additional hardware required. Equations 8.2 and 8.3 specify the received signal strength, P_r, in dBm, when the transceiver is operating at 433 MHz and 868 MHz, respectively. V_{RSSI} is the voltage measured at the RSSI pin.

$$P_r = -51.3 \times V_{RSSI} - 49.2 \tag{8.2}$$

$$P_r = -50.0 \times V_{RSSI} - 45.5 \tag{8.3}$$

Finally, we assume that malicious nodes are capable of HELLO flood attacks and wormhole attacks only. In what follows, a transmission is malicious if the geographical position included in the corresponding message is made up or was transmitted with a power that differs from the one agreed upon by all the other nodes in the system. A node is malicious if it broadcasts a malicious transmission.

Upon receiving a message, a node can classify it as suspicious or unsuspicious, depending on whether the node thinks the transmission is malicious. Given that this classification (suspicious vs. unsuspicious) is done locally at the receiving node, malicious transmissions may not always be classified as suspicious (false negatives), and non-malicious transmissions may be classified as suspicious (false positives).

Suspicious Message Detection by Signal Strength (SMDSS)

Under the model described previously, any node can obtain two values on any transmission it hears. The first value is the expected signal strength of the received signal, which can be computed using the transmission power that was agreed upon for message transmissions in the system and the distance between the nodes that hears the transmission and the source of the transmission itself. The second value is the actual signal strength detected at the listener's transceiver.

In a system where all is well, the two values should match. The same would not be true in most cases; however, if the system is under a HELLO flood attack or a wormhole attack. We make use of this fact to identify suspicious messages in the system.

In our proposed scheme, all transmissions in the network are subject to scrutiny: all nodes monitor all transmissions they hear. Concretely, the following protocol is run locally in each sensor node. For each transmission a node hears, it compares the expected and the actual signal strengths of the received signal, independently of whether it is the intended recipient of the transmission. When the difference between both is greater than a given threshold, the message is regarded as suspicious.

Each node also keeps a local table containing the "reputation" of other nodes in the system. Each entry contains the node id, the number of suspicious votes and the number of unsuspicious votes.

After checking the suspiciousness of a received message, the node updates its table accordingly: if the message is suspicious, it increases the message originator's suspicious count by one; otherwise, the unsuspicious count is increased. Note that the message's originator can be determined, given that its ID is included in the message.

If the message is suspicious, the node takes a further action: it disseminates this information among its neighbors. We describe the dissemination protocol in the next section. A suspicious message is discarded by its intended recipient and not acted upon.

Suspicious Node Information Dissemination Protocol (SNIDP)

Upon detecting a suspicious message, node A broadcasts the identity of the sender S to its neighbors, informing them that S is suspicious. This broadcast also works as an inquiry: those that hear this broadcast (e.g., B) should reply with their opinion (suspicious or unsuspicious) of S. B determines its reply the following way:

- If B is not S's neighbor, i.e., B does not hear transmissions from S, it does not respond;
- If B is a neighbor of S, i.e., B hears transmissions from S, then it responds with "suspicious" if the suspicious count for S in its table is greater than its unsuspicious count; otherwise it responds with "unsuspicious".

A collects all the replies and updates its table accordingly: for each "suspicious" vote it receives, it increases its own suspicious count for S by one; and similarly with "unsuspicious" votes.

Note that B's reply is a broadcast. This means that it could be heard by all its neighbors, including those that are neither S's neighbor nor A's neighbor (i.e., nodes that did not hear either S's malicious transmission or A's broadcast to disseminate the fact that S is suspicious). They all update their tables accordingly.

We clarify a number of our design decisions. First, the SNIDP protocol is executed only when a suspicious message is detected. The assumption here is that, in normal circumstances (we are being optimistic here), all transmissions will be unsuspicious, and the network do not need to incur the overhead of the SNIDP protocol. Second, one might argue that a single "suspicious" vote would be more than enough to render a node suspicious. This reasoning would make our scheme vulnerable to malicious nodes that can also lie. A malicious node could disseminate the false information that a regular node C is suspicious and, with this single vote, effectively eliminate C from the network, potentially causing a massive denial of service in significant parts of the network. Our requirement that a node be considered suspicious only if its suspicious count outnumbers its unsuspicious count makes our scheme more robust against this type of attack.

One might argue that this last design decision could potentially increase the number of false negatives (malicious nodes that are not detected as suspicious) in our system. We believe that this will not be the case, because in most cases, a malicious transmission can fool only a single target among all the neighbors of the malicious node. This means that there will be many more nodes broadcasting warnings saying the malicious node is suspicious than those saying it is not.

PROPOSED MALICIOUS NODE DETECTION MECHANISM

This section proposes features based on malicious node detection and a classification system using neural network classifier, as depicted in Figure 8.1. This proposed system consists of feature extraction and classifications. The features that describe the behavior of the individual node are extracted from each node and these extracted features are trained and classified using a neural network classifier. This classifier classifies the test node into a trust node or malicious node based on the extracted features.

Feature Extraction

In this section, link stability features, probabilistic features, randomness features and credit features are extracted from the test node that is further used to differentiate the test node from malicious nodes.

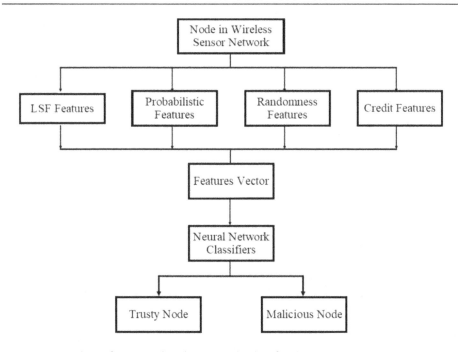

FIGURE 8.1   Flow of proposed malicious node classification system.

Link Stability Features (LSFs)

This feature determines the stability of links between the test node and its surrounding nodes. The positive value of LSF shows that the stability of the link between the test node and its surrounding node is good and there is no possibility of a test node being a malicious node. The negative value of LSF shows that the stability of the link between the test node and its surrounding node is worst and there may be a possibility of a test node being a malicious node. Figure 8.2 shows the extraction process of LSF features for node A by its surrounding nodes.

The LSF features for node A by node B and node C are given as:

$$LSF_{B-A-C} = \frac{(V_1.\ cos\theta_1 - V_2.\ cos\theta_2) \times (V_1.\ sin\theta_1 - V_2.\ sin\theta_2)}{(x_1 - x_2) \times (y_1 - y_2)} \tag{8.4}$$

where

- $(x_1,\ y_1)$ is the location of surrounding node B
- $(x_2,\ y_2)$ is the location of surrounding node C
- (V_1) is the velocity of surrounding node B
- (V_2) is the velocity of surrounding node C
- (θ_1) is the orientation of surrounding node B with respect to node A
- (θ_2) is the orientation of surrounding node C with respect to node B

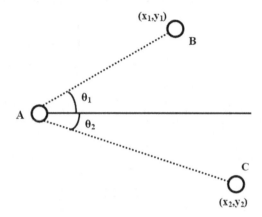

FIGURE 8.2 Illustration of LSF features.

Similarly, the cumulative LSF is computed for node A for all of its surrounding nodes using the following equation:

$$Cumulative\ LSF = \sum_{\in node-pairs} LSF_{\in node-pairs} \qquad (8.5)$$

Probabilistic Features

This feature determines the number of packets correctly transmitted and received on the test node by its surrounding nodes. The abrupt drop in packet transmission or reception indicates that the node is affected by malicious attackers in a WSN environment. The probabilistic feature of the particular node is illustrated in Figure 8.3.

The probabilistic feature of the single node in a WSN is:

$$PF_{node\ B} = \frac{e^{-\alpha_2 t} + e^{-\beta_2 t}}{1 - (\alpha_2 . \beta_2)} \qquad (8.6)$$

where

- α_2 is the number of packets sent by node B
- β_2 is the number of packets received by node B over the certain time period t

The probabilistic feature of the test node A is computed using its surrounding nodes:

$$PF(A) = \sum_{i=1}^{N} PF_{node-i} \qquad (8.7)$$

The number of surrounding nodes is represented by N.

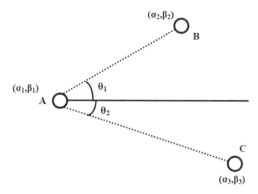

FIGURE 8.3 Extraction of probabilistic features.

Randomness Features

The randomness feature of the individual node in a WSN is given by:

$$R_f = \sum_{i=1}^{N} W_i \cdot (1 - S_i) \tag{8.8}$$

where the weight of the surrounding nodes are represented by W_i and the scaling factor of the surrounding node is depicted by S_i.

The weight of the individual node is based on the computation of the number of packets transmitted, received on the test node within a certain time period t and it is depicted by magnitude function, M_i, and the orientation between the test node with its surrounding nodes and it is depicted by orientation function, W_θ. The weight of the test node is computed using the following equation:

$$W_i = \frac{M_i}{M_i + M_\theta} \tag{8.9}$$

The magnitude function, M_i, of the individual node is given as:

$$M_i = \frac{\alpha_1 \beta_1 + (\alpha_1 - \beta_1)}{\alpha_1 + \beta_1} \tag{8.10}$$

The orientation function, M_θ, of the individual node is given as:

$$M_\theta = \frac{\theta_{A-i} \times r_i}{\theta_{A-i} + 90^\circ} \tag{8.11}$$

The radius between the test node and its surrounding node i is represented by r_i. The orientation between node A and its surrounding nodes is represented by θ_{A-i}.

The scaling factor is an adjustable factor that correlates the weight of the node with its self-properties and the scaling factor of the individual node is given by:

$$S_i = \frac{w_i \cdot r_i}{1 - w_i \cdot r_i} \tag{8.12}$$

Credit Features

Credit features are the value extracted features from each node in WSNs. This feature gives the credits for each individual node and it will also be used to differentiate the non-malicious node from a malicious node in a WSN. The credit feature of the individual node is computed using the following equation:

$$CF_{node} = \frac{S_{p1} + R_{p2}}{1 - (S_{p1} - R_{p2})} \tag{8.13}$$

where

- S_{p1} is the number of packets sent by an individual node
- R_{p2} is number of packets received by an individual node

Classification

Classification is the process of classifying the test node in a WSN into either a malicious node or non-malicious node. In this chapter, a neural network (NN) classifier is adopted in order to classify each node in a WSN to identify its misbehavior functionalities. The NN classifier is categorized into two types: radial NN and feed forward back propagation (FFBP) NN. The classification accuracy of the radial NN is low and it is not suitable for classifying the large number of nodes. Due to this limitation, FFBP neural networks are used in this chapter and it constitutes multiple layers as input, hidden and output layers. Each layer consists of multiple neurons to interconnect with other layers in a NN architecture. In this chapter, one input layer and one output layer with five hidden layers are selected for classification of nodes in a WSN. The number of layers is chosen after several trials and tests. The number of features in a feature vector is equal to the number of neurons in an input layer. Each hidden layer contains 12 neurons with different weight functions. The value of the weight functions are based on the input features. This NN classifier is trained using log-sigmoid activation function with activation values ranging from 0.1 to 0.6 in order to obtain high classification accuracy. This trained NN classifier produces two different classes and class high indicates that the test node is malicious. Class low in the NN classification stage indicates that the test node is non-malicious.

The NN classifier is defined as an information processing system inspired by the structure of the human brain. Inspired by the biological neurons in the brain, NNs consist of a number of interconnected neurons. A neuron is an information-processing unit that receives several signals from its input links, each of which has a weight assigned to it. These weights correspond to synaptic efficiency in biological neurons. Weights are the basic means of the long-term memory in NNs. Neural networks are adaptive, non-linear statistical data modeling or decision-making tools.

NNs can be used to model complex relationships between inputs and outputs or to find patterns in data, thereby making it suitable for brain tumor segmentation. It is composed of a large number of highly interconnected processing elements (neurons) working in unison to solve specific problems. Feed-forward ANNs allow signals to travel one way only, i.e. from input to output. Feed-forward ANNs tend to be straightforward networks that associate inputs with outputs. They are extensively used in pattern recognition. The behavior of an ANN depends on both the weights and the input–output function (transfer function) that is specified for the units. This function can be grouped into one of the three categories:

- linear (or ramp)
- threshold
- sigmoid $f(\alpha) = \dfrac{1}{1 + exp^{-\alpha}}$

The activation function controls the amplitude of the output of the neuron. An acceptable range of output is usually between 0 and 1, or -1 and 1. The functional model illustrating this process is shown in Figure 8.4. The output of the neuron, O_k, is produced due to the outcome of an activation function, A_k, such that:

$$A_k = \sum_{h=1}^{q} W_{kh} P_h \tag{8.14}$$

The classification approaches require only features of the normal and malicious node that are extracted, trained and classified. The other conditions are not required for the classification process like in centralized algorithms. In this way, the classification

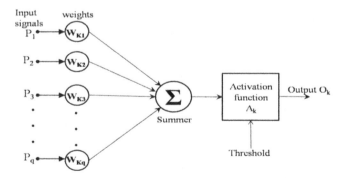

FIGURE 8.4 Practical model of the neural network.

approach is superior to conventional methods for the malicious node detection and mitigation process.

Result and Discussion

Singh et al. (2017) incorporated the fuzzy rules with hybrid methodology to identify the malicious nodes from normal test nodes in a large WSN environment. The authors achieved 99.4% detection rate for a Sybil malicious attack, 98.2% detection rate for wormhole malicious attacks and 99.2% detection rate for hello food malicious node attacks in a WSN. Sharma and Gambhir (2017) developed a methodology for the detection of malicious nodes using a reputation-based cooperative approach. The authors implemented a cooperative technique for differentiating the trusty nodes from untrusty nodes in a WSN environment. Nachammai and Radha (2016) proposed a trust-based approach to detect the untrusty nodes. The authors analyzed their proposed trust methodology against various kinds of attacks such as black hole attacks, gray hole attacks and DoS attacks.

The authors analyzed their performance of the proposed work in terms of detection rate and classification accuracy. Koriata (2016) used the weighted trust evaluation (WTE) technique to differentiate the trusty nodes from malicious nodes in a WSN environment. Sukanesh et al. (2016) proposed an energy-aware malicious node identification technique using dynamic probabilistic flooding (DPF). The rebroadcast probability of each node in a WSN environment is analyzed with respect to various qualities of service parameters.

Turkanović et al. (2014) proposed a key management methodology for heterogeneous wireless sensor networks to achieve high security from attackers. The authors analyzed their performance using flooding attacks in nodes of a WSN environment. Various cryptographic techniques were analyzed on their proposed method to validate the results. The trust behavior of the nodes in a WSN were monitored and compared with reading values in a fixed attribution method in order to avoid the manual error rate during the test period of the malicious node detection process.

The proposed malicious node detection technique is applied on the set of 100 nodes in a WSN environment using the following specifications, as mentioned in Table 8.2. These 100 mobile nodes are randomly spread over the area of 1,500 m × 1,500 m with the mobile velocity of 100 m/s in a WSN. The nodes use DSR protocol to find the shortest distance between source and destination nodes. The initial energy of the individual node is set to 1,200 J and each node consumes 90 mJ of energy for each and every transaction. In this chapter, Network Simulator Version 2 is used to simulate and verify the proposed malicious node detection system. Initially, 10 trust nodes in a WSN are converted into malicious nodes and spread with other trust nodes in a mobile environment. The performance of the entire WSN network is monitored by determining the PDR, detection rate and latency. Then, the number of malicious nodes is increased in this present WSN system in order to prove the robustness of the proposed malicious node detection system.

TABLE 8.2 Initial simulation setup

SPECIFICATION PARAMETERS	INITIAL VALUE
Area of the simulation environment	1,500 m × 1,500 m
Energy	1,200 J per individual node
Moving velocity of the node	100 m/s
Channel	Two-way ground wireless channel
Number of mobile nodes	100
Routing protocol	Dynamic source routing (DSR)

The performance of the malicious node detection system is analyzed in terms of detection rate, PDR and latency.

The detection rate defines the number of malicious nodes detected in a WSN system with respect to the total number of malicious nodes in a WSN environment. The value of detection rate ranges from 0 and 100 and it is measured in percents. The performance of the proposed system is robust if the detection rate reaches more than 90%. Table 8.3 shows the performance results of the proposed system in terms of detection rate with conventional methodologies. The proposed methodology discussed in this chapter achieves a detection rate of 99.1% with the presence of ten malicious nodes and a detection rate of 93.7% in the presence of 50 malicious nodes. This method also achieves a high average detection rate of 96.16%, higher than that of all other conventional methodologies (Figure 8.5).

Each node is analyzed by its packet delivery ratio, as the ratio between number of packets received correctly and the total number of packets. The value of PDR ranges from 0 and 100 and it is measured in percent.

The performance of the proposed system is robust if the PDR reaches more than 90%. Table 8.4 shows the performance results of the proposed system in terms of the PDR with conventional methodologies. The proposed methodology stated in this chapter achieves 98.5% PDR in the presence of ten malicious nodes and 91.4% PDR for the presence of 50 malicious nodes. This proposed method achieves 95.2% PDR as an average value, which is a high detection rate when compared with conventional methods (Figure 8.6).

A malicious node in a WSN frequently transmits the transmission request message to all of its surrounding nodes to interrupt the transmission and reception functions of the surrounding nodes. This degrades the performance of the entire network. The network without malicious nodes consumes less latency for the packet transmission between source and destination nodes. The network with malicious nodes consumes high latency for the packet transmission between source and destination nodes. Table 8.5 shows the performance results of the proposed system in terms of latency with conventional methodologies. The proposed methodology stated in this chapter achieves 20.6 ms of latency for the presence of ten malicious nodes and 36.9 ms of latency for the presence of 50 malicious nodes. This proposed method achieves 28.1 ms of latency as average value, which is low latency when compared with conventional methods.

TABLE 8.3   Performance results on detection rate

NUMBER OF MALICIOUS PEERS	DETECTION RATE (%)			
	PROPOSED WORK	SINGH ET AL. (2017)	KORIATA (2016)	YIM AND CHOI (2012)
10	99.1	95.8	96.4	94.2
20	97.8	93.1	94.3	92.8
30	95.7	91.4	91.8	90.3
40	94.5	85.8	90.1	86.7
50	93.7	81.4	85.7	84.7
Average	96.16	89.5	91.66	89.74

Figure 8.7 shows the graphical illustration of latency for the proposed method with conventional methods. Table 8.6 shows the performance comparisons of the proposed methodologies with conventional methodologies as Singh et al. (2017), Koriata (2016) and Yim and Choi (2012) in terms of detection rate, PDR and latency.

Figure 8.8 shows the graphical illustration of performance comparison for the proposed method with conventional methods.

The presence of malicious nodes in a WSN environment degrades the performance of the other trusty nodes in WSN networks. This presence of malicious nodes also leads to link failures between nodes in a WSN. Hence, this chapter proposes feature-based malicious node detection and classification system using neural network

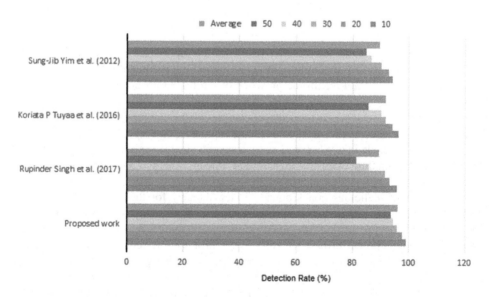

FIGURE 8.5   Graphical illustration of detection rate.

TABLE 8.4   Performance results on PDR

NUMBER OF MALICIOUS PEERS	PDR (%)			
	PROPOSED WORK	SINGH ET AL. (2017)	KORIATA (2016)	YIM AND CHOI (2012)
10	98.5	95.1	96.3	95.7
20	97.5	92.6	93.2	92.1
30	95.1	91.5	91.6	86.5
40	93.5	85.4	86.5	82.6
50	91.4	82.8	84.3	81.7
Average	95.2	89.4	90.3	87.7

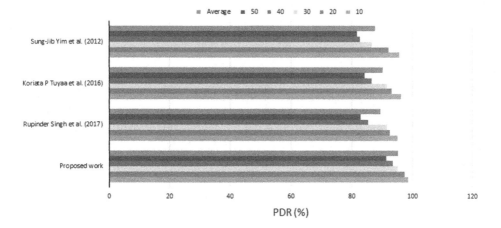

FIGURE 8.6   Graphical illustration of PDR (%).

TABLE 8.5   Performance results on latency

NUMBER OF MALICIOUS PEERS	LATENCY (MS)			
	PROPOSED WORK	SINGH ET AL. (2017)	KORIATA (2016)	YIM AND CHOI (2012)
10	20.6	39.8	25.7	28.6
20	22.8	41.7	27.5	29.6
30	27.5	45.9	29.6	32.9
40	32.7	47.6	33.8	38.5
50	36.9	48.5	35.7	45.7
Average	28.1	44.7	30.4	30.4

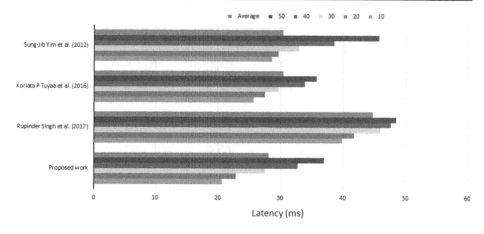

FIGURE 8.7 Graphical illustration of latency.

TABLE 8.6 Performance comparisons with conventional methodologies

METHODOLOGY	DETECTION RATE (%)	PDR (%)	LATENCY (MS)
Proposed method	96.16	95.2	28.1
Singh et al. (2017)	89.5	89.4	44.7
Koriata (2016)	91.66	90.3	30.4
Yim and Choi (2012)	89.74	87.7	30.4

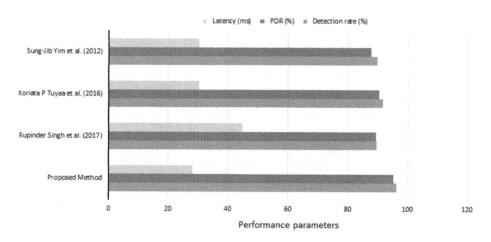

FIGURE 8.8 Graphical illustration of performance comparison.

classifiers. This proposed system consists of feature extraction and classifications as modules. The features that describe the behavior of the individual node are extracted from each node and these extracted features are trained and classified using a neural network classifier. This classifier classifies the test node into a trust node or malicious node based on the extracted features.

The proposed methodology stated in this research work achieves 98.5% PDR for the presence of ten malicious nodes and 91.4% PDR for the presence of 50 malicious nodes. This proposed method achieves 95.2% PDR as an average value, which is a high detection rate when compared with conventional methods. The proposed methodology stated in this research work achieves 99.1% detection rate for the presence of ten malicious nodes and 93.7% detection rate for the presence of 50 malicious nodes.

This proposed method achieves 96.16% detection rate as an average value, which is a high detection rate when compared with conventional methods. The proposed methodology stated in this research work achieves 20.6 ms of latency for the presence of 10 malicious nodes and 36.9 ms of latency for the presence of 50 malicious nodes. This proposed method achieves 28.1 ms of latency as an average value, which is low latency when compared with conventional methods.

In this research work, an efficient link failure detection algorithm is further proposed to detect the link failures in a WSN environment. This link failure detection methodology detects the link failure nodes in both static and dynamic environments. The proposed algorithm works effectively on large-scale sensor networks that detect the failure nodes when compared with conventional methods. The proposed link failure detection algorithm achieves 98.4% PDR and consumes 30.8 ms of latency as performance evaluation metrics.

In this research work, ANFIS classification approach based link failure detection methodology is also proposed in order to classify each link into either strong or weak. The performance of the proposed link failure detection system is analyzed in terms of PDR, latency and detection rate, by varying the number of malicious nodes in a WSN environment. The proposed link failure detection algorithm achieves 99% PDR and also achieves 19.34 ms of latency using the ANFIS classification approach. The proposed methodology stated in this research work also achieves 99.9% detection rate for the presence of 10 malicious nodes and 98.1% detection rate for the presence of 50 malicious nodes.

NOTES

---

1 Chipcon. SmartRF CC1000 single chip very low power RF transceiver. http://www.chipcon. com/files/CC1000 Data Sheet 2 1.pdf, 2003.
2 MICA2 radio stack for TinyOS. http://webs.cs.berkeley.edu/tos/tinyos1.x/doc/mica2radio/ CC1000.html, 2003.

REFERENCES

Atakli, I. M., Hu, H., Chen, Y., Ku, W. S., & Su, Z. (2008). Malicious node detection in wireless sensor networks using weighted trust evaluation. In *Proceedings of the 2008 Spring Simulation Multiconference*, 836–843.

Baig, Z. A., & Khan, S. A. (2010). Fuzzy logic-based decision making for detecting distributed node exhaustion attacks in wireless sensor networks. In *2010 Second International Conference on Future Networks*, 185–189.

Bao, F., Chen, R., Chang, M., & Cho, J.-H. (2012). Hierarchical trust management for wireless sensor networks and its applications to trust-based routing and intrusion detection. *IEEE Transactions on Network and Service Management, 9*(2), 169–183.

Cao, Z., Deng, H., Guan, Z., & Chen, Z. (2012). Information-theoretic modeling of false data filtering schemes in wireless sensor networks. *ACM Transactions on Sensor Networks (TOSN), 8*(2), 1–19.

Celenk, M., Conley, T., Graham, J., & Willis, J. (2008). Anomaly prediction in network traffic using adaptive Wiener filtering and ARMA modeling. In *2008 IEEE International Conference on Systems, Man and Cybernetics*, 3548–3553.

Chang, J.-M., Tsou, P.-C., Woungang, I., Chao, H.-C., & Lai, C.-F. (2014). Defending against collaborative attacks by malicious nodes in MANETs: A cooperative bait detection approach. *IEEE Systems Journal, 9*(1), 65–75.

Chen, R.-C., Haung, Y.-F., & Hsieh, C.-F. (2010). Ranger intrusion detection system for wireless sensor networks with Sybil attack based on ontology. *New Aspects of Applied Informatics, Biomedical Electronics and Informatics and Communications*.

Chen, R. C., Hsieh, C.-F., & Huang, Y.-F. (2010). An isolation intrusion detection system for hierarchical wireless sensor networks. *Journal of Networks, 5*(3), 335–342.

Crosby, G. V., Hester, L., & Pissinou, N. (2011). Location-aware, trust-based detection and isolation of compromised nodes in wireless sensor networks. *IJ Network Security, 12*(2), 107–117.

Curiac, D.-I., Banias, O., Dragan, F., Volosencu, C., & Dranga, O. (2007). Malicious node detection in wireless sensor networks using an autoregression technique. In *International Conference on Networking and Services (ICNS'07)*, 83.

Deng, X.-M., & Xiong, Y. (2011). A new protocol for the detection of node replication attacks in mobile wireless sensor networks. *Journal of Computer Science and Technology, 26*(4), 732–743.

Ganesan, P., Venugopalan, R., Peddabachagari, P., Dean, A., Mueller, F., & Sichitiu, M. (2003). Analyzing and modeling encryption overhead for sensor network nodes. In *Proceedings of the 2nd ACM International Conference on Wireless Sensor Networks and Applications*, 151–159.

George, N., & Parani, T. K. (2014). Detection of node clones in wireless sensor network using detection protocols. *ArXiv Preprint ArXiv:1403.2548*.

Gopalakrishnan, S., & Ganeshkumar, P. (2014). Intrusion detection in mobile ad hoc network using secure routing for attacker identification protocol. *American Journal of Applied Sciences, 11*(8), 1391.

Hill, J., & Culler, D. (2002). *A wireless embedded sensor architecture for system-level optimization*. Citeseer.

Hollar, S. E.-A. (2000). *Cots dust*.

Huo, G., & Wang, X. (2008). DIDS: A dynamic model of intrusion detection system in wireless sensor networks. *2008 International Conference on Information and Automation*, 374–378.

Jadidoleslamy, H. (2011). A hierarchical intrusion detection architecture for wireless sensor networks. *International Journal of Network Security & Its Applications*, 3(5), 131.

Ju, L., Li, H., Liu, Y., Xue, W., Li, K., & Chi, Z. (2010). An improved intrusion detection scheme based on weighted trust evaluation for wireless sensor networks. *2010 Proceedings of the 5th International Conference on Ubiquitous Information Technologies and Applications*, 1–6.

Kahn, J. M., Katz, R. H., & Pister, K. S. J. (1999). Next century challenges: mobile networking for "Smart Dust.", In *Proceedings of the 5th Annual ACM/IEEE International Conference on Mobile Computing and Networking*, 271–278.

Kahn, J. M., Katz, R. H., & Pister, K. S. J. (2000). Emerging challenges: Mobile networking for "smart dust." *Journal of Communications and Networks*, 2(3), 188–196.

Khalil, I., Bagchi, S., & Shroff, N. B. (2008). MOBIWORP: Mitigation of the wormhole attack in mobile multihop wireless networks. *Ad Hoc Networks*, 6(3), 344–362.

Koriata, P. T. (2016). *Enhanced weighted trust evaluation scheme for detection of malicious nodes in wireless sensor networks*. University of Nairobi.

Lee, J., Choi, B., & Kim, E. (2013). Novel range-free localization based on multidimensional support vector regression trained in the primal space. *IEEE Transactions on Neural Networks and Learning Systems*, 24(7), 1099–1113.

Lu, R., Lin, X., Zhu, H., Liang, X., & Shen, X. (2011). BECAN: A bandwidth-efficient co-operative authentication scheme for filtering injected false data in wireless sensor networks. *IEEE Transactions on Parallel and Distributed Systems*, 23(1), 32–43.

Mamun, M. S. I., & Kabir, A. F. M. S. (2010). Hierarchical design based intrusion detection system for wireless ad hoc sensor network. *International Journal of Network Security & Its Applications (IJNSA)*, 2(3), 102–117.

Mao, Y. (2010). A semantic-based intrusion detection framework for wireless sensor network. *INC2010: 6th International Conference on Networked Computing*, 1–5.

Misra, S., Krishna, P. V., & Abraham, K. I. (2010). Energy efficient learning solution for intrusion detection in wireless sensor networks. *2010 Second International Conference on COMmunication Systems and NETworks (COMSNETS 2010)*, 1–6.

Nachammai, M., & Radha, N. (2016). An improved trust based approach for detecting malicious nodes in MANET. *International Journal of Computer Trends and Technology (IJCTT)*, 41(1), 54–58.

Nakul, P. (2013). A survey on malicious node detection in wireless sensor networks. *International Journal of Science and Research*, 2(1), 691–694.

Oh, S. H., Hong, C. O., & Choi, Y. H. (2012). A malicious and malfunctioning node detection scheme for wireless sensor networks. *Wireless Sensor Network*, 4(03), 84.

Papadimitratos, P., & Haas, Z. (2002). Secure routing for mobile ad hoc networks. *Communication Networks and Distributed Systems Modeling and Simulation Conference (CNDS 2002)*, CONF.

Pires, W. R., de Paula Figueiredo, T. H., Wong, H. C., & Loureiro, A. A. F. (2004). Malicious node detection in wireless sensor networks. In *18th International Parallel and Distributed Processing Symposium, 2004. Proceedings*, 24.

Rajasegarar, S., Leckie, C., & Palaniswami, M. (2008). Anomaly detection in wireless sensor networks. *IEEE Wireless Communications*, 15(4), 34–40.

Rappaport, T. S. (1996). *Wireless communications: principles and practice* (Vol. 2). Prentice Hall PTR: New Jersey.

Sa, M., & Rath, A. K. (2011). A simple agent based model for detecting abnormal event patterns in distributed wireless sensor networks. *Proceedings of the 2011 International Conference on Communication, Computing & Security*, 67–70.

Sei, Y., & Ohsuga, A. (2013). Need only one bit: Light-weight packet marking for detecting compromised nodes in WSNs. *Proc. 7th SECURWARE*, 134–143.

Sharma, S., & Gambhir, S. (2017). CRCMD&R: Cluster and reputation based cooperative malicious node detection & removal scheme in MANETs. *2017 11th International Conference on Intelligent Systems and Control (ISCO)*, 336–340.

Singh, R., Singh, J., & Singh, R. (2017). Fuzzy based advanced hybrid intrusion detection system to detect malicious nodes in wireless sensor networks. *Wireless Communications and Mobile Computing, 2017*.

Stallings, W. (2006). *Cryptography and network security, 4/E*. Pearson Education India.

Sukanesh, R., Edsor, E., & Aarthylakshmi, M. (2016). Energy efficient malicious node detection scheme in wireless networks. *2016 10th international conference on intelligent systems and control (ISCO)*, 1–6.

Sun, B., Shan, X., Wu, K., & Xiao, Y. (2012). Anomaly detection based secure in-network aggregation for wireless sensor networks. *IEEE Systems Journal*, 7(1), 13–25.

Thakre, B., & Sonekar, S. V. (n.d.). *An algorithmic approach for the detection of malicious nodes in a cluster based adhoc wireless networks*.

Tiwari, M., Arya, K. V., Choudhari, R., & Choudhary, K. S. (2009). Designing intrusion detection to detect black hole and selective forwarding attack in WSN based on local information. *2009 Fourth International Conference on Computer Sciences and Convergence Information Technology*, 824–828.

Turkanović, M., Brumen, B., & Hölbl, M. (2014). A novel user authentication and key agreement scheme for heterogeneous ad hoc wireless sensor networks, based on the Internet of Things notion. *Ad Hoc Networks*, 20, 96–112.

Vasiliou, A., & Economides, A. A. (2006). MANETs for environmental monitoring. *2006 International Telecommunications Symposium*, 813–818.

Warneke, B., Last, M., Liebowitz, B., & Pister, K. S. J. (2001). Smart dust: Communicating with a cubic-millimeter computer. *Computer*, 34(1), 44–51.

Xu, Z., Hsu, H., Chen, X., Zhu, S., & Hurson, A. R. (2012). AK-PPM: An authenticated packet attribution scheme for mobile ad hoc networks. In *International Workshop on Recent Advances in Intrusion Detection*, 147–168.

Yan, K. Q., Wang, S. C., & Liu, C. W. (2009). A hybrid intrusion detection system of cluster-based wireless sensor networks. *Proceedings of the International MultiConference of Engineers and Computer Scientists*, 1, 18–20.

Ye, F., Luo, H., Lu, S., & Zhang, L. (2005). Statistical en-route filtering of injected false data in sensor networks. *IEEE Journal on Selected Areas in Communications*, 23(4), 839–850.

Ye, F., Yang, H., & Liu, Z. (2007). Catching "moles" in sensor networks. *27th International Conference on Distributed Computing Systems (ICDCS'07)*, 69.

Yim, S.-J., & Choi, Y.-H. (2012). *Neighbor-based malicious node detection in wireless sensor networks*.

Yu, C. M., Tsou, Y. T., Lu, C. S., & Kuo, S. Y. (2013). Localized algorithms for detection of node replication attacks in mobile sensor networks. *IEEE Transactions on Information Forensics and Security*, 8(5), 754–768.

Yu, S. M., & Kim, S.-L. (2011). Optimal detection of spatial opportunity in wireless networks. *IEEE Communications Letters*, 15(4), 395–397.

Zhang, Q., Zhou, X., Yang, F., & Li, X. (2007). Contact-based traceback in wireless sensor networks. *2007 International Conference on Wireless Communications, Networking and Mobile Computing*, 2487–2490.

The Distributed Signature Scheme (DSS) Based on RSA

9

INTRODUCTION

The distributed signature scheme (DSS) is another important security service. It enables sensor nodes to communicate securely with each other. The main problem is to establish a secure signature between communicating nodes. However, some special features (i.e., resource constraint, impracticalness of protecting or monitoring each individual node physically as well as their applications which usually being supported by many components such as routing and localization) of sensor networks make it particularly challenging to provide security services for sensor networks. This chapter describes a secret distribution scheme for sensor networks that achieves automatic secret redistribution. The goal is to support distributing the secret among new members joining a sensor network without involving a trusted agent or intervention from the user. Our analysis indicates that our new schemes have some nice features compared with the previous methods. In particular, the system is efficient. Second, it guarantees automatic key distribution after initializations. Third, it is not urgent for key distribution and, finally, it automatically interact nodes coalition.

Wireless sensor networks have recently emerged as important means to study and interact with the physical world. A sensor network typically consists of a large number of tiny sensor nodes and possibly a few powerful control nodes (also called base stations). Many protocols and algorithms (e.g., routing, localization) will not work in hostile environments without security protection (Liu & Ning, 2007).

The use of aggregation in a WSN allows an increase in the efficiency and significantly survivability of sensor nodes. In this presentation, many aspects of the WSN are being examined including security and efficient data aggregation (Zhu et al., 2004; Estrin et al., 1999; Hu & Evans, 2003; Madden et al., 2002; Przydatek et al., 2003;

DOI: 10.1201/9781003257608-9

241

Shrivastava et al., 2004). For example, we will use a base station (BS) to define the integral characteristic of any part of a WSN; and assign one of the nodes as an aggregator for clear elaboration and understanding of our presentation. The node will gather the needed information from the area, calculate the aggregation functions (i.e., average, min, max) and transfer this value to the BS. By doing so, this will facilitate the decrease of total transmission cost rather than with the use of an aggregator. But, all in all there is a need of special and reliable aggregation algorithms when it comes to node failing fulfilling their tasks, e.g., when the adversary can capture the nodes and change their functionality or the aggregator is compromised and brings total destruction to its function, i.e., when an aggregator is compromised and sends the wrong information to the BS. For solving this kind of problem, special cryptography procedures can be used (Eschenauer & Gligor, 2002; Chan et al., 2003; Hwang & Kim, 2004; Liu et al., 2005; Schneier, 2007; Gura et al., 2004). Some of the solutions cited might allow the BS to define an incorrect aggregation result with a high probability. And in this case the aggregation might be called reliable.

It's clear that it's necessary to provide reliability requirements to transmit some extra data from the aggregator to the BS. In this case, we argue that the data capacity (size) should be minimized with given reliability. In the existing reliability aggregation protocols at present, the size of extra data used is sufficiently high. This sets conditions and motivations for further interest in creating new reliable aggregation protocols, though it should be noted that creating special protocols for a WSN also have some shortcomings, mainly the high number of keys to be kept by each sensor. However, in providing reliable aggregation in a WSN, the key management protocol issues should also be realized. The present solutions used for classical networks are unable to implement some of these options to a WSN due to the sensors' limitations and unfeasibility of using the sensors' infrastructure.

When it comes to providing security services in sensor networks, it also proves to be a very challenging task. With the same lane of creating reliability in data aggregation, we introduce our finding to solve the problem of scheme distribution for signing the accurate information within nodes participating in transmitting the final information to the BS. Having this kind of mechanism will allow a substantial decrease in energy consumption by eliminating the transmission of fake packets within the sensor networks, meanwhile enhancing the accuracy of security.

In this chapter, we have presented a DSS design based on RSA (well-known encryption system used in a large amount of applications). Our scheme has three advantages. First, the mathematics presentations are proven secure. Second, the scheme is efficient; third, together, we have proposed a secure, efficient proactive RSA-based scheme with three security properties that did not exist in previous schemes.

RELATED WORK

There are a few different notions of signature related to distributed signatures.

Threshold Signatures

Threshold signatures have received considerable attention (e.g., see Damgård & Dupont, 2005; Desmedt, 1987; Desmedt & Frankel, 1989; Gennaro et al., 1996, 2001, 2008; Li et al., 2007; Stinson & Strobl, 2001). A signature can be created from the participation of any t or more signers among n potential signers. When $2t - 1 \leq n$, the scheme can be made robust. To realize robustness, Gennaro et al. (1996) proposed two approaches to verify RSA signature fragments, which are based on the non-interactive information checking protocol, and undeniable signature requiring interactions between the verifier and the signers. The robust threshold RSA signature schemes also have been discussed in a random oracle model (Gennaro et al., 2008; Li et al., 2007) and without random oracles (Li et al., 2007; Damgård & Dupont, 2005). There is also a threshold version for digital signature standard (DSS) signatures (Gennaro et al., 2001).

Distributed Signatures

A RSA-based DSS for general access structures was proposed by Herranz et al. (2003). A RSA-based scheme in the standard model was given by Damgård and Thorbek (2006), which introduced linear integer secret sharing to distribute RSA secret keys. Stinson and Strobl (2001) generalized discrete-logarithm-based Schnorr's signature (Pointcheval & Stern, 2000; Schnorr, 1991) into a threshold version. Distributed Schnorr's signature was studied by Herranz and Sácz (2003), which also served as a building block for constructing a distributed proxy signature (Herranz & Sáez, 2003, 2004). However, these schemes are analyzed in the random oracle model.

Mesh Signatures

As a generalization of ring signatures, mesh signatures (Boyen, 2007) can be generated by a qualified set of valid atomic signatures with anonymity. The only construction known (Boyen, 2007) has complexities linear in the number of signers. In fact, the corresponding arborescent monotone access structure is a linear combination of threshold gates, as both AND and OR gates are special cases of threshold access structures. However, this scheme (Boyen, 2007) cannot support monotone access structures without arborescent representations. Both distributed signature and mesh signature can be used to express that the signers are from a qualified group. A mesh signature can be generated by a single signer, while a distributed signature is usually generated by multiple signers.

Attribute-Based Signatures

In attribute-based signatures (Maji et al., 2011), each signer is assigned a set of attributes. A signer can generate a signature if the claim predicate is satisfied by the attributes. Both monotone (Maji et al., 2011; Herranz et al., 2012) and non-monotone access structures (Okamoto & Takashima, 2011, 2013) can be realized by span programs. Like distributed signatures, the scheme has collusion resistance such that signers cannot create a signature that none of them are qualified to, even if they pool their attributes together. Unlike distribute signatures, an attribute-based signature is generated by a single signer (with a qualified set of attributes). The claim-predicate can be different for each signature, which inherently makes the signature more complex, either in terms of signature size or underlying assumption. For example, the schemes of Okamoto and Takashima (2011, 2013), which are based on decisional linear assumption, produce signatures of lengths that increase linearly with the complexity of the access structure. The attribute-based signature scheme with threshold access structure due to Herranz et al. (2012) is constant-size, yet based on a non-static assumption. Bellare and Fuchsbauer (2014) considered a more general primitive known as a policy-based signature, which allows a signer to generate a signature on some message that fits in some policy, while the privacy of the policy is preserved.

RSA-BASED SECURE SCHEMES

Blakley and Shamir invented secret sharing schemes independently. In Blakley's scheme (Gennaro et al., 2008), the intersection of m of n vector spaces yields a one-dimensional vector that corresponds to the secret. The Wong et al. scheme (Wong et al., 2002) is one of several to catch a dealer that attempts to distribute invalid shares. Desmedt and Jajodia (1997) also present a protocol to perform non-interactive verifiable secret redistribution (VSR) that mitigates these problems in static sensor networks. VSR divides the sensor field into control groups each with a control node. Data exchange between nodes within a control group happens through the mediation of the control head that provides the common key. The keys are refreshed periodically and the control nodes are changed periodically to enhance security. SECOS enhances the survivability of the network by handling compromise and failures of control nodes. Gennaro et al. present a verification of a signature using a regular public key and a standard verification procedure; hence, the verifier of a signature does not need to be aware of the form (centralized or distributed) in which the signature was generated, or the parties involved, nor does the signature increase in size as a function of the number of signers.

Our DSS scheme differs from previous VSR schemes in that it achieves automatic secret redistribution without the use of agents. Also, unlike in VSR schemes, with signature setting actions, node members can associate independently in our DSS. However, secret key distribution protocol is un-interactive and doesn't require agent participation after scheme initialization.

Kong et al. proposed a proactive RSA scheme for large-scale, ad hoc networks (Kong et al., 2003; Luo et al., 2004). In their scheme, every node in an ad hoc network has a secret share of the secret key (the private key d). Nodes within one-hop distance jointly perform issuing certificates and refresh their secret shares. The scheme is efficient. Unfortunately, the scheme has proved faulty (Narasimha et al., 2003). All the previous schemes (Blakley, 1979; Eschenauer & Gligor, 2002; Chan et al., 2003) can be considered special instances in this framework. Also, Rui-shan et al. (Zhang & Chen, 2007), have presented a new proactive RSA scheme for ad hoc networks, which include four protocols, the initial key distribution protocol, the share refreshing protocol, the share distribution protocol and the signature generation protocol. Their work is mainly based on the use of an efficient proactive threshold RSA signature scheme. The initial key distribution protocol is used to distribute the initial secret shares to $2t + 1$ R nodes. Before distributing the secret key, they assume that a setup process has been carried out in which the RSA key generation took place and the RSA key pair has been computed, whereby in our work the agent is used to initialize the distributed signature's scheme and, hence, the remaining process is independently operated.

By instantiating the components in the previous frameworks, we further develop our DSS based on RSA with an automatic signature setting procedure that provides coalition between (nodes) members and system with a self-organizing property, i.e. the agent is not involved after initialization and during the secret distribution process.

RSA-BASED DSS

Using only symmetric algorithms with the authentication of sending data from sensors to the BS has some disadvantages as well, e.g., only the BS might be able to authenticate the final report sent by the aggregator toward the BS. This means there is a chance of a compromised node being sent into a network and, by chance, this fake packet might only be detected or thrown off by the BS at the end point. With accomplishment of the process, the sensor node's resources would have been consumed by sending the fake packet.

For sensor networks with more powerful nodes, solving this kind of problem can be based on the use of a distributive asymmetric signature. This sort of signature assumes the distribution of "digital signature of asymmetric algorithm secret key" by a threshold circuit (scheme) key distributed between the all scheme members. Also, this scheme assumes the presence of a protocol that allows coalition from a given number of members to compute a digital signature for a given message in a distributed manner. Regarding the fake packet filtering task in a WSN, the digital asymmetric signature algorithm can be used as follows.

The agent chooses and distributes a digital signature's chosen algorithm secret key between all the sensors and, hence, all the sensors are initialized by the public key. By sending the aggregation result to the BS, the results are signed by a given number of sensors using a signature distribution protocol. Furthermore, each sensor, retransmitting a data packet by using a public key, can check the packet itself and, if the signature does not surpass the checking, it is automatically ejected from the network.

Distributed Signature Features

To effectively work as a system, distributed signature protocols should have some features:

- Independent work of the members during the initialization of signature. If the number of members is increased, this feature is enabled to not initialize this protocol again. Also, it reduces the signature setting delay.
- Self-organization, i.e., the system should be able to work automatically after initialization.
- Distribution of the new projection of the secret should be non-interactive.

For the interactive protocol, assuming the process of data exchange between working (nodes) members is an essential shortcoming due to limited traffic capacity existing in today's many WSNs, additionally it increases energy consumption, whereas the synchronization in a WSN is necessary. The schemes that can guarantee security are suitable for WSN security at present.

A DSS with two features described previously can easily be established based on an El-Gammal or DSS digital signature (ElGamal, 1985). Unlike these digital signatures, based on a RSA digital signature, no existing work, to the best of our knowledge, has addressed the issue of developing distributed signature schemes with the previously listed features at the moment. However, a RSA digital signature has one important feature that does not exist in El-Gammal and DSS schemes. For the RSA signature, the signature checking procedure is substantially accelerated if a public key value is correctly chosen. This characteristic provides a significant advantage for RSA distributed signatures used in WSNs.

By the definition of the scheme, for the system model assumes that we have n nodes and one malicious node (note that for this example we will use only one malicious node, though in reality, our approach should be able to withstand up to $t - 1$ compromised nodes). Also, the system has a trusted agent that initializes the scheme. For this case, the agent chooses a RSA secret key and distributes this key safely between the nodes, providing the (t, n) — threshold scheme. After this initialization, the participation of the trusted agent is not needed. Assuming that the malicious user can compromise $s < t$ of nodes and since the malicious user is able to break the multiple signature scheme, he/she could execute an attack by a chosen message (we call it a chosen-message attack, CMA); therefore, he/she could request any of n node members to invoke a signature protocol for any chosen message. In this situation, the malicious user's aim is either tamper the message signature which he/she did sign or disrupt a wrong message signed by another member.

RSA-Based Secret Key Distributions Main Approaches

In existing works based on a distributed RSA signature, there are three main approaches as far as the RSA-based secret key distribution is concerned.

- In the first approach, the secret key d is distributed according to the Shamir secret scheme distribution. The system working according to this approach is impossible without a trusted agent participating.
- In the second approach, the level in the secret scheme distribution has been added. Firstly, the secret is distributed between n nodes additively, and then every received projection is distributed by a threshold circuit. Such schemes are interactive and are unable to work without an agent.
- In the third approach, there is a secret key d distributed. But this kind of separation brings vulnerability to the distributed scheme. Moreover, this approach doesn't assume independent working members' nodes coalition during signature establishment.

Thus, each of these approaches have some functional limitation and do not employ at least one of the features formulated previously.

The scheme of secret distribution (sharing) is one of the DSS components. In particular, the Shamir scheme can be used as a scheme of secret distribution. In the Shamir scheme, there is polynomial function f(x):

$$f(x) = (f_0 + f_1 x + f_2 x^2 + ... + f_{t-1} x^{t-1}) mod \qquad (9.1)$$

in which $f_0 = S$—secret, i.e., secret key, $f_1. .....f_{t-1}$ — *random* values, *t*—*number* of the secret's projections (sub-keys) or number of coalition members and *P*—*prime number*. Each member of the protocol gets the secret projection as $ss = f(id)$, where id is the member's ID. Any coalition K of t members could restore (recover) the secret $f_0 = f(0)$ using the Lagrange interpolation:

$$f(0) = \sum_{u \in K} ss_u l_u(0)(mod\ P) \qquad (9.2)$$

where $l_u(x)$ are Lagrange coefficients.

For the Shamir scheme to be used in a distributed RSA signature, it's necessary to choose the secret S and module P. For a distributed RSA signature, secret key d is the secret. Relative to module *P,* there are two ways, either make it public, e.g., $P = N$ or make it secret, i.e., $P = \phi(N)$ or $P = \lambda(N)$. If P is known (e.g., RSA module N), that brings information leaks and interdependency of coalition member actions during the distribution of signature setting procedure running. If P is a secret value (e.g., $P = \lambda(N)$ or $P = \phi(N)$), that gives the system the possibility of not being self-organized according to the next statement.

STATEMENT 1: In the case of using module P and this P module is unknown to members, then it's necessary to have a trusted agent for secure project distribution to a new member.: It is necessary to ignore the use of the module P approach to eliminate the disadvantages listed previously. However, the projection distribution procedure without an agent remains interactive. In addition, abandonment of P increases the projection size eventually to the complexity of signature setting. It's easy to get a higher estimation of the secret projection size (R) by using:

$$R \le \log(N) + (t - 1)k + 1 \qquad (9.3)$$

where N—*RSA module*, t—*coalition size* (number of members), k—*user* ID length. For example, for user ID length $k = 48$ bit and coalition size $t = 10$, the projection size R will not be over $\log(N) + 48(t - 1) + 1 \approx 1500$ bit, which means there is an increase of signature setting complexity of approximately 1.5 times.

OUR APPROACH ON SCHEME ESTABLISHMENT

We propose to modify a secret distribution scheme by getting rid of the interaction in the distribution procedure of a new projection without anagent (statement 1) and reduce the size of the secret projection. We put into consideration a prime number $Q > \max(id_i)$. We estimate the secret projection $f(x, y)$ as follows:

$$f(x, y) = \sum_{i=0}^{t-1} \sum_{j=0}^{t-1} f_{i,j}(x^i \bmod Q)(y^j \bmod Q) \qquad (9.4)$$

It's impossible to use the Lagrange interpolation with this kind of secret distribution function. Instead, it's essential to solve the combined linear equations.

For secret recovering, each coalition member node u calculates its function value with $x = 0$ getting:

$$f(0, id_u) = f_0 + f_1(y \bmod Q) + f_2(y^2 \bmod Q) + \ldots + f_t(y^t \bmod Q) \qquad (9.5)$$

with $y = id_u$ and $f_0 = f_{0,0}$. Having t values of a given function, the secret can be recovered by solving the following combined equations:

$$
\begin{bmatrix} f(xi_1) \\ f(xi_2) \\ \vdots \\ f(xi_t) \end{bmatrix} = G \begin{bmatrix} f_0 \\ f_1 \\ \vdots \\ f_{t-1} \end{bmatrix}
$$

where

$$G = \begin{bmatrix} (xi_1)^0 \; mod \; Q & (xi_1)^1 \; mod \; Q & \cdots & (xi_1)^{t-1} \; mod \; Q \\ (xi_2)^0 \; mod \; Q & (xi_2)^1 \; mod \; Q & \cdots & (xi_2)^{t-1} \; mod \; Q \\ & \vdots & & \\ (xi_t)^0 \; mod \; Q & (xi_t)^1 \; mod \; Q & \cdots & (xi_t)^{t-1} \; mod \; Q \end{bmatrix} \qquad (9.6)$$

Each coalition member calculates its function value with $x = id_{new}$ getting:

$$f(id_{new}, id_u) = s_0 + s_1(y \; mod \; Q) + \ldots + s_{t-1}s_1(y^{t-1} \; mod \; Q) \qquad (9.7)$$

with $y = id_u$ for the projection to be distributed to new members without an agent. The secret projection $s_0, s_1, \cdots, s_{t-1}$ for a new user can be calculated from the following combined equations:

$$\begin{bmatrix} s_{new}(xi_1) \\ s_{new}(xi_2) \\ \vdots \\ s_{new}(xi_t) \end{bmatrix} = \begin{bmatrix} s_0 \\ s_1 \\ \vdots \\ s_{t-1} \end{bmatrix} \qquad (9.8)$$

The following statement is true for a proposed secret distribution scheme according to statement number 2.

STATEMENT 2: For the modified secret distribution scheme the following are true:

I. Scheme has threshold (t) and it is safe;
II. The procedure of projection distribution in a scheme is non-interactive and doesn't request agent participation;
III. The procedure of projection distribution is safe;
IV. The size of each projection is no larger than $\log(N) + k + t$.

The new RSA DSS based on a proposed modified secret distribution scheme includes three steps.

Scheme Initialization

The agent generates the prime number $Q > \max(id)$.

The agent generates public RSA key $N = pq$ and $e > Q$, where e— prime number and p and q are random prime numbers. Then, the agent generates a secret key d as follows: $ed = 1 \; mod \; \Phi(N)$.

$\Phi(N) = (p - 1)(q - 1)$, where e and d are public and close parts of the key. (N, e) — public key's part, d—closed.

The agent generates a function:

$$f(x, y) = \sum_{i=0}^{t-1} \sum_{j=0}^{t-1} f_{i,j} (x^i \bmod Q)(y^i \bmod Q) \tag{9.9}$$

where $f_{0,0} = d$ and coefficients $f_{i,j} \in Z_N$ (Z_N is a set of prime numbers) were randomly chosen with the $f_{i,j} = f_{j,i}$ condition.

Each node u gets the function $s_u(x) = f(x, id_u)$ as a secret key projection.

Generation of Distributive Signature

The coalition K of t members is chosen (cluster). Each node calculates a partial signature by the equation $s_u(m) = m^{s_u(0)} \bmod N$, where m is a hash-function value of signing message, $u \in K$.

a. After getting t partial signatures, the signature's collector makes the matrix G for coalition K members and reverses it over the rational number field.
b. The signature collector calculates $G' = \lambda G^{-1}$, where λ is the least common multiple of all elements of matrix G^{-1}. Then the signature collector calculates:

$$S'(m) = \left(\prod_{j=1}^{t} (S_{uj}(m))^{g'_{ij}} \right) \bmod N \tag{9.10}$$

c. Using the extended Euclid algorithm, the collector finds x and y from $x\lambda + ye = 1$.

$$S(m) = ((S'(m))^x\, m^y) \bmod N \tag{9.11}$$

d. Calculating of the signature as

$$f(id_{new}, id_u) = s_{new}(id_u) = s_0 + s_1(y \bmod Q) + \cdots + s_{t-1}(y^{t-1} \bmod Q) \tag{9.12}$$

with $y = id_u$.

Key Projection Distribution to New User

a. For getting a secret key projection, the new node u has to find coalition K from t as already initialized nodes and report them to its own id_{new}.
b. Every coalition member u calculates its own function value with $x = id_{new}$, getting:

c. The new node finds its secret projection $(s_0, s_1, \cdots, s_{t-1})$ from the combined linear equations:

$$\begin{bmatrix} s_{new}(xi_1) \\ s_{new}(xi_2) \\ \vdots \\ s_{new}(xi_t) \end{bmatrix} = G \begin{bmatrix} s_0 \\ s_1 \\ \vdots \\ s_{t-1} \end{bmatrix} \tag{9.13}$$

Thus, the secret key projection distribution to a new node does not request agent participation and it is not interactive.

For a proposed scheme, it can be seen that it allows generating a correct RSA-based signature, and the next statement is true.

STATEMENT 3: The proposed distributed signing scheme provides a high security guarantee and is even safer as a RSA.

SUMMARY

In this chapter, we developed a RSA-based DSS with independent member node behavior, signature signing setting and un-interactive projection distribution protocol secret key with no agent participation. The proposed DSS, unlike existing schemes, has the following advantages:

- Nodes in clusters can associate independently during the signature distributing;
- Secret key distribution protocol is non-interactive and doesn't require agent participation after scheme initialization.

As one of the possible future directions, we observed that sensor nodes have low mobility in many applications. Thus, it may be desirable to develop location-based schemes so that the nodes can directly establish a signature setting automatically.

REFERENCES

Bellare, M., & Fuchsbauer, G. (2014). Policy-based signatures. *International Workshop on Public Key Cryptography*, 520–537.

Blakley, G. R. (1979). Safeguarding cryptographic keys. *1979 International Workshop on Managing Requirements Knowledge (MARK)*, 313–318.

Boyen, X. (2007). Mesh signatures. *Annual International Conference on the Theory and Applications of Cryptographic Techniques*, 210–227.

Chan, H., Perrig, A., & Song, D. (2003). Random key predistribution schemes for sensor networks. *2003 Symposium on Security and Privacy, 2003*, 197–213.

Damgård, I., & Dupont, K. (2005). Efficient threshold RSA signatures with general moduli and no extra assumptions. *International Workshop on Public Key Cryptography*, 346–361.

Damgård, I., & Thorbek, R. (2006). Linear integer secret sharing and distributed exponentiation. *International Workshop on Public Key Cryptography*, 75–90.

Desmedt, Y. (1987). Society and group oriented cryptography: A new concept. *Conference on the Theory and Application of Cryptographic Techniques*, 120–127.

Desmedt, Y., & Frankel, Y. (1989). Threshold cryptosystems. *Conference on the Theory and Application of Cryptology*, 307–315.

Desmedt, Y., & Jajodia, S. (1997). *Redistributing secret shares to new access structures and its applications*. Citeseer.

ElGamal, T. (1985). A public key cryptosystem and a signature scheme based on discrete logarithms. *IEEE Transactions on Information Theory, 31*(4), 469–472.

Eschenauer, L., & Gligor, V. D. (2002). A key-management scheme for distributed sensor networks. *Proceedings of the 9th ACM Conference on Computer and Communications Security*, 41–47.

Estrin, D., Govindan, R., Heidemann, J., & Kumar, S. (1999). Next century challenges: Scalable coordination in sensor networks. In *Proceedings of the 5th Annual ACM/IEEE International Conference on Mobile Computing and Networking*, 263–270.

Gennaro, R., Halevi, S., Krawczyk, H., & Rabin, T. (2008). Threshold RSA for dynamic and ad-hoc groups. *Annual International Conference on the Theory and Applications of Cryptographic Techniques*, 88–107.

Gennaro, R., Jarecki, S., Krawczyk, H., & Rabin, T. (1996). Robust and efficient sharing of RSA functions. *Annual International Cryptology Conference*, 157–172.

Gennaro, R., Jarecki, S., Krawczyk, H., & Rabin, T. (2001). Robust threshold DSS signatures. *Information and Computation, 164*(1), 54–84.

Gura, N., Patel, A., Wander, A., Eberle, H., & Shantz, S. C. (2004). Comparing elliptic curve cryptography and RSA on 8-bit CPUs. *International Workshop on Cryptographic Hardware and Embedded Systems*, 119–132.

Herranz, J., Laguillaumie, F., Libert, B., & Ràfols, C. (2012). Short attribute-based signatures for threshold predicates. *Cryptographers' Track at the RSA Conference*, 51–67.

Herranz, J., Padró, C., & Sáez, G. (2003). Distributed RSA signature schemes for general access structures. *International Conference on Information Security*, 122–136.

Herranz, J., & Sáez, G. (2003). Verifiable secret sharing for general access structures, with application to fully distributed proxy signatures. *International Conference on Financial Cryptography*, 286–302.

Herranz, J., & Sáez, G. (2004). Revisiting fully distributed proxy signature schemes. *International Conference on Cryptology in India*, 356–370.

Hu, L., & Evans, D. (2003). Secure aggregation for wireless networks. *2003 Symposium on Applications and the Internet Workshops, 2003. Proceedings*, 384–391.

Hwang, J., & Kim, Y. (2004). Revisiting random key pre-distribution schemes for wireless sensor networks. In *Proceedings of the 2nd ACM Workshop on Security of Ad Hoc and Sensor Networks*, 43–52.

Kong, J., Zerfos, P., Luo, H., & Zhang, L. (2003). Providing Robust and Ubiquitous Security Support for MANET. *ACM Workshop on Security of Ad Hoc and Sensor Networks*.

Li, J., Yuen, T. H., & Kim, K. (2007). Practical threshold signatures without random oracles. *International Conference on Provable Security*, 198–207.

Liu, D., & Ning, P. (2007). *Security for wireless sensor networks (Vol. 28)*. Springer Science & Business Media.

Liu, D., Ning, P., & Li, R. (2005). Establishing pairwise keys in distributed sensor networks. *ACM Transactions on Information and System Security (TISSEC)*, 8(1), 41–77.

Luo, H., Kong, J., Zerfos, P., Lu, S., & Zhang, L. (2004). URSA: Ubiquitous and robust access control for mobile ad hoc networks. *IEEE/ACM Transactions On Networking*, 12(6), 1049–1063.

Madden, S., Franklin, M. J., Hellerstein, J. M., & Hong, W. (2002). TAG: A tiny aggregation service for ad-hoc sensor networks. *ACM SIGOPS Operating Systems Review*, 36(SI), 131–146.

Maji, H. K., Prabhakaran, M., & Rosulek, M. (2011). Attribute-based signatures. *Cryptographers' Track at the RSA Conference*, 376–392.

Narasimha, M., Tsudik, G., & Yi, J. H. (2003). On the utility of distributed cryptography in P2P and MANETs: the case of membership control. In *11th IEEE International Conference on Network Protocols, 2003. Proceedings*, 336–345.

Okamoto, T., & Takashima, K. (2011). Efficient attribute-based signatures for non-monotone predicates in the standard model. *International Workshop on Public Key Cryptography*, 35–52.

Okamoto, T., & Takashima, K. (2013). Decentralized attribute-based signatures. *International Workshop on Public Key Cryptography*, 125–142.

Pointcheval, D., & Stern, J. (2000). Security arguments for digital signatures and blind signatures. *Journal of Cryptology*, 13(3), 361–396.

Przydatek, B., Song, D., & Perrig, A. (2003). : Secure information aggregation in sensor networks. In *Proceedings of the 1st International Conference on Embedded Networked Sensor Systems SIA*, 255 265.

Schneier, B. (2007). *Applied cryptography: protocols, algorithms, and source code in C*. John wiley & sons.

Schnorr, C.-P. (1991). Efficient signature generation by smart cards. *Journal of Cryptology*, 4(3), 161–174.

Shrivastava, N., Buragohain, C., Agrawal, D., & Suri, S. (2004). Medians and beyond: New aggregation techniques for sensor networks. *Proceedings of the 2nd International Conference on Embedded Networked Sensor Systems*, 239–249.

Stinson, D. R., & Strobl, R. (2001). Provably secure distributed Schnorr signatures and a (t, n) threshold scheme for implicit certificates. *Australasian Conference on Information Security and Privacy*, 417–434.

Wong, T. M., Wang, C., & Wing, J. M. (2002). Verifiable secret redistribution for archive systems. In *First International IEEE Security in Storage Workshop, 2002. Proceedings*, 94–105.

Zhang, R., & Chen, K. (2007). An efficient proactive RSA scheme for large-scale ad hoc networks. *Journal of Shanghai University (English Edition)*, 11(1), 64–67.

Zhu, H., Bao, F., & Deng, R. H. (2004). Computing of trust in wireless networks. *IEEE 60th Vehicular Technology Conference, 2004. VTC2004-Fall. 2004*, 4, 2621–2624.

Index

abnormality detection, 215
active attacks, 215, 32
Active Query Forwarding in Sensor Network
    (ACQUIRE), 11
ad-hoc networking, 20
angle of arrival (AoA), 178, 182
angulations, 78
application layer, 4, 37
APTEEN, 143
attack-resistant location estimation, 191
attenuation, 78
attribute-based signatures, 243
authentication, 26, 68, 174
availability, 27, 58, 66, 174

bandwidth, 24, 117
bandwidth limitation, 45
battery source, 5
beacon suite, 190
black hole attack, 158
braided multi-path routing protocol, 51, 154
buffer size limitation, 46

CDMA, 141
certification authority, 68
channel error rate, 21
classification, 217, 224, 230
cluster key, 10, 70
cluster-based pre-distribution, 110
collective bandwidth, 48
collective latency, 48
collective packet loss, 48
collusion resistance, 117
combinatorial design-based pre-distribution, 106
compact size, 23
complementary metal oxide semiconductor
    (CMOS), 4
confidentiality, 25
continuous model, 48
credit features, 230

data aggression, 132
data confidentiality, 66
data delivery model, 132
data freshness, 27, 66
data integrity, 26, 66

data link layer, 36
data rate, 20
delay trade-off, 46
Denial of Service (DoS), 33, 159
deployment knowledge-based pre-distribution, 103
direct behavior trust, 86
direct data trust, 83
directed diffusion, 135
distributed signature scheme, 241
distributed signatures, 243
DRBTS, 188, 193

ECRA, 145
efficiency metric, 117
end-to-end path key establishment, 69
energy-aware pre-distribution, 107
energy-aware routing protocol, 155
event-driven model, 48

false beacon location attack, 182
false node, 34
fault tolerance, 2
flexibility metric, 117
flooding, 37, 133

geographic adaptive fidelity (GAF), 150
geographic and energy aware routing (GEAR), 150
geographic protocol, 149
gossiping, 133
GPS-based localization, 175, 207
gradient-based routing (GBR), 11, 139
grey hole attack, 160
grid-based pre-distribution, 102
group key, 10
group-based probabilistic pre-distribution, 99

Hello flood attack, 33, 77, 159
hierarchical geographical adaptive fidelity
    (HGAF), 152
hierarchical routing, 140
HiRLoC, 180, 194
historical behavior trust, 86, 87
historical data trust, 85
hypercube-based pre-distribution, 106

ID-based pre-distribution, 107

impersonation, 184
individual key, 10
information throughput, 48
infrastructure-centric, 189
integrity, 26, 174
intermittent connectivity, 21
isolating aberrant nodes, 69

key management, 34, 68, 97
key pool-based pre-distribution, 97
key pre-distribution, 69, 118
key space-based pre-distribution, 99
key-establishment latency, 69

latency, 2
lateration, 78
LEACH, 141
LEAP protocol, 9
LED sensors, 4
link stability features (LSFS), 227
localization, 28, 171
location-based pre-distribution, 109
location-based routing, 149
location-reference attack, 185

matrix-based pre-distribution, 104
memory, 5, 117
memory limitations, 19
mesh signatures, 243
microcontroller, 5
microelectromechanical system (MEMS), 4
minimum energy communication network
        (MECN), 149
misuse detection, 215
mobile WSNs, 6
mobility, 23, 117
μTESLA, 9
multilateration, 173
multimedia WSNs, 6
multi-path multi-speed protocol (MMSPEED), 154
multi-path routing protocols, 96, 152

network key, 70
network layer, 4, 36
node malfunction, 33
node outage, 33
node replication attacks, 34
node revocation, 117
node subversion, 33
node-centric, 187
nodecentric routing protocol, 140
non-repudiation, 174

packet size, 20
pair-wise key-based pre-distribution, 98

pairwise shared key, 10
passive attacks, 214
physical attacks, 34
physical layer, 4, 35
polynomial-based probabilistic pre-distribution, 104
power consumption, 2, 132
power efficiency, 22
power source, 5
power-efficient gathering in sensor information
        systems (PEGASIS), 142
privacy, 174
probabilistic features, 228
production cost, 3, 132
propagation, 78

Quality of Service (QoS), 41
query-driven model, 48

randomness features, 229
range change attack, 182
range-based localization, 175
range-free localization, 179
received signal strength indicator (RSSI), 178
recharge ability, 18
regional relative trust, 84
reliability, 23, 44, 55
replay attack, 184
resilience, 117, 132
responsiveness, 23
robust positioning system (ROPE), 179, 192
routing attacks, 32, 156
rumor routing, 138

scalability, 3, 23, 99, 118, 132
secure localization, 28, 67, 77, 174
security metrics, 117
selective forwarding, 32
self-organization, 67, 246
sensor key, 70
sensor protocol for information via negotiation
        (SPIN), 135
sensors, 4, 5, 22
sensors nodes, 5
SeRLoC, 67, 190
sink node, 1, 6, 83, 88, 154
sinkhole attack, 32
sleep patterns, 19
small minimum energy communication network
        (SMECN), 150
SNEP, 7, 111
specification-based detection, 215
spin protocol, 7, 136
SPINE, 192
suspicious message detection by signal strength
        (SMDSS), 225

suspicious node information dissemination protocol (SNIDP), 225
Sybil attack, 32, 158, 184

TEEN, 143
terrestrial WSNs, 7
threat model, 81
threshold signatures, 243
throughput, 2
time difference of arrival (TDOA), 178
time of arrival (TOA), 178
time synchronization, 28, 68
TL-LEACH, 142
topology, 3
transceiver, 2, 5
transmission media, 3

transmission range, 19, 194
transport layer, 4, 37
tree-based pre-distribution, 105
triangulation, 77, 172
trilateration, 173
trust evaluation model, 83
trust list, 88
trust model, 82

ultra-wideband (UWB), 177, 189
unattended operations, 20
underground WSNs, 6
underwater WSNs, 6

wormhole attack, 29, 159, 185